The Big Book
of Comedies

The
Big Book
of Comedies

*25 one-act plays, skits, curtain
raisers, and adaptations for
young actors*

Edited by
Sylvia E. Kamerman

Publishers   PLAYS, INC.   *Boston*

CAUTION

Library of Congress Cataloging-in-Publication Data

The big book of comedies.

   Summary: A collection of twenty-five dramatic pieces, including one-acts, skits, curtain raisers, and adaptations, for ages from the middle grades through high school.
   1. Children's plays. 2. Comedy. [1. Plays]
I. Kamerman, Sylvia E.
PN6119.9.B54   1989   808.82′41   89-8774
ISBN 0-8238-0289-2

Manufactured in the United States of America

Contents

Junior and Senior High

Middle Grades

Skits and Curtain Raisers

Adaptations

The Big Book
of Comedies

Junior and Senior High

Fitness Is the Fashion

by Anne Coulter Martens

Aerobics, sit-ups, and push-ups put a strain on a budding romance. . . .

Characters

LIZ, *a college student*
CHARLES, *her intellectual brother, 16*
MRS. SMITH ⎱
MR. SMITH ⎰ *their parents*
GRANNY, *their grandmother*
JAY BARLOW, *playground supervisor*
TESS, *a pretty troublemaker*
JOAN ⎫
SANDY ⎬ *teenagers*
BOB ⎭
MRS. MILLIGAN, *a neighbor*
OFFICER CANNON
OTHER TEENAGERS

TIME: *A summer morning.*
SETTING: *Smiths' family room. Sofa is against wall up center. At left is cassette player with several tapes nearby; in front of it is*

coffee table holding magazines, bowl of fruit, and plate of cookies. Desk, telephone, and chair are at right. Other furniture has been pushed toward walls to make room for exercising in center. Exercycle and weight scale are down right. Ankle or wrist weights, jump ropes, etc., are piled on table left. Door left leads outside; door right to other rooms.

AT RISE: *Lively popular music is playing loudly.* CHARLES *is relaxing on sofa, reading a book. Everyone else is exercising to music, directed by* JAY BARLOW: SANDY *is on exercycle;* MRS. SMITH *is doing aerobics;* JOAN *is using weights; and* BOB *is doing push-ups.* JAY *goes from one to the other, first joining in aerobics, then using weights, then doing push-ups. As he does so he counts the time in a loud voice.*

JAY: Stretch—those—muscles. That's—the—spir—it. One—two—three—four. Try—to—do—more! (LIZ *hurries in, grabs weights from table, waves to* JAY *and joins in.*)

LIZ (*In same rhythm*): I—was—busy!

JAY (*Standing near her*): Busy—Lizzie? (LIZ *smiles at him; and they continue to exercise to music. After a few moments, telephone rings; no one pays any attention.* GRANNY *enters, pauses in doorway, and shouts.*)

GRANNY: The telephone is ringing! (*Music and exercising continue.* GRANNY *shouts in time to music.*) Phone—is—ring—ing! (CHARLES *reaches for knob of stereo and turns down volume.*) Will you all stop this racket? (*All relax, sprawling on floor, as* GRANNY *picks up phone.*) Hello. . . . Yes, she is. One moment. (*Turns*) Liz, it's for you. (LIZ *goes to phone.* GRANNY *addresses others.*) If you ask me, you all get too carried away with this physical fitness nonsense.

MRS. SMITH (*Stretching*): You ought to join us.

GRANNY: That'll be the day!

CHARLES: I'm with you, Granny. I have better things to do. Like reading.

JOAN: Shakespeare? Really, Charles!

LIZ (*Into phone*): Hello? . . . Oh, hi, Tess. . . . No, I'm not driving to the playground today. Jay's bringing me. . . . (*Annoyed*) Well, I guess so, Just a minute. (*To* JAY) It's Tess Daly. She wants to know if she can get a ride with you to the playground.

JAY: Does she have car trouble?

LIZ: Apparently.

JAY: Sure, I'll pick her up.

LIZ (*On phone*): Tess, Jay says he'll pick you up. . . . But we're right in the middle of our exercise class, and . . . well, Jay and my mother and my brother Charles and some of his friends.. . . . O.K., then. I'll see you. (*Hangs up. To* JAY) She knows you're here, and she's coming over to watch.

JAY: That's nice.

CHARLES: "All the world's a stage." I guess Tess wants to see the show.

LIZ: Charles, must you quote Shakespeare to us all the time?

JOAN: He's just lazy.

CHARLES (*Reaching for cookie*): Watching other people work is my favorite sport.

BOB: A little exercise wouldn't hurt you.

CHARLES: I prefer to exercise my brain.

JOAN (*To* JAY): Reading and eating are Charlie's main activities.

CHARLES (*Quoting*): "O! that this too too solid flesh would melt!" *Hamlet.*

JAY (*Chuckling*): Charles, you're a hopeless case.

GRANNY: Smart, that's what he is. Like me. (*Moves to exit*) I'm going to sit on the porch and wait for the mail.

MRS. SMITH: Are you expecting something important?

SANDY (*Teasing*): Maybe a letter from a boy friend, Mrs. Smith?

GRANNY: At my age? Don't be silly, Sandy.

JAY: You're a fine-looking woman, Mrs. Smith. You just need a little exercise to tone you up.

GRANNY: Don't try that line on me, young man!

MRS. SMITH: I suppose you're hoping to hear from your friend who went to Florida . . . Bella, wasn't it?

GRANNY: Right. I hope the trip wasn't too much for her.

MRS. SMITH: I hope so, too, but she *is* seventy-six.

GRANNY: Age is relative, Alice. (GRANNY *exits.* MRS. SMITH *slumps into chair.*)

MRS. SMITH: Jay, I have to tell you, I'm a little tired.

JAY: You have to work up to this kind of thing gradually. (*To others*) O.K., everybody, take five! (SANDY, JOAN, *and* BOB *go downstage.*)

JOAN: Charles, don't be such a stick-in-the-mud. Come on outside with us and get some fresh air.

CHARLES (*Sighing heavily; rising*): I'd rather be reading, but I suppose Shakespeare can wait for five minutes or so. (*He puts down book and follows* SANDY, JOAN, *and* BOB *out.* LIZ *sits on exercycle.*)

MRS. SMITH: I'm going to try that thing one of these days. (*To* JAY) Jay, it's wonderful of you to give us an hour of your time every morning. Do you know I've lost five pounds already? I just bought a new dress, and it's a whole size smaller than the ones I've been wearing.

JAY: That's great, Mrs. Smith.

LIZ: When Dad comes home from his business trip, maybe he'll join us, too.

MRS. SMITH: It would do him a world of good. (*Thoughtfully*) You know, I was thinking of asking Mrs. Milligan, our new neighbor, if she'd like to join our exercise class, but she's always so busy weeding those petunias of hers.

LIZ: She does have a beautiful garden. . . . By the way, Mom, what time do you expect Dad home?

MRS. SMITH (*Rising from chair and starting right*): Sometime before noon. He said he'll just take a cab from the airport. He has lots of work to do this afternoon—and then a school board meeting tonight. (*At door*) Want anything from the kitchen?

LIZ *and* JAY (*Together*): No, thanks. (MRS. SMITH *exits right.*)

LIZ: Dad will be so pleased when he hears about all this.

JAY (*Worried*): I hope he likes the idea.

LIZ: Jay, what's the matter with you? You seem sort of upset today.

JAY: Just the usual. I like my summer job as playground supervisor . . .

LIZ (*Teasing*): Especially when you have volunteer helpers like me?

JAY (*Smiling*): Absolutely! But the summer's almost over, and

I'm still not sure of having a Phys. Ed. job at the high school this fall.

LIZ (*Confidently*): You'll get it, Jay. Don't worry.

JAY: But there are six applicants for one vacancy. How do I know they'll pick *me*?

LIZ: Because of your good record in college. And because you're doing a great job as playground supervisor.

JAY: Well, I'm trying. (GRANNY *enters, holding letter.*)

GRANNY: Well, my letter came. Bella says she's having a marvelous time.

LIZ: That's nice, Granny.

GRANNY (*To* JAY): When you told the group to take five, did you mean five laps around the house?

JAY: No. Why do you ask?

GRANNY: Well, they're all running around the house right now. Except for Charles, of course. He was lying on the hammock for a while, and now he's rummaging through the pantry for something to eat.

LIZ: I'm not surprised!

JAY: I'd better go round everyone up so we can get started again. (*Looks at watch*) The playground opens at ten. (CHARLES *enters right, eating banana.*)

CHARLES (*As he goes to sofa and plunks down on it*): "If music be the food of love, play on." That may be all right for Orsino in *Twelfth Night,* but I like something more substantial. (*Picks up book and begins to read. Doorbells rings.* LIZ *opens door to* TESS, *who is attractively dressed.*)

TESS (*Brightly, as she enters*): Hi, everyone. I thought the exercise class was still going on.

JAY: We took a short break. It's going to begin again in about two minutes. Care to join us?

TESS (*Posing*): In this outfit? Sorry, Jay, not this time. (*Sits down*)

JAY: I'm going to get the others. Be back in a minute. (*Exits left*)

TESS: He's so cute. (*To* GRANNY, *who is busy reading letter*) Don't you think so, Mrs. Smith?

GRANNY (*Reading letter*): Hm-m-m? A little young for me, Tess.

Listen to this. Bella's been in Florida only one week, and already she's met (*Quotes*) "a very distinguished gentleman"!

CHARLES (*Not looking up from book*): Rich, too?

GRANNY: According to Bella, he has a nice pension.

TESS (*To* LIZ): Speaking of pensions, has Jay been talking to your father about the Phys. Ed. job?

LIZ: No, Dad's away on business. (*Annoyed*) And anyway, Jay would never do such a thing!

TESS (*Rising and going to door*): Are you sure about that?

LIZ: What do you mean?

TESS (*Laughing*): Liz, don't be so naive! And remember, *I* saw Jay before *you* did. (*Exits*)

GRANNY: You'd better keep an eye on that girl, Liz.

LIZ: Both eyes! (*Hurries out*)

GRANNY (*To* CHARLES): Bella says she saw this nice-looking man sitting on a bench, so she sat down beside him and started talking.

CHARLES: Bella must be a fast worker.

GRANNY: Well, she has no common sense at all.

CHARLES: "The lady doth protest too much, methinks."

GRANNY: Oh, Charles, you and your Shakespeare! (*Phone rings.* GRANNY *answers it.*) Hello? . . . Oh, hello, Mrs. Milligan. . . . (*Shocked*) What? Oh, that's too bad. . . . Now, Mrs. Milligan, it's nothing to get so excited about. You know how petunias just keep on growing in spite of everything, and . . . (*Surprised*) Why, she just hung up! She's furious. (*Shakes her head*)

CHARLES: What's the matter, Granny?

GRANNY: Mrs. Milligan says Bob, Joan, and Sandy trampled her petunias while they were running around the house.

CHARLES: She sounds like a real pain.

GRANNY (*Going right*): Tell the kids when they come in, will you, Charles? I have things to do right now.

CHARLES: Sure.

GRANNY (*Glancing at letter again*): Do you know what Bella's P.S. says? (*Reading*) "We're practically going steady!" (*Exits right as* LIZ *enters left*)

LIZ (*Annoyed*): I don't like what Tess said about Jay.

CHARLES: Feeling a little jealous, Sis?

LIZ: Suppose she *did* see Jay first? He was so anxious to meet me that he came over and introduced himself!

CHARLES: And *you* don't even have a pension!

LIZ (*Impatiently*): Charles, what do *you* know about . . . things?

CHARLES: Love, you mean? (*Quoting*) "Men have died from time to time, and worms have eaten them, but not for love."

LIZ: So?

CHARLES: So, what if I don't have much practical experience? I can use my brain.

LIZ: I've heard enough about that wonderful mind of yours. (*Musing*) You know, I also don't like Tess's implication that Jay would try to use Dad's position on the school board to get the Phys. Ed. job. I mean, Jay met Dad only once, when he delivered his application to the high school. (MRS. SMITH *enters, carrying dress on hanger.*)

MRS. SMITH: What do you think of this dress, Liz?

LIZ: I love it, Mom. It's going to look wonderful on you.

MRS. SMITH: I'd like to lose another couple of pounds before I wear it. (*Puts dress on chair, starts stretching*) Well, I'm ready to get started again. Where's Jay?

LIZ: He just went out to get the others. (JAY *enters.*)

JAY: Those kids were running around like crazy.

CHARLES: Oh, that reminds me. There was a phone call . . .

LIZ (*Ignoring* CHARLES): Jay, there's something I want to ask you . . . (SANDY, JOAN, *and* BOB *enter, followed by two or three* OTHER TEENAGERS.)

SANDY: Jay, I hope you don't mind, but we brought some more recruits.

JAY: That's fine, but if this keeps up we'll have to get a bigger place. (*To* LIZ) Liz, can your question wait till later?

LIZ: I guess it'll have to. (SANDY *puts tape into recorder.* TESS *enters left.*)

TESS (*To* JAY; *oozing charm*): It's so nice of you to use your free time like this, Jay. You don't mind if I watch, do you? I'll just stand over here out of the way.

JAY: O.K., Tess. (*To* CHARLES) Charlie, how about joining us?

CHARLES: Thanks, Jay, but I'd rather curl up with a good book. (JAY *passes out weights.*)

MRS. SMITH (*Looking at exercycle*): I wonder if I dare try out the exercycle?

LIZ: Why not? (*Helps her mother onto it*)

JAY: All right, everybody, in time to the music. Give it all you've got! (SANDY *hits "play" button and loud music is heard.* JAY *starts to count rhythmically.*) One—two—three—four! Reach—to—the—floor! (*Continues counting, as members of group do various exercises: toe touches, knee bends, push-ups, etc. No one but* TESS *notices* MR. SMITH *enter, down left, carrying briefcase and suitcase. He stops short, obviously surprised.*)

MR. SMITH (*Shouting above the music*): What's going on here? (*No one answers, and he raises his voice.*) What in the world is all this? (TESS *turns down volume of music, so that suddenly* MR. SMITH *is shouting in near silence.*)

CHARLES: Hi, Dad! Welcome home.

LIZ (*Going to him and hugging him*): Hi, Dad. Good to see you.

MRS. SMITH (*Getting off exercycle and crossing to* MR. SMITH): Why, Ted! I didn't expect you so early.

MR. SMITH: Alice, will you tell me what's going on here?

LIZ (*Quickly*): Dad, you remember Jay Barlow, don't you?

JAY: We met when I applied for the Phys. Ed. job. (*Shakes* MR. SMITH's *hand*) Good to see you, Mr. Smith.

MR. SMITH (*Curtly*): Hello. Nobody has answered my question yet.

CHARLES: They're all getting physically fit, Dad.

LIZ: And it was Jay's idea. Isn't it great?

MRS. SMITH: Ted, look at me. I'm a whole size smaller.

SANDY: Come on, Mr. Smith, touch your toes! (*Goes to tape player and turns up volume again.* JAY *resumes his counting,* MRS. SMITH *returns to exercycle, others continue exercising, and* MR. SMITH *goes to door right, dodging carefully around others. Suddenly, loud knocking is heard on door left.*)

MR. SMITH (*Shouting*): Will someone please answer the door? (*Exercising continues.* TESS *goes to door and opens it.* MRS. MILLIGAN *storms in with* OFFICER CANNON.)

CANNON (*Loudly*): All right, break it up! Break it up! (SANDY *turns off music, and they all freeze.*)

MRS. MILLIGAN: I told you, Officer. This place is a zoo!

MRS. SMITH: Why, Mrs. Milligan!

MR. SMITH: Is something wrong?

MRS. MILLIGAN (*Angrily*): For two whole weeks this has been going on every morning! Shrieking and laughing and playing records. Not to mention running all over my petunias. Officer, I demand that you *do* something!

MRS. SMITH (*Getting off exercycle*): But Mrs. Milligan, we're just—

MRS. MILLIGAN: I can see what you're doing. Creating a public nuisance, that's what this is!

JAY (*Quietly*): Take five, kids. (SANDY, JOAN, *and* BOB *exit left.*)

CANNON: Mrs. Milligan seems to have a legitimate complaint. Destruction of property and operating an exercise salon without a license. (*To* MR. SMITH) Do you have a license to operate, sir?

MR. SMITH: Do *I* . . . (*Bellowing*) Who's responsible for this? (*There is a moment of silence. All look toward* JAY.)

MRS. SMITH: Well, Ted, when Jay came over one night to see Liz, he talked so much about physical fitness that I suggested . . .

JAY (*Quickly*): Mr. Smith, it was my idea to start an exercise group.

MRS. MILLIGAN: Well, Officer, you've seen for yourself. Now I'm ready to sign that complaint. (*Goes right*) In a quiet place where I can hear myself think! (*Exits*)

CANNON: I'm sorry, Mrs. Smith. Nothing personal about this, you understand. (*Exits right*)

MRS. SMITH: How dare that Mrs. Milligan file a complaint against us! (*Exits right*)

JAY: It's against me, because I'm responsible.

MR. SMITH (*Angrily*): I go away for a few days on business, and when I come back I expect to find a peaceful, happy home. And what do I find? (*To* JAY) You, young fellow, are irresponsible!

JAY: If there's a fine, I'll pay it, Mr. Smith.

LIZ: Dad, Jay was only doing us a favor.

MR. SMITH (*To* JAY): If this is your idea of a favor, I wish you'd go do favors for someone else. (*Starts to exit*)

JAY (*Stiffly*): I really meant no harm, sir. (MR. SMITH *exits.*)

TESS (*Amused*): That was quite a scene!

JAY: Hardly an amusing one! (*Exits*)

LIZ: You think it's funny, Tess?

TESS: Not at all. I think it's a shame, after Jay went to so much trouble to make a good impression on your father.

LIZ: *What* did you say?

TESS: You heard me. Why else do you suppose he got acquainted with you so fast?

LIZ (*Angrily*): Are you trying to imply that Jay is friendly to me because my father's on the school board?

TESS: Of course. Why else?

LIZ: That's just not so! (JAY *re-enters.*) When Jay first talked to me, he didn't even *know* Dad was on the school board! (*To* JAY) Did you, Jay?

TESS: How could he help knowing? I told him!

LIZ (*Almost pleading*): Jay, you *didn't* know, did you?

JAY (*Unhappily*): Yes, I did, Liz.

TESS (*Brightly, to* JAY): I'm sure you can find a Phys. Ed. job in some other high school. (*At door left*) I'll wait for you out in your car, Jay. (*Exits*)

LIZ: But, Jay, you acted so surprised when I told you!

JAY: I didn't want you to think that was why I came over to talk to you.

LIZ: But it *was*! All the time you were being so nice to me, and coming here to meet Mother, and starting this class . . . all that time you were planning to make a good impression on my father!

JAY: It wasn't that way at all!

LIZ (*Angrily*): What an idiot I've been. Just go!

JAY: Liz, listen to me!

CHARLES (*Quoting*): "Though she be but little, she is fierce."

LIZ (*Coldly*): Tess is waiting! (*She exits right. Angry and frustrated,* JAY *pounds a fist into his hand.*)

CHARLES: Things sure are a mess, aren't they? "Lord, what fools these mortals be!"

JAY: If Liz thinks that about me . . . if she thinks I'm a conniving . . .

CHARLES: You mean you're not?

JAY: I never gave a thought to impressing your father! I'm just not like that!

CHARLES: But you sure managed to do it—the wrong way. Too bad. You're a good guy, Jay.

JAY (*Shrugging*): Oh, well, I've lost out on the job and Liz. (*Starts collecting weights, jump ropes, etc., and putting them in carrying case*)

CHARLES: Oh, Jay, don't forget your badminton racquets—they're on the back porch. (JAY *gives him a dirty look and exits left.* CHARLES *sits up, takes an apple, and bites into it.*) MRS. SMITH *and* MRS. MILLIGAN, *who is still miffed, enter right.*)

MRS. SMITH: I assure you it won't happen again, Mrs. Milligan.

MRS. MILLIGAN: I would hope not! I thought I had moved into a civilized neighborhood!

CHARLES: You know what, Mom? You're lucky.

MRS. SMITH: Why's that, Charles?

CHARLES: You already lost five pounds so you can fit into that gorgeous new dress. (*Points to dress*)

MRS. MILLIGAN (*Surprised*): How many pounds?

MRS. SMITH: Five. My husband and I are going to a big party next week, and I used that as an incentive for losing some weight and getting in shape. (*Picks up dress, holds it up*)

MRS. MILLIGAN: You lost five pounds in only two weeks?

CHARLES: Well, she dieted a little, and the exercise really helped.

MRS. SMITH: Besides, it was fun, working out with the young people. Made me feel like a kid again.

MRS. MILLIGAN (*Thinking*): Hm-m-m . . . (*She turns and looks at tag on dress, sighs.*) Oh, my, only a couple of years ago I wore the same size, myself. (*Shakes head*) This young Phys. Ed. fellow . . . what's his name?

CHARLES: Jay Barlow.

MRS. MILLIGAN: Maybe he didn't have such a bad idea after all. (*After a pause*) Mrs. Smith, I'm a very quick-tempered woman, but when I make a mistake, I'm just as quick to admit it. (CANNON *and* MR. SMITH *enter right.*) Officer Cannon, I've decided to withdraw my complaint.

MRS. SMITH (*Pleased*): Oh, that's very good of you, Mrs. Milligan!

MRS. MILLIGAN (*To* CANNON): I'm sure I can get used to a little noise—especially since I intend to join that class myself!

MR. SMITH: Am I hearing you correctly, Mrs. Milligan?

CHARLES: Jay's out on the porch, if you want to tell him.

MRS. MILLIGAN (*Starting left*): He's a smart young fellow, and I'm sure he's a wonderful teacher. (*Exits left*)

CANNON: I'm glad she withdrew the complaint, because I'm an exercise nut, myself. The police department even has a regular aerobics program, and the classes are always filled. Well, I'm glad this worked out for everybody. Be seeing you around. (*All ad lib thanks and goodbyes, and* CANNON *exits left.*)

CHARLES: It's funny the officer put it like that, Dad—"Be seeing you around." You *are* sort of round in the middle.

MRS. SMITH: Charles!

MR. SMITH (*Protesting*): Round in the middle? That's nonsense! I'm as fit as I was twenty years ago.

CHARLES: *Sure* you are, Dad.

MRS. SMITH (*Sternly*): Charles, don't laugh at your father just because he has a little spare tire.

MR. SMITH: *Who's* got a spare tire? (MRS. SMITH *examines him critically, and turns away, smiling.*) I weigh the same as the day I got out of college!

CHARLES: Are you sure about that, Dad?

MR. SMITH: I'll prove it to you! (*Goes to scale, hesitates, then steps on it. He reads weight, gives a slight gasp, then steps off quickly.*) This can't be accurate!

MRS. SMITH: Ted, you know that scale never lies.

CHARLES: Don't worry, Dad. Lots of people your age have a spare tire. Shakespeare called it an "unbounded stomach."

MRS. SMITH: I was getting one myself. (*Raises her arms and stretches and bends*) And look at Charles.

CHARLES (*Stung*): What do you mean, look at Charles? (*Jumps up, puffing out his chest*) There's not an ounce of fat on me . . . well, maybe one or two ounces. (*He does some knee bends, and* MR. SMITH *tries to touch his toes, without success.* JAY *enters, carrying two racquets.*)

JAY: Has anyone seen the box for these racquets? (LIZ *enters right.*)

LIZ: Are you leaving, Jay?

JAY: You told me to go home, didn't you?

MR. SMITH (*Quickly*): Hold on, Jay. Don't run off. I'm just beginning to realize that you had quite an impact here. Fact is, I'm proud of your initiative.

JAY: You are?

MR. SMITH: We need teachers of your caliber on our faculty. I want you to know that you'll have my recommendation at the school board meeting tonight.

JAY (*Surprised*): Why . . . thanks very much, Mr. Smith. (SANDY, JOAN, BOB, *and* OTHER TEENAGERS *drift in. They stand, listening.*)

MR. SMITH (*Clearing his throat*): Now, about these morning gym classes. We may as well continue them here for the rest of the summer.

JAY (*Pleased*): Whatever you say, sir.

MR. SMITH: But in the fall, what would you say to a night class for adults, held in the high school gym? Mrs. Smith and I have quite a few friends who might join.

JAY: That would be terrific! (*To* LIZ) Liz . . .

LIZ (*Turning her back to him*): Didn't you forget? Tess is waiting.

JAY: Let her wait. (*To* SANDY) Sandy, music, please!

SANDY: You bet! (*As* SANDY *is about to put tape into player,* GRANNY *runs in, wearing leotard and tights.*)

GRANNY: Don't start without me!

LIZ: Granny!

GRANNY: All I need is a little toning up. Then *I'm* going to Florida.

CHARLES: In the words of the immortal bard, "All's well that ends well!" (SANDY *turns on player. As* JAY *begins to count, everyone begins to exercise to music.* GRANNY *climbs on exercycle and gives it her all.* MRS. SMITH *does toe touches.* MR. SMITH *uses weights.* LIZ *watches, smiling, and crosses center. After a moment,* MRS. MILLIGAN, *wearing shorts and T-shirt, enters with* CANNON, *and they join in.* JAY *works his way toward* LIZ, *as he counts. At her side, he starts doing arm exercises, nods at her to join him. She hesitates.* TESS *enters and goes toward* JAY. *Before she reaches him,* LIZ *joins* JAY *in exercise, beaming at him. Seeing this,* TESS *shrugs and exits. Music and exercising continue as curtain falls.)*

THE END

Joe White and the Seven Lizards

by Claire Boiko

Magic and mischief in the major leagues. . .

Characters

NARRATOR
JOE WHITE
FAITHFUL FENELLA
MIKE VIDEO, *sports announcer*
BRAGGART MCTAGGART
SHADOW, *his manager*
PITCHER
GHOST UMPIRE
LEFTY ⎫
RIGHTY ⎪
SLIDER ⎪
GLIDER ⎬ *the Leaping Lizards*
GROUNDER ⎪
SINKER ⎪
SCREWBALL ⎭

GROUNDSKEEPER
PHOTOGRAPHER
SIGNMAKER
BATTER
RUNNER
CATCHER
THIRD BASEMAN
OUTFIELDER
GIRL ROOTERS
THREE VOICES

SCENE 1

BEFORE RISE: NARRATOR, *in baseball uniform, enters through curtain, center, carrying a book. He addresses audience.*

NARRATOR: What you are about to see is a legend. Now, most legends begin: "Once upon a time, there was a beautiful princess." Right away, the boys go outside for a game of catch. Princesses are all right in their place, but they don't do much. Now, the kind of story most boys would like to hear begins in a setting like this . . . (NARRATOR *opens his book and sits at a side of stage down right. Curtains open.)*

* * *

TIME: *Just before the World Series.*

SETTING: *A baseball field, with empty tiers of seats on backdrop. There are chairs up left and right in a single row. In front of chairs are dugout benches. Pitcher's mound is down left. Home plate with batter's screen is right and a scoreboard at rear which reads,* WORLD SERIES—WESTERN HEMISPHERE VS. EASTERN HEMISPHERE.

AT RISE: JOE WHITE, *in ragged polo shirt and baggy baseball pants, enters up right, carrying baseball bats wrapped in cellophane and tied with satin bows. He drops them at home plate, and pretends to swing a bat.*

NARRATOR: Our story begins with a real hero. You've heard of "Snow White and the Seven Dwarfs"? Now listen, as the sequel to Snow White comes to life. Here is "Joe White and the

Seven Lizards." (*He opens book and begins to read.*) Once upon a World Series, there was a poor little overworked bat boy named Joe White. Now, Joe White wanted to become the Player of Year, but he didn't stand a chance. There were always those voices!

1ST VOICE (*Offstage*): Joe White! Get to work. Clean off home plate. Braggart McTaggart's coming to batting practice. (JOE *takes cloth out of his pocket and dusts off home plate.*)

2ND VOICE (*Offstage*): Joe White! Line up the bats. (Joe *lines up bats in a neat row.*)

3RD VOICE (*Offstage*): Joe White! Sound the fanfare. Here comes Braggart McTaggart! (JOE *takes small trumpet out of his pocket.* GIRL ROOTERS *enter with pennants, sit left.* SIGNMAKER *enters, holds up sign reading,* BRAGGART MCTAGGART—GREAT-EST OF THE GREAT!, *and also sits left.* JOE *sounds a fanfare.* ROOTERS *cheer. From off right,* PHOTOGRAPHER, *holding camera to his eye, backs onstage, snapping* BRAGGART MCTAGGART, *who swaggers on followed by* SHADOW *and* MIKE VIDEO. PITCHER *enters down left, bowing as* JOE *hands* MCTAGGART *a bat.* CATCHER *enters up right, also bowing to* MCTAGGART, *who tips his cap.* ROOTERS *continue cheering, until* MCTAGGART *motions airily for them to stop.*)

MCTAGGART (*To* JOE): Boy—is this a fresh bat?

JOE: Oh, yes, sir, Mr. McTaggart. Sanitized and sterilized.

MCTAGGART: Good. Don't ever give me a used bat.

JOE: Oh, no, sir.

MCTAGGART (*Motioning* JOE *away*): Move. I'm going to swing now. (PITCHER *winds up, but does not throw.* MCTAGGART *poses swinging, as* PHOTOGRAPHER *snaps a picture.* MCTAGGART *puts his bat down and waves* PITCHER *away.* PITCHER *bows and exits left.*)

MIKE VIDEO: One minute, please, Mr. McTaggart. Just one minute. I've waited months to interview you.

MCTAGGART: Another interview? That's six interviews I've given today. One minute, you say? Well, I'll ask my manager, Shadow. Hey, Shadow, can I spare a minute?

SHADOW: O.K. One minute. I'll time you. (*He looks at his watch.*)

MIKE VIDEO: Thank you, thank you, Mr. McTaggart. Now there's one thing that millions of fans are eager to know. You never go to spring training, and you never practice, but you are the Player of the Year. How did you manage that?

McTAGGART: I'm a natural. Why should I go to spring training? It interferes with fishing.

MIKE VIDEO: Another thing. How do you keep in shape? It's a well-known fact that you eat twenty ice cream sodas a day— yet you batted .400 this year. How did you do it?

McTAGGART (*Loftily*): I'm a genius, of course. (*Spelling it*) G-e-n-y-u-s-s. Genius.

MIKE VIDEO: Maybe, but your fans seem to think you have a secret.

McTAGGART (*Winking at* SHADOW, *who winks back*): A secret? Well, now, as a matter of fact—

SHADOW: Time!

McTAGGART (*Pushing* MIKE VIDEO *downstage, by the shoulders*): Isn't that a shame. Time for you to go. Batting practice is over.

MIKE VIDEO (*Protesting*): But you haven't hit the ball once.

McTAGGART: Oh, I don't come to hit balls. I come to have my picture taken and give the girls cheering practice. (*He waves to* ROOTERS.) All right, girls, I'm giving autographs in the clubhouse.

ROOTERS: Hooray! (ROOTERS *and* SIGNMAKER *exit up left, as* CATCHER *exits up right.* McTAGGART, *still pushing* MIKE VIDEO, *followed by* SHADOW, *crosses down right. He stops and turns to* JOE WHITE.)

McTAGGART: Hey, you—

JOE WHITE: Yes, sir?

McTAGGART: My fanfare. I get a fanfare coming and a fanfare going.

JOE WHITE: Sorry, sir. (*He sounds a fanfare.*)

McTAGGART: That's better. I don't feel as if I've been any place until I hear that fanfare. (*He swaggers off right, followed by* MIKE VIDEO *and* SHADOW. JOE *crosses to pitcher's mound and warms up.*)

NARRATOR: And that's how it was, down at the stadium. Joe White never had a moment to practice from the time the sun touched the flag at the top of the stadium, until it cast long

shadows over center field. But for a few moments every evening, just before sundown, he was alone and free. How he
worked! (JOE *pantomimes the action.*) He practiced his over-
hand and underhand, low balls, high balls, slow balls, and fly
balls. Did I say alone? Not quite. (FENELLA *enters up left.*)
Because Joe White had one fan, Faithful Fenella. (FENELLA
sits center in rooting section.)

FENELLA: Hooray for Joe White! (*She applauds vigorously.*)

JOE: Thank you, Faithful Fenella. Would you like to pitch a few?

FENELLA: I'd be glad to, Joe. Anything at all, Joe. (*She crosses to
pitcher's mound.* JOE *picks up bat used by* MCTAGGART *and
pounds the plate.*)

JOE: Play ball, Fenella. (FENELLA *winds up like a windmill.
Sound of a slide whistle is heard. She pantomimes throwing.*
JOE *swings. Sound of a loud pop is heard.* FENELLA *watches
imaginary ball sailing over audience.*)

FENELLA (*Pointing*): Look at that! Right over the back fence.

JOE: It should have been higher.

FENELLA: But I don't think any fielder could jump thirty feet,
Joe.

JOE: A person can't be overconfident, Fenella. Say—I'm hungry.
Do you have an apple?

FENELLA: Right here, Joe. I just happen to have one in my purse.
(*She crosses to* JOE *and hands him an apple.*)

JOE: You know what they say—"An apple a day keeps the outfield away." I wonder how Braggart McTaggart keeps his
pitching arm in shape? He never practices, yet he's surefire.
He must have a secret.

FENELLA: Well, whatever that secret is, it can't beat hard work
and fair play. Someday, Joe White, you'll be Player of the Year.
(*Curtain*)

* * * * *

SCENE 2

BEFORE RISE: NARRATOR *addresses audience.*

NARRATOR: Little did Joe White dream that Braggart McTaggart
did indeed have a secret most foul. That same night, when all

good ball players were asleep, Braggart McTaggart and his sneaky manager, Shadow. . . . (*Curtains open.* NARRATOR *exits.*)

SETTING: *Same as Scene 1, but lights are dim.*

AT RISE: *Shadow sidles in right, beckoning for* McTAGGART *to follow. They cross center.* FENELLA *enters up right, sees them, and unseen, huddles in one of rooting chairs and watches.*

McTAGGART: The World Series begins soon, Shadow. We have to figure out how to hex and hoo-doo the Eastern Hemisphere team.

SHADOW: Isn't it lucky I'm your manager, Master? You were a third-rate, bench-warming pitcher until you found me. My magic and my magic alone made you Player of the Year. Remember how you found me?

McTAGGART: I'll never forget it. Somebody threw a soda bottle at the umpire, and I caught it. When I opened it—there you were. My own personal genie—casting spells on the other teams. Ha ha! (FENELLA *pantomimes astonishment.*)

SHADOW: Do you think anybody suspects that I'm the power behind the throw?

McTAGGART: Of course not. People only have to look at me to believe that I'm the greatest of the great. Right?

SHADOW: There's only one way to find out for sure.

McTAGGART: You mean there's a doubt? Who knows for sure?

SHADOW: The Ghost Umpire.

McTAGGART: What Ghost Umpire?

SHADOW: The Ghost Umpire who haunts the World Series Stadium. He walks the outfield and stalks the infield. He hovers eternally above home plate. He knows for sure.

McTAGGART: Get him! Ask him! I must know for sure.

SHADOW (*Calling*): Ghost Umpire! You are summoned to appear for an instant replay! (GHOST UMPIRE *enters right and walks behind home plate.*)

GHOST UMPIRE (*In a sepulchral tone*): I come. I see all. I know all. I tell all.

SHADOW: Go ahead. Ask him.

McTAGGART (*Very assured*):
Umpire, Umpire, at the plate,
Who's the greatest of the great?
UMPIRE (*Sternly*):
Take care, McTaggart, you've made an error.
Your hex and hoo-doo hold no terror;
For a bat boy plays by night,
Greatest of the great is young—Joe White!
(FENELLA *claps her hands softly.*)
McTAGGART (*Staggered*): No! A bat boy. I don't believe it!
SHADOW: You'd better believe it. The Ghost Umpire never lies.
McTAGGART: I want to see Joe White in action!
SHADOW: Right away, Master. (*Calls off*) Joe White, come to the
field, Joe White, come to the field! (JOE *runs in from left, sees*
McTAGGART *and blows a fanfare on his trumpet.*)
McTAGGART: Stop that! I don't feel like a fanfare right now.
SHADOW (*Putting his arm around* JOE; *with oily kindness*): So
you're the famous bat boy? We've heard great things about
you, Joe.
JOE (*Surprised*): You have?
McTAGGART: Well, not exactly *great* things. The fact is, I don't
think you can throw a ball without dropping it. Here, pitch
one to me. (*In pantomime he throws a ball to* JOE, *who crosses
to pitcher's mound and warms up.* SHADOW *crosses to dugout,
and* FNELLA *ducks down again.*)
JOE: Yes, sir, Mr. McTaggart. (McTAGGART *picks up bat.*) That's a
used bat, Mr. McTaggart.
McTAGGART: Never mind. I can't wait to see you pitch.
UMPIRE: Play ball! (JOE *winds up and pitches. Sound of slide
whistle.* McTAGGART *steps back, as* UMPIRE *catches ball.*) Stee-
rike one! (*He throws back to* JOE.)
McTAGGART: Beginner's luck. (JOE *winds up and pitches again.
Sound of slide whistle.* McTAGGART *swings,* UMPIRE *catches.*)
UMPIRE: Stee-rike two! (*He throws back to* JOE.)
McTAGGART: The light was in my eyes.
SHADOW: Light? It's nine p.m.
McTAGGART: Well, Shadow, why don't you make some magic?

SHADOW: All right, all right. (*As* JOE *winds up,* SHADOW *makes motions. Sound of slide whistle.* MCTAGGART *swings,* UMPIRE *catches.*)

UMPIRE: Stee-rike three!

MCTAGGART: He struck me out! What happened?

SHADOW: I don't know. It's as if he's immune to magic.

UMPIRE: Hex and hoo-doo ne'er outweigh

Practice, hard work, and fair play,

And an apple every day! (*He exits up right.*)

SHADOW: We're in trouble, Master, unless you get rid of Joe White.

MCTAGGART: You're right, and the sooner the better. I've got an idea. Hex me up a long-term contract.

SHADOW (*Puzzled*): A long-term contract? (*Getting the idea*) Oh—yes. Right away, Master. (*He produces long roll of paper and pen from up his sleeve.*)

MCTAGGART (*Beckoning*): Joe—oh, Joe White. Come here. (JOE *crosses to* MCTAGGART *and* SHADOW. FENELLA *cautiously peeks out.* MCTAGGART *slaps* JOE *on shoulder, as* JOE *winces.*) That was great pitching, Joe. The Western Hemisphere needs you. Here. (*He hands him pen and contract.*) Sign this contract. It's for a little team we've started out in the West. (FENELLA *shakes her head violently.*)

JOE (*Signing paper, as* FENELLA *wrings her hands*): In the West! That sounds great. Thanks, Mr. McTaggart. You've got a heart as big as your head. When do I start?

SHADOW: Immediately. Maybe sooner. Stand over here on the mound. (JOE *crosses to mound.*) Wind up for a pitch. (JOE *winds up.*) Now! (*He chants*).

Wind up, wind up, young Joe White;

Pitch yourself clear out of sight.

Pitch yourself, at my behest,

Over the stands and way out—West!

(*Sound of a tremendous wind.* JOE *spins around and around. Lights flicker on and off. During quick blackout,* JOE *exits. When lights come back up,* MCTAGGART *and* SHADOW *are shaking hands.*)

McTAGGART: You did it! But will he stay out there permanently?

SHADOW: Of course. Unless—

McTAGGART: Unless what? (SHADOW *looks around uneasily.* SHADOW *takes* McTAGGART *down center.* FENELLA *creeps behind them, listening intently.*)

SHADOW: That soda bottle! What did you do with it after you let me out?

McTAGGART: I threw it away somewhere in the stadium.

SHADOW: You must find it. If somebody finds that soda bottle and blows across the top three times like this (*He acts out blowing across top.*)—you will lose all your magic powers and become a third-rate bench-warmer again.

McTAGGART (*Horrified*): No!

SHADOW: I will be forced back into the bottle, to await a new master.

McTAGGART (*Horrified*): No, no!

SHADOW: And Joe White will return to the pitcher's mound, as great as he was two minutes ago.

McTAGGART: No! No! No! (*He calls offstage.*) Groundskeeper! (GROUNDSKEEPER *runs in up left, clicks his heels, and salutes* McTAGGART.)

GROUNDSKEEPER: At your service, Mr. McTaggart.

McTAGGART: Groundskeeper, you must find each and every soda bottle in this stadium before the series starts.

SHADOW (*Threatening*): Each and every soda bottle—or else.

GROUNDSKEEPER: Yes, sir. Each and every soda bottle. How many are there?

McTAGGART: 50,000. Smash them to smithereens. I don't want a smither left. (GROUNDSKEEPER *nods.*) Well, what are you standing there for? Go!

GROUNDSKEEPER: Yes, sir. (*He zigzags up left, looking for bottles, and finds one under dugout.*) I found one! (*He exits up left. Sound of bottle smashing.*)

McTAGGART: One down!

SHADOW: 49,999 to go!

McTAGGART: We'll outsmart Joe White yet. I feel like celebrating. How about a double-dip ice cream soda?

SHADOW: Make it a triple. (*They laugh, and exit down right.*

FENELLA *crosses center.*)

FENELLA: So that's their foul secret. An enchanted soda bottle. Oh, Joe. I won't let you down. I'll find that bottle and bring you back. I promise. (*She turns and looks under dugout, finding a bottle. She blows across it three times, waiting expectantly. When nothing happens, she sighs.*) Oh dear. Nothing at all. One down, 49,998 to go! (*Curtain*)

* * * * *

SCENE 3

BEFORE RISE: *Prop boy puts cactus with sign reading,* DEATH VALLEY. LOWEST POINT IN THE U.S. *down right.* JOE *enters down left, holding his head. He looks around, bewildered.*

JOE: Wow! They certainly make fast jets these days. (*He sees cactus.*) Death Valley. I must be out West. (*He looks at contract.*) Let me see my contract. Hm-m-m. I signed myself up for twenty years! I've heard of long-term contracts, but this is the limit. What's my team? Oh. The Leaping Lizards. (*Looks up*) The Leaping Lizards? I've heard of the Cubs and the Orioles, but who in the World Series are the Leaping Lizards? (LIZARDS *enter single file, down right. They wear ragged uniforms and carry dilapidated fielders' mitts with torn fingers, and gnarled bats.*)

LIZARDS: Greetings, Joe White. We are your team. The Leaping Lizards. In batting order we are—(*Each doffs his cap in turn*)

LEFTY: Lefty.

RIGHTY: Righty.

SLIDER: Slider.

GLIDER: Glider.

GROUNDER: Grounder.

SINKER: Sinker.

SCREWBALL: (*Tossing his cap in the air and catching it*): Screwball!

JOE: Pleased to meet you. (*He looks at them closely.*) Where'd you get these uniforms?

LIZARDS: From the ragbag.

LEFTY: I'm sorry, Joe. You've been sent out to the Cactus League.

SCREWBALL: That's even further out than the Bush League.

GLIDER: We're too minor for the Little Leagues.

LEFTY: They call us the Be-little League.

GROUNDER: Our batting average is zero-zero-zero and a half.

SINKER: We almost batted in a run two years ago.

SLIDER: And we made over three hundred errors—

RIGHTY: In our last game.

SCREWBALL: Welcome, Joe White. (*Pumps* JOE's *hand.*)

LIZARDS: Welcome seven times seven, Joe White.

LEFTY: Stay here with us, Joe. We won't let Braggart McTaggart get you ever again.

RIGHTY: We'll help you, Joe. You can practice with us.

SLIDER: Pitch (*He pitches.*)

GLIDER: Catch. (*He catches.*)

GROUNDER: Run bases. (*He runs in place.*)

SINKER: Bat. (*He swings.*)

LEFTY: Field! (*He pretends to catch a high fly.*)

SCREWBALL: You'll work hard and play fair.

LIZARDS: We'll make you the Player of the Year. What do you say, Joe White?

JOE: I say, let's do it! Does anybody have an apple? (LIZARDS *cheer and lead* JOE *off. Prop boy removes cactus.*)

* * *

SETTING: Same as Scene 1.

AT RISE: FENELLA *enters left, purse in one hand and a basket full of bottles in the other. She blows three times across one of the bottles, then shakes her head, discouraged.*

FENELLA: 24,999. (MCTAGGART, SHADOW, *and* GROUNDSKEEPER *enter down right.* FENELLA *sees them and hides watching.*)

GROUNDSKEEPER: But I tell you, Mr. McTaggart, I *am* looking for bottles. I've found exactly half of them—25,000. But somebody else must be looking for them, too.

MCTAGGART: Well, don't stand there making excuses. Go find the rest. (GROUNDSKEEPER *salutes and runs off.*) Somebody else? Who else?

SHADOW: I'll find out, Master. Never fear. But why did we return to the field?

McTaggart: Now that Joe White's out of the way permanently, I want to hear the good news from the Ghost Umpire. Get him for me, Shadow.

Shadow (*Calling*): Ghost Umpire! You are summoned to appear for an instant replay.

Umpire (*Appearing up right and crossing to behind home plate*): I come. I see all. I know all. I tell all.

McTaggart:
Umpire, Umpire at the plate,
Now who's the greatest of the great?

Umpire:
Out in the West, so far away,
A bat boy works out every day,
His star is rising high and bright,
The Player of the Year will be—Joe White!

McTaggart (*Enraged*): No! I won't believe it! Not that fumble-thumbs! Not Joe White! (Fenella *claps her hands delightedly.* Shadow *sees her, sneaks up and grabs her, pulling her down center.*)

Shadow: Aha! A spy. I found a spy.

McTaggart: Aw, that's only Faithful Fenella, Joe White's friend. Blow her to the moon or some place.

Shadow: Not so fast, Master. She's going to help us get rid of Joe White forever.

Fenella: I won't help you. Never!

Shadow (*Grabbing her purse*): What's this—a purse! Let's have a look. (*He takes out apple.*) Ah, an apple.

Fenella: Give that back. That's Joe's apple. It keeps the outfield away.

Shadow: An apple, eh? You know, McTaggart, I think it's time dear old Joe had some fresh fruit. (McTaggart *nods and winks.*) A nice red apple with some spice on it. (McTaggart *guffaws.*)

Fenella: Spice? Joe doesn't like spice in his apples.

Shadow: He'll never know, my dear. One bite of my special apple and he's out. O-U-T. Out for good.

McTaggart: I understand. Out. O-U—? O-U—?

SHADOW: T. T for Terminated! (*They laugh as* FENELLA *runs off, crying. Curtain*)

* * * * *

SCENE 4

BEFORE RISE: *Prop boy puts out cactus.* JOE *enters right, tossing ball.* LIZARDS *enter, cheering.*

LEFTY: Come on, Joe. Let's go.

LIZARDS: Let's go, Joe! Let's go, Joe!

JOE: Do you really think I'm ready to play in the World Series, fellows?

LEFTY: Affirmative, Joe.

RIGHTY: Certainly, Joe.

SLIDER: Undoubtedly, Joe.

GLIDER: Unquestionably, Joe.

GROUNDER: Yes, siree, Joe.

SINKER: You bet, Joe.

LEFTY: Incontrovertibly, Joe.

JOE: Screwball? What do you think? (*He calls offstage.*) Hey, Screwball! (SCREWBALL *dashes on right, breathless, with a package in his hands.*)

SCREWBALL: Unanimous, Joe! (*He takes a deep breath, then takes his place at end of line.*) Here—special delivery. (*He hands package to* GLIDER, *who hands it to next* LIZARD. *Each gives it a little shake, and listens to it.*)

GLIDER: It says "Handle with Care."

SINKER: It says "Perishable."

GROUNDER (*Looking under it*): It says "This Side Up." (*He turns it over.*)

SLIDER: It rolls like a round rock.

RIGHTY: Hm-m-m. It's postmarked from back East. That's mighty strange.

LEFTY: The handwriting looks sinister. It says "From you-know-who" on the label.

JOE: What can it be? Who do I know who's known as you-know-who? (*He opens box and holds up apple.*) An apple. Now I know who. Faithful Fenella. (*He sits down right.* LIZARDS *sit beside him.*)

LEFTY: Don't eat it, Joe.

RIGHTY: It might be rotten.

JOE: Fenella wouldn't give me a rotten apple. I'll just wipe it off before I eat it. (*He carefully polishes apple. Prop boy removes cactus.* JOE *and* LIZARDS *hold their positions on stage. Prop boy puts soda bottle down center.* FENELLA *enters through curtain center, as* GROUNDSKEEPER *enters down left. Both spy bottle at same instant.*)

FENELLA: Mine!

GROUNDSKEEPER: Mine! (*They tug at bottle.* FENELLA *manages to blow across the top twice. There is sound of two loud gusts of rushing wind. As* MIKE VIDEO *enters through curtain, center,* FENELLA *and* GROUNDSKEEPER *hold their positions, tugging at bottle.*)

MIKE VIDEO (*On microphone*): Ladies and gentlemen, what excitement! Until two seconds ago, Western Hemisphere, led by mighty Braggart McTaggart, had this series sewed up. It's the bottom of the ninth, Eastern Hemisphere is at bat, and there are two outs. It should be a shutout—the score is Western Hemisphere one, Eastern Hemisphere, zero. But there were a couple of cold gusts of wind, and Braggart McTaggart just seemed to fold up. He allowed runners at first, second, and third. The batter has three balls, no strikes, and now, the next pitch is coming up. The world is asking—why doesn't the manager put in a relief pitcher! (*Curtains open.*)

* * *

SETTING: *Same as Scene 1. Backdrop shows a crowded stadium, and scoreboard reads,* WESTERN HEMISPHERE—1, EASTERN HEMISPHERE—0.

AT RISE: ROOTERS *are seated up left and right. At third base,* RUNNER *stands ready to take off for home plate.* THIRD BASEMAN *hovers beside him. At home plate,* BATTER *holds bat up.* CATCHER *stands expectantly behind him, and* GHOST UMPIRE *stands up right, a mask concealing his face.* McTAGGART *wipes his face. Beside him is* SHADOW, *slumped over, as if very weak.* MIKE VIDEO *crosses down right.*

MCTAGGART (*To* SHADOW): Help me, blast you! Pour on the magic. You know I can't pitch for beans!

SHADOW: I can't. I'm getting weaker and weaker. Somebody must have found the magic soda bottle. I've got to sit down, Master. (*He totters to dugout and sits with his head in his hands.*)

UMPIRE: Play ball!

ROOTERS: Go, McTaggart, go! Go, McTaggart, go! (SIGNMAKER *puts out a sign reading,* PLAY BALL! MCTAGGART *winds up and drops ball.*)

ROOTERS: Boo-oo! Boo-oo!

MCTAGGART: Who said that! Who booed Braggart McTaggart! That does it. (*He throws down his mitt and stalks off down left.*) I quit!

MIKE VIDEO (*Into his mike, dramatically*): Ladies and gentlemen, this is absolutely the most dramatic moment in baseball history. Braggart McTaggart has walked off the pitcher's mound. If the Western Hemisphere does not replace McTaggart in three seconds, the game will be forfeited, and Eastern Hemisphere will win the World Series. Listen—even the Rooters are counting the seconds.

ROOTERS: One!

JOE (*Downstage*): I'm going to eat this apple. I don't care what anyone says. (*He stands, holding apple upraised as* LIZARDS *reach out their arms to him.*)

LIZARDS: No, Joe!

ROOTERS: Two! (FENELLA *tugs at bottle with all her might. She frees it and raises it to her lips.*)

FENELLA: Now—for the third and last time! (*She blows across the bottle. Sound of a loud rushing of wind.* LIZARDS *exit right.*)

ROOTERS: Three! (*Lights flicker on and off, then black out, and come up as* SHADOW *exits up left.* JOE *runs to mound, his hand with apple still upraised, as if he is ready to pitch.*)

UMPIRE: Play ball! (JOE *winds up and pitches apple.* BATTER *swings. Sound of slide whistle, followed by a loud pop.* ROOTERS *cheer and wave pennants.* SIGNMAKER *puts out a sign reading,*

SHUTOUT! THIRD BASEMAN *and* CATCHER *run to slap* JOE *on shoulders.* BATTER *and* RUNNER *exit up right, sadly.*)

MIKE VIDEO: What a moment! A young, unknown relief pitcher trapped the batter on the Eastern Hemisphere team into hitting a high fly. Western Hemisphere caught the fly easily, and wrapped up the World Series. What a moment! What a game! What a pitcher!

UMPIRE (*Lifting his mask*):
Hard work and fair play,
Always and ever win the day!
(ROOTERS *cheer and applaud.* THIRD BASEMAN *and* CATCHER *make a chair seat and lift* JOE, *bringing him down center.* FENELLA *hands* GROUNDSKEEPER *the bottle.*)

FENELLA: It's all yours now! (GROUNDSKEEPER *exits left.*)

JOE (*Waving his cap*): Thank you, Lizards. Thank you, fans. And thank you—Fenella! (*Players put him down.* FENELLA *hugs* JOE.)

FENELLA: You were wonderful, Joe. I have a surprise for you.

JOE: What?

FENELLA (*Bringing an apple out of her purse*): A juicy, red apple. (JOE *winks at her, and takes a bite out of apple. They exit up left,* MIKE VIDEO *crossing after them.*)

MIKE VIDEO: Wait—wait. A million fans want to hear from their new hero. (*Into microphone*) I'm sorry, folks, but the mysterious pitcher has just been carried away in triumph by one of his fans. However, here's the outfielder who caught that pop fly and saved the series for Western Hemisphere. (OUTFIELDER *enters down left.*) Tell the folks—how do you feel about that last amazing catch?

OUTFIELDER: Oh, the catch was fine, but . . . (*Hesitates, then holds up mitt*) how in the world did I get a mitt full of applesauce? (*Curtain, as* NARRATOR *enters from center curtain. He closes his book.*)

NARRATOR: And that is the story of Joe White and the Seven Lizards. If you think carefully, you may remember having heard it all, somewhere, before. Oh, yes. You may be wondering about what happened to Shadow, the evil genie. Listen! (*Sound of a bottle smashing*) Any more questions? Braggart

Hayloft with ladder against it is left. At right are six curtained horse stalls that serve as bedrooms for the family; each has a wooden name plaque over it. Table with odd chairs, couch, easy chair and chest of drawers with cracked mirror hanging over it complete the setting. A view of the countryside can be seen through open door, center.

AT RISE: JAMES HOLLOWAY, *wearing an artist's smock, stands at easel, alternately painting and dabbling at it.* JILL *is furiously polishing saddle.* PETER, *his clothes and hair sprinkled with hay, descends ladder from loft, a hen held firmly under his arm.* JENNIFER *stands in front of mirror, tying bow in her hair.* TOMMY *lies on stomach under couch with only his legs visible.*

PETER: I had an awful time catching this sneaky old hen. I wish she wouldn't come barging in here every time we open the barn door.

JILL: Poor Hannah! I expect she just wants to lay her eggs in the hayloft again. After all, it used to be hers until we chickens came here to roost.

JENNIFER (*Pouting*): We aren't chickens, even if I do look like one in this crazy old mirror. It makes my face all squiggly. I wish I had the one in the gold frame that hung over my dressing table at home.

JILL: Oh, Jennifer, hush—(*Glancing appreciatively toward her father, who paints on unheeding*) *This* is our home now, and it's great. After all, old Mr. Jimson lets us ride his horses and keep all the eggs Hannah lays in the barn. (PETER *places hen outside and shuts door.* TOMMY *wriggles into view.*)

TOMMY (*Shrieking, as he jumps to his feet*): I have him! I have him! (*He holds up a mouse by the tail.* JENNIFER *screams and leaps on a chair.*)

PETER (*Grinning*): This barn is certainly full of livestock! (MR. HOLLOWAY *paints on serenely, as* JENNIFER *continues to yell.*)

JILL: Jennifer, will you be quiet? It's just a mouse. And Tommy, hold him properly. How would you like to be suspended head down by the tail?

TOMMY (*Indignantly*): I haven't got a tail. (ROSEANNE *enters, carrying mail.*)

ROSEANNE (*Firmly*): Tommy, take that mouse outdoors at once, and let it go. (*Disgusted,* TOMMY *goes to door and lets mouse go.*) And Jennifer, get off that chair. It belonged to Great Aunt Clara, and it's an heirloom. (*To* MR. HOLLOWAY) Dad, I hope they weren't disturbing you.

MR. HOLLOWAY (*Vaguely, turning toward them*): Who—me? Oh, no, I don't think so, Roseanne, my dear. As a matter of fact, I was far away in Spain (*Pointing to painting*), in this lovely old castle by the sea. (ROSEANNE *looks at painting despairingly.*)

ROSEANNE: Dad, don't you think the summer people might buy your paintings more often if they had more—well, local color? Barns and New England countryside and things like that? (PETER *is removing hay from his hair and clothes and scattering it carelessly on the floor.* TOMMY, *attempting to perform somersaults, knocks over a number of canvases.* JENNIFER *is trying to turn mirror upside down.*)

MR. HOLLOWAY (*Oblivious to children, waving hands vaguely*): The studios and art shops are full of local color. One gets tired of looking at it—especially when the real thing is all around. But take a castle in Spain—ah, there is the stuff of dreams, of romance, of poetry for the soul!

ROSEANNE (*Sighing as she looks through mail*): People don't seem very romantic around here. All we get are bills . . . except this letter (*Holding out letter*) from Aunt Harriet. (MR. HOLLOWAY *looks up, startled, runs hand nervously through hair.*)

MR. HOLLOWAY: From Harriet? Now what? (*Takes letter and absentmindedly stuffs it into his pocket*)

ROSEANNE (*Patiently*): We'll never find out what she wants unless you read it.

MR. HOLLOWAY (*Looking pained*): Must I? We'd all probably be happier if I didn't, you know.

PETER: Dad, we don't mind if she calls you the black sheep of the family.

JENNIFER (*Throwing her arms around his neck*): We don't care if Uncle Brad is a Senator and Uncle Wilbur is a bank president.

JILL: And *we* love castles in Spain, even if they don't sell very well. (*Glaring at* ROSEANNE)

JENNIFER (*Bravely*): And living in a barn, even though it is full of—of livestock!

MR. HOLLOWAY (*Capitulating*): Oh, all right. (*Removing letter from his pocket*) You may read it, Roseanne, if you think we must. I will continue with my painting while the light is right. (*Children huddle around* ROSEANNE, *as she tears open envelope.*)

ROSEANNE (*Reading aloud*): "Dear James, I trust that you will be pleased to hear that I am coming for a visit. (*Children groan.*) Now that I am a widow, I can turn my attention to the welfare of my nieces and nephews, who are sorely in need of it. (MR. HOLLOWAY *stops painting.*) If I find them intelligent, obedient, and respectful, I shall take them back to my Boston townhouse in the fall to live with me (*Children groan again.*), where they can be brought up properly and do credit to the family name. Your sister, Harriet." (*Children look dismayed.*)

MR. HOLLOWAY (*Beginning to pace back and forth*): You see, I told you we'd be sorry if you read it, Roseanne.

ROSEANNE: But, Dad, we had to know she was coming. Now we can plan for this—this emergency properly. (MR. HOLLOWAY *shrugs unhappily and returns to easel.*)

JILL (*Scornfully*): This ought to be easy. We'll just be as stupid, disobedient, and disrespectful as possible.

PETER: We'll let Hannah lay her eggs in the hayloft whenever she feels like it and cackle proudly even if it's the middle of the night.

TOMMY: And I'll put a mouse in Aunt Harriet's bed.

ROSEANNE (*Sternly*): You'll do no such thing, any of you! You'll act the way Mother would want you to if she were alive and be a credit to Dad's upbringing.

JENNIFER (*Virtuously*): I wouldn't want to be naughty. Aunt Harriet always sends me pretty clothes at Christmas and on my birthday. (*Smoothing down ruffles on her dress with obvious satisfaction*)

ROSEANNE: Jennifer's right. We should be grateful for all the nice things Aunt Harriet *has* done for us. Her intentions are good.

JILL (*Dismayed*): But Roseanne, we're going to fall right into her trap if we act that way. Being grateful and everything.

ROSEANNE: I don't think so. (*In an adult manner*) Virtue is its own reward, children. When she sees what a good job Dad is doing, she will probably go home satisfied.

PETER (*Ominously*): But suppose she isn't satisfied—what then?

TOMMY: Yeah—what then?

JILL (*Darkly*): Aunt Harriet never gives up.

PETER: That's right. We'd better have another plan ready, just in case.

ROSEANNE (*Coldly*): Have you any suggestions? (PETER *glances toward* MR. HOLLOWAY, *who stares distractedly out window. He beckons children to him.*)

PETER (*Huskily*): Sure, I have an idea. What is the one thing in the world Aunt Harriet is afraid of?

JILL (*Triumphantly*): I know—ghosts!

PETER: Exactly—ghosts!

JENNIFER (*Fearfully*): G-g-ghosts?

TOMMY (*Squealing*): Ghosts!

ROSEANNE (*Thoughtfully*): That's true. She won't stay in a place that's supposed to be haunted, ever since she and Uncle Leo were frightened out of their beds by a ghost in an old English manor house. But unfortunately, there *are* no ghosts in our barn.

PETER: That's easily solved. We'll provide our own—with winding sheets and dragging chains and mysterious music in the dead of night. (*He picks up a flute from chest and blows a few weird notes.*)

ROSEANNE (*Dubiously*): I wouldn't want to frighten Aunt Harriet. That wouldn't be nice at all.

PETER: Don't worry. We'll be very easy on her—just a teeny weeny little ghost.

TOMMY (*Jumping up and down*): I want to be a teeny weeny little ghost and wear a sheet!

JENNIFER (*Romantically*): I could be the ghost of the Indian maiden who jumped to her death from Lover's Leap up by the lake.

PETER (*Interrupting*): Now, hold on. We can't overdo this thing or Aunt Harriet will catch on. We must make careful plans.

ROSEANNE: If only this barn were really haunted—not that I believe in ghosts, of course.

MR. HOLLOWAY (*Turning*): Do you know, children, that this castle I'm painting is an ancient one that really exists on an island off the coast of Spain? (*Turns to look at painting*) I visited it once, and since then I've carried the picture of it in my mind. Today it is not much more than a crumbling ruin. . . . Nobody has lived in it for many years because it's rumored to be haunted.

JILL: Really and truly haunted?

TOMMY: By a teeny weeny little ghost, Daddy?

JENNIFER: Of course not, silly. (*Dreamily*) Probably by a beautiful young maiden.

MR. HOLLOWAY: You're right, Jennifer. The story goes that a lovely, dark-eyed Spanish princess named Felicia was slain there by a jealous suitor and was doomed to roam in search of her true love through the years.

JENNIFER (*Dreamily*): It's far more romantic than the legend of the Indian maid.

ROSEANNE: I must admit it makes the picture come to life, Dad. (*In surprise*) Why, I can almost see Felicia with a lace mantilla over her head, standing in the shadows of that deep window. (*She goes over and peers closely at painting, then steps back, looking puzzled.*) I guess I only imagined it. How strange!

MR. HOLLOWAY: Not so strange. Many people visiting the old castle have thought they saw Felicia, only to find her melting into the shadows when they approached more closely. If she comes to haunt my painting, so much the better for me—it will make it all the more valuable. I'll probably sell it for a great deal of money one of these days. And then we can all go and live in a castle of our own in Spain. (*He resumes his painting.*)

ROSEANNE (*Softly, shaking her head*): Poor Dad!

PETER: Just the same, it's wonderful how he gave us such a great idea without even realizing it.

JILL: You could say our barn is really haunted now, couldn't you?

We'd just sort of be helping Felicia out if we ghosted for her. (JENNIFER *runs to chest of drawers and removes white lace scarf, which she throws fetchingly over her head, posing with hands on hips like a Spanish dancer.*)

ROSEANNE (*Firmly*): Nevertheless, we must try my plan first. Better to win by fair means than foul. We'll begin by giving the barn a thorough cleaning. (*Children groan.*)

JILL (*Plaintively*): But I have to give Black Prince a rubdown.

PETER: And I promised Johnny Weaver I'd go fishing with him.

JENNIFER: And I simply must wash my hair. I'm sure Felicia must have had gorgeous, silken locks.

TOMMY (*Edging toward door*): I guess I'd better go find that sneaky old hen before she tries to get into the barn again.

ROSEANNE (*Calmly*): Very well. In that case, I'll go lie in the hammock under the apple tree and read a book. (*Children regard her in open-mouthed astonishment.*)

JILL: But—but, Roseanne, we can't have Aunt Harriet come and find the place in such a mess!

PETER (*Indignantly*): I should say not. Why, she'd blame it all on poor Dad. (*He grabs broom and begins sweeping.*)

JENNIFER: I'm certainly not going to let Daddy down. (*She flings off scarf, puts on apron that is hanging on chair, starts picking up.*)

TOMMY: Neither am I. I want to help, too. (ROSEANNE *smiles.*)

JILL : Come on, we'll all pitch in. (*Dramatically*) A change of scene must now take place or the Holloway family will all lose face. (*Quick curtain*)

* * * * *

SCENE 2

TIME: *Late evening the following day.*

AT RISE: *Barn looks neat and attractive, with curtains at smaller window and drawn burlap drapes at large studio window. Table has white cloth and vase of flowers on it. Canvases have been neatly stacked beneath loft and one on easel covered from view.* MR. HOLLOWAY'S *plaque has been replaced by one labeled*

AUNT HARRIET, *and his plaque hangs from loft. Children are seated around table in nightclothes and bathrobes, with open books propped up in front of them.* AUNT HARRIET, *also in night attire, is striding back and forth.*

AUNT HARRIET: A fine kettle of fish—human beings sleeping in horse stalls, and your father planning to bed down in the hay like a tramp when he comes in from his noctural wanderings. Very likely that dreadful hen will find her way up there, too.

JILL (*Saucily*): Well, we can always be sure of having fresh eggs, Aunt Harriet!

AUNT HARRIET: Don't be impudent, Jill, and attend to the geography lesson I assigned you, or you will never be able to meet the Boston school requirements in the fall. It's high time I took charge of you.

JENNIFER (*Anxiously*): But Aunt Harriet, we don't need to meet the Boston school requirements here in Lindale. (AUNT HARRIET'S *expression softens as she regards* JENNIFER *and strokes her hair fondly.*)

AUNT HARRIET: Ah, but you will, dear, when you come to the city to live with me. Wait till you see the charming room I have for you, Jenny, all in pink and white, with a frilly dressing table and a gilt-edged mirror. And a closet big enough to hold lots and lots of pretty dresses. (JENNIFER *heaves a long sigh.*)

ROSEANNE (*Firmly*): We are quite happy where we are, Aunt Harriet. We hoped you'd be pleased with the way Dad was bringing us up.

JENNIFER (*Resolutely*): We couldn't bear to be separated from Daddy, Auntie.

AUNT HARRIET: Nonsense—you're too young to know what's good for you. No Holloway has ever lived in a barn.

PETER: Dad's proud of us, and that's what counts.

TOMMY: Pretty soon we're going to live in an old castle in Spain, aren't we, Roseanne? Daddy said so.

AUNT HARRIET: A castle in Spain, indeed! That sounds like another one of your father's foolish dreams.

JENNIFER: Not foolish, Aunt Harriet. Dreams of romance, of— of—(*Trying to remember her father's words*) of poetry for the soul!

AUNT HARRIET: Poetry for the soul—fiddlesticks!

JILL (*Thoughtfully*): I don't suppose you'd know anything about that, would you, Aunt Harriet?

AUNT HARRIET (*Sharply*): Well now, I wouldn't say that. When I was a girl I was once courted by a young man with poetical leanings. He used to call me (*A little wistfully*) his dark-eyed señorita, and threatened to lock me up in the castle of his heart. (*Tartly*) Is that romantic enough for you?

JENNIFER (*Wide-eyed*): I never knew Uncle Leo was a poet!

AUNT HARRIET: Dear me, not him, child. Your uncle was a solid citizen, not a penniless scribbler. My parents soon made me see the error of my ways.

JENNIFER (*Sadly*): What happened to the poet, Aunt Harriet? Did he pine away?

AUNT HARRIET (*Snapping*): He did not. He married and tried to raise a family on pipe dreams—like your father.

PETER (*Eagerly*): The painting Dad's working on now is no pipe dream. He expects to be offered a great deal of money for it.

JILL (*Mysteriously*): You see, it has something extra special about it.

AUNT HARRIET (*Skeptically*): Indeed! Is that why he keeps it so carefully covered?

ROSEANNE: In a way—yes. Would you like to see it?

AUNT HARRIET: I certainly would. I am consumed with curiosity. (ROSEANNE *removes covering as others watch eagerly. Disdainfully; shaking her head*) I might have known—just another of his tumble-down castles—with no proper plumbing, of course.

ROSEANNE: There's more to it than meets the eye, Aunt Harriet.

AUNT HARRIET (*Crossly*): What is so special about it, may I ask?

PETER: You can sense it. Just keep looking at it, Auntie.

AUNT HARRIET (*Looking at painting; hesitantly*): Well, I must admit I didn't notice that shadowy figure in the window at first. Why, it almost looks as if it were moving! How ridiculous! (*Straightening up*) I must be imagining things.

JILL: Oh, but you're not!

TOMMY: Don't be scared, Aunt Harriet—it's only a teeny weeny ghost.

JENNIFER (*Dreamily*): The ghost of a beautiful Spanish princess.

AUNT HARRIET: A ghost—nonsense. A trick of the lantern light, I expect. (*Stepping closer to painting*) There now, just as I thought. I can't see the ghost—er, I mean, the shadow—now at all!

PETER: That's a habit ghosts have—appearing and disappearing!

JILL (*Innocently*): You aren't afraid of ghosts, are you, Aunt Harriet? (PETER *slips off right, unnoticed.*)

AUNT HARRIET: Certainly not! Besides, whoever heard of a ghost haunting a painting? (*Suddenly, picture is jerked off easel and lands on floor. This is accomplished by a wire attached to lower corner that runs offstage.* AUNT HARRIET *shrieks and* JENNIFER *giggles hysterically.*)

JILL (*Calmly; replacing painting*): Don't worry, Auntie. Things like this happen all the time. We're quite used to them. (PETER *slips back on stage.*)

AUNT HARRIET (*Sharply*): Things like what?

JILL (*Shrugging*): Things one can't account for.

PETER: Things that come and go in the night—strains of music—

JENNIFER (*Dramatically*): The sights of a beautiful maiden!

TOMMY: Things that squeak!

ROSEANNE (*Noticing that* AUNT HARRIET *is alarmed*): Perhaps we'd better go back to our geography lesson. (*Soothingly*) We wouldn't want to frighten Aunt Harriet, would we?

ALL: Oh, no!

TOMMY: Anyway, it's only a teeny weeny little ghost, Auntie.

AUNT HARRIET: I've heard quite enough about ghosts, though I dare say it's James's fault for putting such fanciful ideas into your heads. Best to cover the canvas again before your imaginations completely run away with you.

PETER (*Darkly*): We've found out that it doesn't do much good to cover it, Aunt. The—the presence makes itself felt whether you can see it or not.

AUNT HARRIET (*Throwing her hands up in exasperation*): Here we go again. I can see we'll get no more geography done tonight. So, off to bed, all of you. (*Children move slowly to their stalls, grinning slyly. They close curtains.* AUNT HARRIET *puts out lantern, leaving only one on near painting. She goes into her stall and draws curtains. Curtains at smaller window are drawn aside, and* SEÑOR JOSÉ GARCIA *leaps nimbly into room and approaches easel on tiptoe. As he is about to lift covering, faint, eerie notes on a flute are heard. Startled, he conceals himself behind drapes at studio window.* AUNT HARRIET *steps out of her stall, her face smeared with cold cream. She peers around nervously.*) This place gives me the creeps. I could swear I heard music—ghostly music. (*With a shudder*) There, I've let them put ideas into my head now. I almost wish I were back in Boston in my own bed, but I'm not one to turn my back selfishly when duty calls. (*She strides to painting and boldly whips off cover.*) Ghosts—hah! (*Walks determindedly back to her stall and jerks curtain closed.* SEÑOR GARCIA *emerges from behind drapes and studies painting eagerly.*)

SEÑOR GARCIA (*With Spanish accent*): Si, it is the truth—she is there waiting for me in the shadows, just as my astrologer foretold. Ah, Felicia, my beautiful señorita, can it be that we are really to meet again after all these centuries? Give me some sign, I implore you. (*A long shuddering sigh is heard, and* SEÑOR GARCIA *dodges behind drapes again, as* AUNT HARRIET *sticks her head out from stall.*)

AUNT HARRIET (*Nervously*): Who—who's there?

JILL (*Peering out*): Did you call, Auntie?

AUNT HARRIET: I thought I heard voices!

JILL: Oh, don't let that bother you, Aunt Harriet. We all hear them now and then. We call them The Voices that Pass in the Night . . . instead of ships, you know.

AUNT HARRIET: Er—ah, yes—Ships that Pass in the Night—I mean Voices. Good—good night, Jill.

JILL: Good night, Auntie. (*They withdraw.* SEÑOR GARCIA *emerges again.*)

SEÑOR GARCIA (*Looking puzzled*): This is a strange household—people that sleep in horse stalls (*Shrugging expressively*), and Ships that Pass in the Night, and—(*Looking at painting closely*) miracles! Ah, Felicia, my little dove (*Waving his finger roguishly*), do not try to play hide and seek with José. Come out, come out, wherever you are. (JENNIFER *emerges from her stall, wrapped in a sheet with lace scarf over head and shoulders. She moves stiffly, arms extended out in front of her, her eyes fixed straight ahead as if sleepwalking.* SEÑOR GARCIA *stares at her, his mouth agape. He claps his hand to his head.*) No! Can this be Felicia? How the graveyard has changed her! (*As* JENNIFER *approaches him, he dodges behind curtain. She circles around easel and heads back to her stall.* AUNT HARRIET *steps out just in time to catch a glimpse of* JENNIFER, *gives shriek of terror and falls on the floor in a faint.* SEÑOR GARCIA *comes out from behind curtain, steps gingerly over her body and faces audience.*) What a mess! Can it be that my astrologer has made a mistake? For centuries the stars have predicted our meeting—mine and Felicia's. But now I find she is not my type! (*Raising his hands toward heaven*) What am I to do? (TOMMY, *dressed as a ghost, steps out of his stall.* SEÑOR GARCIA *stumbles backward in astonishment.*) Not another—it is too much!

TOMMY: Don't be scared, mister. I'm just a teeny weeny little ghost. Who are you?

SEÑOR GARCIA: It is what I am beginning to ask myself. (MR. HOLLOWAY *enters, wearing smock, carrying his palette and paint box under his arm.* TOMMY *hides behind drapes.*)

MR. HOLLOWAY (*Absent-mindedly*): Good evening, sir, good evening. A beautiful night for painting beneath the stars.

SEÑOR GARCIA: Now I have heard everything! Painting beneath the stars in the dead of night! It is even worse than I thought. I am trapped in a madhouse.

MR. HOLLOWAY: Oh, no, you may leave any time you like. The door is unlocked. (*Seeing* AUNT HARRIET *on floor*) Ah, now what has happened to dear Harriet?

SEÑOR GARCIA (*Franctically*): I had nothing to do with it, señor, I assure you. She fainted, and I can hardly blame her. I feel a little faint myself.

MR. HOLLOWAY (*Observing him closely*): Well, I can see why. That costume does look a trifle warm for this time of year. A fancy party in the village, I presume?

SEÑOR GARCIA (*Drawing himself up haughtily*): I am Señor José Garcia, Spain's most famous bullfighter, and the descendant of an illustrious family. (*He doffs his matador's cap and makes a sweeping bow.*)

MR. HOLLOWAY (*Chuckling*): Oh, you're very good! You must have been the hit of the party.

SEÑOR GARCIA (*Restraining himself*): You do not understand what I say, señor. I am who I say I am—(*Aside; desperately*) at least I think I am! I came here from Spain on a good will tour. (*Takes papers from pocket and hands them to* MR. HOLLOWAY.) Here are my credentials.

MR. HOLLOWAY (*Perusing papers; bewildered*): But why are you including me—a poor struggling artist—on your tour?

SEÑOR GARCIA: It is because of you I am here. My astrologer has foretold that the painting of the ancient castle on your easel holds the secret to my past and future. If the prophecy is correct, I am willing to pay a great deal of money to possess it. It is why I have come secretly like a thief in the night to ascertain the truth of it before making an offer. But—alas— (*Despairingly, he covers his face.*)

MR. HOLLOWAY (*Sighing*): It did not come up to your expectations, señor?

SEÑOR GARCIA (*Excitedly*): It more than came up to my expectations, señor—it came alive! The spirit of Felicia, the ghost of my true love, she who was to bring me luck in the bull ring, she is—alas! What can I say? (*JENNIFER appears again, sleepwalking.*) There, you see what I mean, señor, she is a mere child! I would have to watch out for her instead of attending to my good fortune.

MR. HOLLOWAY (*Laughing*): Why, that is my daughter Jennifer. She frequently walks in her sleep. (*JENNIFER rubs her eyes, stretches and yawns.*)

SEÑOR GARCIA (*Dazed*): Wearing a wedding gown, señor, and the veil of a bride?

TOMMY (*Coming out from behind drapes*): Mr. Bullfighter, these are just sheets from our beds. We're not really ghosts. We just wanted to scare Aunt Harriet.

MR. HOLLOWAY (*Looking at* HARRIET; *amused*): Well, you succeeded.

SEÑOR GARCIA (*Muttering*): A madhouse! But then, all artists are mad, and the same must be true of their families. (*Points toward painting*) Ah, my poor Felicia, what a ghastly mistake to have made. My most humble apologies. But you will soon be mine, never fear. (*Other children have gathered on stage.*) I will make you an offer, señor. What do you say to five thousand dollars for your painting, eh?

MR. HOLLOWAY: (*Looking suddenly very startled*): Did he say—five—thousand dollars?

CHILDREN (*Together*): Five—thousand—dollars!

SEÑOR GARCIA (*Hastily, appearing to mistake their astonishment*): You are right, señor—it is not enough. I beg a thousand pardons. Your painting is worth at least ten thousand dollars. When I meet the angry bull, I must have all the good fortune I can possess. (*Pleadingly*) Will you accept ten, señor, ten thousand dollars? See, I have my checkbook and pen right here. (*Fishing them out of his sash*) And you have already seen my credentials.

MR. HOLLOWAY: Ten thousand dollars! (*He falls into faint beside AUNT HARRIET.*)

AUNT HARRIET (*Sitting up abruptly*): He accepts, señor. Make the check payable to my favorite brother (*Dramatically*), James Sylvester Holloway! (*She leaps nimbly to her feet and stands over him at table as he writes check.*)

PETER: Dad's no longer the black sheep of the family.

JILL: He's more famous than Uncle Brad or Uncle Wilbur! (*As children talk excitedly, SEÑOR GARCIA carries painting off.*)

ROSEANNE (*Reproachfully*): Isn't anyone thinking of poor Dad? Somebody get a glass of water, quick! (*JILL gets pitcher from chest of drawers and pours glass.*)

AUNT HARRIET (*To JILL*): Give me that water, child. I'll bring him around in short order. (*She flings water in MR. HOLLOWAY's face. He sits up abruptly, shaking water from head.*)

MR. HOLLOWAY (*Dazed*): What happened?

ROSEANNE (*Soothingly*): Are you all right, Dad? You fainted. (*Children help him up.*)

PETER: I guess I would have fainted, too, if I had been offered ten thousand dollars.

AUNT HARRIET (*In businesslike tone*): Nonsense—a great artist like your father has to expect rich rewards for his labors. If it had not been for my presence of mind, heaven knows what might have happened. Now, off to bed, everyone. We will have to be up extra early in the morning to study our geography. (*Children groan.*) The geography of Spain, of course. We will all need to know everything there is to know about *that* country, won't we? (MR. HOLLOWAY *and his children cheer.*) As for me, I will go to Spain as good will ambassador from the United States. Of course (*Smirking*), I shall consider it my duty to follow the bullfights—all the best ones, that is! (*She sings the words, "Toreador—toreador," from the opera "Carmen," and the children, catching the spirit, join in noisily as curtain falls.*)

THE END

Society Page

by Joan and Pearl Allred

Cynical newspaperwoman changes her mind about love. . . .

Characters

VIOLET PEMBERTON, *society editor*
JANICA REED, *her assistant*
FRANCIE GERBER, *recent bride*
MRS. JESPERSON, *her mother*
JIMMY HARPER, *photographer*
BARBARA LAKE, *businesswoman*
SALLY SUMNER, *socialite*
CLIFTON DWYER, *her fiancé*

SETTING: *Cluttered office of a newspaper society department. Two large desks stand at center, each with a chair, wastebasket overflowing with papers. On desk are phone, jars of glue, word processor or typewriter, wire basket with papers and large photos. There are two chairs near desks. Door right leads outside, door up left with sign on it reading* NO ADMITTANCE, *leads to darkroom. Door down left opens into small office. Water cooler is up left.*

AT RISE: JANICA REED *sits at one desk, busily typing;* VIOLET PEMBERTON *sits at other desk talking on phone and taking notes on a pad.*

VIOLET (*On phone*): No, of course not. Naturally you don't want to cause any hurt feelings, so we won't mention how many guests came. Why don't we say "a few intimate friends"—that way nobody will be upset about being left out . . . How does this sound: "Japanese lanterns and masses of roses formed a gala summer setting when Dr. and Mrs. Howard Norbert entertained for a few intimate friends at their charming home in Hillcrest Heights last Thursday evening . . ." Good . . . Oh, yes, of course. We'll give it a good position at the top of the column. (*While* VIOLET *is on the phone,* FRANCIE GERBER *and* MRS. JESPERSON *enter and walk toward center right.*)

JANICA (*Looking up*): May I help you?

MRS. JESPERSON: Are you the society editor?

JANICA (*Gesturing toward* VIOLET): Ms. Pemberton is on the phone right now. I'm her assistant. How can I help you?

MRS. JESPERSON (*Suspiciously*): Well—(*She gropes through purse and takes out small, dog-eared picture.*) We want to put this photo in the Sunday paper. (*Hands picture to* JANICA.)

JANICA: I see. Won't you sit down? (FRANCIE *and* MRS. JESPERSON *sit.* JANICA *examines picture closely.*) Hm-m. It's a little dark. Is that the bride to the left?

MRS. JESPERSON (*Irritated*): Well, it's not the bridgegroom.

JANICE (*Peering closely at picture*): I see the bridegroom now, behind a basket of ferns.

FRANCIE: My husband's cousin took the pictures. He does nice work, but it was a little dark in the church.

JANICA (*Smiling; to* FRANCIE): You're the new bride, then?

FRANCIE: Yes.

JANICA: Well, we'll see what the photo lab can do with this, but I can't promise it will be very clear. Do you have the wedding details written down? (MRS. JEFFERSON *fumbles through her purse again and hands scrap of paper to* JANICA, *who reads.*) "In one of the most gorgeous affairs of the season, Frances Jesperson, daughter of Mr. and Mrs. Joe Jesperson, married

Mr. Vern Gerber of this city." (*Looks up*) Do you want to include the names of the bridegroom's parents?

FRANCIE (*Accusingly*): See, Mother, I told you they'd want to know that.

MRS. JESPERSON: Well, don't come crying to me about it, Francie. It's your own fault for not finding out the details before Vern went off on his fishing trip.

JANICA (*Surprised*): He went on a fishing trip right after his marriage?

MRS. JESPERSON: Yes. He said he had to recover from the wedding. (*To* FRANCIE) Now, think hard, Francie. Try to remember if Vern ever said anything about his parents.

FRANCIE: I know he must have mentioned them, but it slipped my mind. (*Hopefully*) He used to live in Nebraska. (*To* JANICA) Do you know anyone in Nebraska?

JANICA: I'm afraid not.

MRS. JESPERSON: Never mind. Just leave them out.

JANICA: Whatever you like. (*Looks at paper again*) Everything else seems to be here. (FRANCIE *and* MRS. JESPERSON *rise.*) Congratulations, Mrs. Gerber. (FRANCIE *smiles and exits with her mother.* JANICA *shakes her head.*) I give that marriage one month.

VIOLET (*Hanging up phone*): You know, Janica, we have twenty-four weddings already this week. I can't imagine where on earth we'll find the space to put all the announcements. June is such a lovely, romantic month, but the brides keep us almost too busy to enjoy it. (*Sighs*)

JANICA: Romantic! Wait till next year—all these starry-eyed brides will realizing they made a big mistake.

VIOLET: Now, Janica. Don't be so cynical!

JANICA (*Laughing*): Oh, you're impossible, Violet. You must have written up five thousand weddings since you came on the society staff of this paper, and you still get excited over an engagement.

VIOLET: I like to see people happy. Especially young people. (*Thumbs through papers*) What do you think of this picture for the first page of your section? (*Holds up large sheet of paper*)

Pine View Lake in the background, with that nice young Bob
Turner helping Laurel Evans into the canoe.

JANICA: I thought you were using Marsha Walker in that spot.
(*Warningly*) Her mother isn't going to like this. I hear she
handpicked Bob long ago, and she hasn't let him out of her
sight since he got home from Yale.

VIOLET: You're telling me! But I don't care, Marsha's had her
share of the limelight and I'm going to focus a little on Laurel.
She's such a dear—and much more Bob's type than Marsha.
(*Dreamily*) Who knows? Pine View on a Sunday afternoon—
all that scenery—nice boy—pretty girl—

JANICA (*Laughing*): Violet, you're incorrigible!

VIOLET (*Starting to dial phone*): I don't believe in leaving things
to chance. (*Into phone*) Hello, Ruby? . . . Violet Pemberton
here. How are you? . . . Oh, you have the lists ready. Good.
(*Gets pad and pencil*) O.K. Shoot. (*She continues to talk on
phone, as* JIMMY *enters, carrying some galley proofs, camera
tripod, and other photographic equipment, which he sets on
floor, then puts pile of galleys on* JANICA'*s desk.*)

JIMMY (*Sitting next to desk*): Just a few galleys. They're not half
pretty enough for you. I wish I could afford emeralds.

JANICA: They're beautiful, Jimmy dear. Just the kind of galleys
I've always wanted. (*Sighs*) As you can plainly see, I'm surrounded with work this morning, so please don't try to distract
me. This is June, the season of love and romance and marriage—and nervous breakdowns in the society department.

JIMMY: Don't worry. In fact, I'm on my way to an important
assignment right now. (*Pats camera*) But I stopped by to con-
tribute a little story for your Sunday page.

JANICA (*Groaning*): Not another wedding!

JIMMY: Just an engagement. Put a piece of paper in your typewriter and I'll dictate it. (*She does so. He stands, walks
around, and looks over her shoulder.*) "The season's loveliest
and most radiant bride—"

JANICA: Oh, stop. They all begin that way.

JIMMY: You're interrupting my train of thought. (*Clears throat,
then resumes*) "The season's loveliest and most radiant bride

(*Pause*) will exchange vows at the end of the month." (*Pauses while* JANICA *types*) Got that?

JANICA: Yes. Go ahead.

JIMMY: "Friends learned today (JANICA *resumes typing.*) of the engagement of Janica Reed to James C. Harper, Jr. (JANICA *abruptly stops typing, glares at* JIMMY, *who continues.*) Announcement is made by the parents of the bride-elect, Mrs. and Mrs. —" (*Suddenly*) Hey! why did you stop?

JANICA: Oh, Jimmy, you lunatic! (*Snatches paper from typewriter, crumples it, and throws it in wastebasket*) You left out one important thing. Quote, "This announcement comes as a total surprise to Ms. Reed, who has not said 'yes'!" Unquote.

JIMMY: A mere formality.

JANICA: Jimmy, please get this straight. I have no intention of becoming a bride, yours or anyone else's, this year, or next year, or maybe any year.

JIMMY (*Complaining*): Why are you so uncooperative? I feel extremely engaged. But there should be two of us.

JANICA: Jimmy, you need to find some sweet, young girl who hasn't been over-exposed to love and youth and spring. (*Turns away, puts fresh sheet of paper in typewriter, and resumes work, ignoring* JIMMY. VIOLET *hangs up phone, greets* JIMMY.)

VIOLET: Hello, Jimmy. How are you?

JIMMY: Fine, thanks, Violet. Only I'm not gaining any ground with your assistant here. (*Strikes romantic pose*) What she feels for me isn't love!

JANICA (*Primly*): It's a much more stable emotion, Jimmy.

JIMMY: Don't tell me. (*With exaggerated innocence*) Could it be friendship?

VIOLET: Friendship often blossoms into you-know-what. (*Lowering her voice*) Janica's allergic to the word *love*. All my assistants get that way in June.

JIMMY: Well, I'll work on her, Vi. Do you want to know something in strict confidence? That unyielding woman over there has done things to me.

VIOLET (*Amused*): Like what, Jimmy?

JIMMY: It used to be that just the mention of the word "commit-

ment" would start me hitting the trail. But since I met Janica,
I'm a changed man. All I can think of is a house and garden
and white picket fence and everything that goes with it.

VIOLET (*Laughing*): June's got you, too, Jimmy!

JANICA (*Plaintively*): Why don't you just steal quietly away,
Jimmy? I've got to concentrate on my hearts and flowers.

JIMMY: I will if you'll give me one little bit of encouragement.

JANICA (*Firmly*): The answer is no!

JIMMY (*Sighing*): I was afraid you'd say that. Well, so long. (*He
waves, then saunters out, whistling cheerfully.*)

VIOLET: There's something about Jimmy you don't appreciate,
Janica.

JANICA (*Absently*): What?

VIOLET: Oh, I don't know. Maybe it's the way he combs his hair, or
the way he sort of lopes when he walks. (*Dreamily*) He makes
me think of somebody I knew once. (*Pause*) A long time ago, of
course. He didn't believe in careers for women, and I was
determined I'd prove I could resist him. (*Dryly*) I did.

JANICA (*Briskly*): And a good thing, too. Instead of being tied
down, here you are: a happy, well-balanced individual, able to
do what you want, when and where you want, and with whom
you want. Nobody to tie you down.

VIOLET (*Wistfully*): Janica, you're right about that. Nobody at all.

JANICA: That's for me—the free life. I'm not going to let senti-
mentality lead me into any traps.

VIOLET: How old are you, Janica?

JANICA: Twenty-one. Old enough to follow a good example when
I see one—and this department is full of good examples.
(*Phone rings and she answers.*) Society. (*Long pause*) Is it an
article we already have, Mrs. Snyder? . . . You'd just like a
correction? . . . All right. (*Talking as she writes*) "Ms. Lulu
Snyder will marry David H. Butler on June 21." That's instead
of "Ms. Lulu Snyder will marry J. G. Welthorpe," right? . . .
Oh, think nothing of it. Every woman has a right to change
her mind. Goodbye, Mrs. Snyder. (*Hangs up*) Out with
Welthorpe, in with Butler!

VIOLET (*Gathering up papers*): Janica, will you hold the fort for a
few minutes? I'm expecting Barbara Lake.

JANICA: Oh, is Barbara back in town?

VIOLET: Yes, she just came back yesterday. (*Rummaging through papers on desk*) Now, where did I put those proofs? Oh, here they are. (*Pauses and looks at watch*) Oh, no! I completely forgot that Sally Ann Sumner and her fiancé are due here any minute to tell me the plans for their wedding. Hm-m. That could be awkward.

JANICA: Why? I can talk to Barbara till you're through.

VIOLET: That's not the point. Clifton Dwyer, Sally's fiancé, was practically engaged to Barbara before she went East to study music. Everyone says she never got over him.

JANICA: Oh, Vi, you know how the people in this town exaggerate. Besides, Barbara's not the type to pine over a man.

VIOLET: Don't be so sure. If ever I saw two people simply *made* for each other, it's Cliff and Barbara.

JANICA (*Wryly*): Arranged in heaven, I suppose.

VIOLET: I mean it. Here's Cliff Dwyer, within a year of his Ph.D., and you watch—if he marries Sally Sumner, he'll never get his degree.

JANICA: Why not?

VIOLET: Sally Sumner's a spoiled brat. She wanted Cliff only because he was a change from her country club set, and he was a challenge for her. The idea of Sally as a professor's wife is ridiculous.

JANICA: What can you to do about it?

VIOLET (*Sighing*): Nothing, I suppose. But, it's a shame. All Sally wants is novelty—and Cliff's a novelty to her.

JANICA: Well, it's their affair, not ours.

VIOLET (*Sighing*): You're right, Janica. The announcement's practically in the paper. If only Barbara had come home sooner. (*Shakes her head*) I'm afraid it's too late now to do anything.

JANICA (*Suspiciously*): Violet Pemberton! I believe you deliberately planned this meeting.

VIOLET (*Innocently*): Who me? I swear it's pure coincidence. But if they do just sort of—well, happen to run into each other here, be tactful, won't you?

JANICA: Tact, she says! (*Goes to water cooler for drink, stands with her back to exit as* BARBARA LAKE *enters,* JANICA *turns and sees her.*) Barbara, you look wonderful! (*They shake hands.*)

BARBARA: If I do, it's because I've just had my first vacation in three years. (*Laughingly*) But now it's back to the salt mines.

JANICA: I think it's great that you're opening a music studio here.

BARBARA: Thanks, Janica. Keep you fingers crossed for me, will you?

JANICA: I certainly will.

BARBARA (*Looking around*): Is Violet around? She was going to do a piece on me—"Local girl makes good," that sort of thing.

JANICA: She'll be back in a minute. Will you sit down? (BARBARA *sits.* JANICA *starts straightening papers on desk.*) Brides! June brides!

BARBARA: Is anyone I know taking the fatal step?

JANICA: Well, let me see, Margaret Blaine—did you know her? Oh, and Patricia Lester.

BARBARA: I know Patricia.

JANICA: And, of course, you've heard about the big Sumner splurge next week.

BARBARA: No, I haven't.

JANICA: Sally Sumner is marrying Clifton Dwyer.

BARBARA: Oh. (*Uncomfortable pause*) I didn't know it was final. I used to date Clifton—but, of course, that was a long time ago. High school romance.

JANICA: Actually, Sally and Clifton are due here any time now, Violet tells me.

BARBARA (*Hastily*): In that case I think I really should come back another time. (*Gets up, as* VIOLET *enters*)

VIOLET (*Cordially*): Barbara Lake! (*Grasping her by the arm*) Come right over here and tell me all about yourself. We're quite excited about your new venture, and I'm giving you a good spot in Sunday's paper, even if I have to throw out a bride to do it.

JANICA: Don't believe her, Barbara. If anyone threw out a bridal picture around here, it'd have to be over Vi's dead body. (*All laugh.*)

VIOLET: I have some of the facts already—musical training at Julliard . . . a year in Paris . . .

BARBARA: Let's not make it sound too glamorous, Vi. People might expect too much from me.

VIOLET: You're too modest, Barbara. Why don't we go into my private office so we can talk without being interrupted. (*They exit down left. After a short pause,* CLIFTON DWYER, *laden with parcels, and* SALLY SUMNER *enter.* CLIFTON *drops one of the packages.*)

SALLY: Mother won't be very pleased with your dropping her favorite perfume, Clifton.

CLIFTON: Your mother isn't going to be happy about anything I do, period!

JANICA (*Getting up*): Why don't you put some of those packages over here?

CLIFTON (*Gratefully*): Thanks a lot. (*He walks over to* JANICA's *desk, puts down packages, picks up the one he dropped and throws it into wastebasket.*) I'm afraid I'm the proverbial bull in the china shop, but there's no use crying over spilled Chanel.

JANICA: Won't you both sit down? Violet will be with you right away.

SALLY (*Peevishly*): You go ahead and sit down, Clifton. (*He does so.*) I don't like to be kept waiting. After all, this wedding is Violet's big story, and if she can't keep appointments, I'll just leave her some lists or something, and let her make the best of it. I have them with me . . . (*Reaches for purse, realizes she doesn't have it*) Oh, dear. I must have left my purse in the restaurant. (*To* CLIFTON) Be a love, Clifton, and run back and get it for me. (*She sits down on chair near desk.* CLIFTON *sighs, gets up wearily, and exits.*)

JANICA (*Sweetly*): It must be nice to have someone go about with you to take care of all these last-minute details. So few men are that way.

SALLY (*Also sweetly*): Oh, do you think so? I find most of them quite—shall we say—tractable?

JANICA: You're lucky.

SALLY (*Haughtily*): You might look at it that way. The men I've gone out with usually describe *themselves* as lucky.

JANICA: I see. I've been hearing nice things about your fiancé—his work in science. He's getting close to his Ph.D., isn't he?

SALLY: Not really. He has a full year to go. A year too long if you ask me.

JANICA: I always thought a Ph.D. and a college professorship were rather nice myself.

SALLY (*Huffily*): It might satisfy some, but can you see *me* as the wife of an impoverished professor? (*Pause*) I have a strong feeling that my Dad's going to offer Clifton a job in Sumner Bottling Works—and I'm sure he'll accept.

JANICA (*Amazed*): You mean after all these years of working for something he loves he'd give it up—just like that?

SALLY: As I told you, I've always found men (*Pausing just perceptibly*) tractable. (*Phone rings, and as* JANICA *answers,* SALLY *picks up newspaper from desk.*)

JANICA (*Into phone*): Society. . . . Yes, Mrs. Cartwright. The annual breakfast . . . Thursday, one o'clock . . . just a brief notice now and the story later . . . Fine. . . . You're quite welcome. (*During the last part of* JANICA's *conversation,* VIOLET *and* BARBARA *emerge from the inner office.* JANICA *hangs up, watches following action while pretending to work.*)

VIOLET: I'll let you know, Barbara. Either Alex or Jimmy will do a good job on the pictures of the studio.

BARBARA: You've been awfully sweet, Vi. This ought to give my enterprise a real shot in the arm. I'll see you soon.

VIOLET: Oh, wait a minute, will you? (*Puts hand on* BARBARA's *arm while she greets* SALLY) Sally, how are you?

SALLY: A little shopworn at the moment.

VIOLET (*Cordially*): Do you two know each other? Sally Sumner—Barbara Lake. (*They murmur greetings.*) Barbara's setting up a music studio here in town.

SALLY (*Bored*): How nice. (CLIFTON *reenters, carrying* SALLY's *purse, which he hands to her.*)

VIOLET: Cliff! How are you? You remember Barbara Lake, don't you?

CLIFTON (*With genuine pleasure*): Barb! How are you? It's been ages. (*Clasping her hand*)

BARBARA (*Nervously*) I didn't expect to see you here.

CLIFTON: It's not my natural habitat. Sally—you must know Barb. You were both at Westover.

SALLY (*Sweetly*): I think Barbara was a little before my time.

BARBARA: Eons, I imagine. Westover is part of my long ago past.

VIOLET (*Briskly*): Sally, I've kept you waiting long enough. Let's go into the other office. (*To others*) We won't be long. (*Quickly*) Oh, Jan, be a love and bring in that layout. We'll all look at it together.

JANICA (*Slyly*): O.K., but it'll be a squeeze. (*To* BARBARA *and* CLIFTON) That office was originally designed as the city editor's clothes closet. (BARBARA *and* CLIFTON *laugh.*)

VIOLET: Barbara, do you mind waiting? I need a few more details about the photos. (*She starts left, pushing* JANICA *and* SALLY *ahead of her.*) We won't be long. (*They exit down left.*)

CLIFTON (*Nervously*): We might as well sit down while we're waiting.

BARBARA: I suppose so. (*They sit.*)

CLIFTON: It's been a long time, Barb.

BARBARA (*Formally*): Yes, hasn't it?

CLIFTON (*Uneasily*): I don't think you've changed at all since the last time I saw you.

BARBARA (*Lightly*): How disappointed my father would be to hear that—after all the money he's spent on me the past years! The least he could expect would be that old friends would stand back in amazement.

CLIFTON: Old friends. (*Sighs*) Yes, I suppose we are.

BARBARA (*Quickly*): I've been hearing interesting things about your research. I saw your piece in *Scientific Monthly*.

CLIFTON (*Pleased*): You saw that? I don't know many people outside the science world who read it.

BARBARA: I daresay I'll soon be saying I knew you when.

CLIFTON (*Suddenly serious*): When what?

BARBARA: Well . . . when we took that science class together—remember?

CLIFTON (*Moving closer to Barbara*): How could I forget? You know, Barb, we really had some good times together . . .

BARBARA (*Suddenly*): Cliff—please—(*She gets up and tries to speak lightly, but does not look at him.*) Bridegrooms are supposed to look forward, not back.

CLIFTON (*Standing*): I guess you're right. (VIOLET *and* SALLY *emerge from office.* JIMMY *saunters in, whistling, and pauses at* VIOLET's *desk.*)

VIOLET: Jimmy, do you know everyone—Barbara, Clifton, and Sally? (JANICA *comes out of inner office holding papers.*)

JIMMY (*To* BARBARA *and* CLIFTON): Nice to meet you. Hello, Sally.

SALLY (*Flirtatiously*): Of course I know Jimmy. He's one of my favorite photographers. I don't know anyone else who has his finesse.

JIMMY: Why, thanks, Sally.

JANICA: You shouldn't spoil him, Sally. He's conceited enough already.

JIMMY (*To* SALLY, *who is smiling at him*): You see? I'm not appreciated around here. (*Gathers photographic equipment*) See you later. I've got to develop some film.

SALLY (*Putting her hand on* JIMMY's *arm*): Jimmy, do you have any pictures of the garden tea? How did they turn out?

JIMMY: Sorry, Sally. They're not ready yet. I'm going to work on them right now.

SALLY: You are! (*Eagerly*) Could I watch? I've always wanted to see inside a darkroom.

JIMMY (*Quickly*): You wouldn't like it. It's dark and has lots of smelly chemicals. I'll show you the pictures tomorrow. (*Starts toward darkroom*)

SALLY (*Pouting*): But I want to see them now. (JIMMY *stops.* SALLY *crosses to him, looks up at him.* JANICA *gives her a disgusted look and bangs down a paperweight.*)

JIMMY (*Grinning in* JANICA's *direction*): Sorry, Sally, that darkroom is tiny—there's room for only one person in there.

SALLY (*Insistently*): You can't stop me, Jimmy.

CLIFTON: Just a minute, Sally. We're—

SALLY (*Cutting him off*): Oh, don't be stuffy, Clifton. I won't be

long. You wait right here. (*Takes* JIMMY *by the arm*) Let's go,
Jimmy.

JIMMY (*Shrugging*): O.K. I give up. But just this once. (*They exit.*
CLIFTON *picks up newspaper and starts to read.* JANICA, *annoyed, begins to cut and paste galleys.*)

BARBARA: Well, Vi, thanks again. I—

VIOLET: Oh, Barbara, could you spare a few minutes more? I'd
like a silhouette to go with the photos of your studio, and you
have such a nice profile.

BARBARA (*Hesitating*): You mean—right now?

VIOLET: If Alex is free, I certainly would appreciate it.

BARBARA: If it helps you, Vi, O.K.

VIOLET: Thanks, Barbara. (*Picks up phone*) Photography, please
. . . Hello, Alex? Would you have time to take a quick shot for
me? We've got space for a little art work. . . . I'd like a silhouette of a man and a woman, with a few stars. . . . Five
minutes? (*To* BARBARA) Do you mind waiting five minutes,
Barbara? (BARBARA *shakes head. Into phone*) O.K. Thanks,
Alex. (*Hangs up.*)

CLIFTON (*Looking at watch*): It's getting late. I really have to be
going. (*Crosses to darkroom. Knocks on door. Calls*) Sally!
Let's go!

SALLY (*In muffled tone*): I can't come out right now. The film's
developing. (CLIFTON *returns to chair, looks agitated.*)

BARBARA: She's very enthusiastic about learning new things,
isn't she?

CLIFTON (*Grimly*): Yes, she is.

BARBARA: At least she'll never let you stagnate, Cliff. She'll
probably keep you from turning into one of those ivory-tower
professors.

CLIFTON (*Wryly*): She'll probably keep me from turning into any
professor at all. (*Suddenly*) Say, Barb, as long as we're both
waiting, would you like to get a soda next door?

BARBARA: Well, sure, if we have time. (*To* VIOLET) Violet, is that
all right?

VIOLET: Of course Alex will wait. (BARBARA *and* CLIFTON *exit.*)

JANICA: Violet Pemberton! You should be ashamed of yourself!

VIOLET (*With mock innocence*): Ashamed of myself? Why?

JANICA: I never saw so many match-making schemes. And this couple is practically married.

VIOLET (*Firmly*): Not until next Saturday. Until then, all's fair.

JANICA (*Puzzled*): I don't understand why you care so much. You never get any thanks for your pains.

VIOLET (*A bit sadly*): I guess I care about other people's weddings because I'll never have one of my own. (*Suddenly*) What do you think I'll do tonight when I get home, Janica?

JANICA (*Shrugging*): I don't know. Anything you want to, I guess.

VIOLET: Did it ever occur to you that a whole lifetime of planning little things to amuse yourself gets monotonous? (*Pause*) You know, at the end of a day here, when I stand outside my apartment with the key ready to open the door, I think, what if I should find the living room all messed up—a coat thrown on the couch, toys on the floor, and somebody there waiting for me. Isn't it silly? That seems like the most wonderful thing in the world. Then I open the door. It's all so neat, so quiet. (*More briskly, with a forced smile*) I've turned into a sentimentalist.

JANICA (*Subdued*): I guess I never thought of it just that way, Violet.

VIOLET (*Brightly*): But you're a stronger person than I was at your age, Janica. Maybe you'll be able to make your life work out exactly as you expect. Maybe you'll figure out how not to be lonely.

JANICA (*Desperately*): It's just seeing the foolishness of these elaborate weddings, Violet, looking ahead and wondering what will happen to their hopes and dreams. I just wish I knew for sure. (*Sits perplexed, glances unhappily at darkroom door. Phone rings.*) Society. . . . Yes, Mrs. Snyder. . . . (VIOLET *giggles.*) Yes, I remember. . . . No, I haven't made the correction yet. Now, let's see? How do we stand? . . . Your daughter's marrying J. G. Welthrope after all? Then we'll just let the story we go as we originally had it. . . . Yes, I understand. (*Hangs up*) Yea, Welthorpe! He finally won out. (BARBARA *and* CLIFTON *enter, carrying soft drink cans.* CLIFTON *goes to the darkroom door, knocks.* BARBARA *sits down.*)

BARBARA: Is Alex ready for me yet, Vi?

VIOLET: It shouldn't be more than a few minutes longer.

CLIFTON (*Calling*): Sally! Are you coming?

SALLY (*From darkroom*): In a minute, Clifton! (CLIFTON *starts to pick up* SALLY's *packages, drops one; there is the sound of breaking glass. He picks it up and with an angry gesture, throws it into the wastebasket.*)

CLIFTON (*Sarcastically*): The rest of the beauty treatment, I suppose. (*He suddenly puts the rest of the packages back down on the chair, brushes his hands.*) That's it. I'm through being a Boy Scout. (*Turns to others*) It's been pleasant seeing you—and thanks for everything, Barb.

VIOLET (*Quickly*): Cliff, I know this is a terrible imposition, but could you wait just a few minutes and let Alex take your silhouette with Barb's? (*Cajolingly*) I don't think there's another good-looking man in the building at this hour—except Jimmy—and (*Wickedly*) he seems to be quite busy.

CLIFTON (*Dubiously*): I don't know, Violet. What's the picture for?

VIOLET: Just a little art work for the feature page.

BARBARA: Come on, Cliff. Be a good sport.

CLIFTON: Well, all right.

VIOLET: Thanks so much. (*Picks up phone*) Photography, please . . . Alex, are you ready? . . . O.K. I'll send them right in. (*Hangs up; to* BARBARA *and* CLIFTON) Just down the hall, third door on the right. (*They exit, and she smiles slyly at* JANICA.) Don't you say a word, Janica.

JANICA: My lips are sealed. (*Starts gathering photos from desk, and puts them in large envelope*) I'll leave these bridal photos here for Jimmy, and then I guess I'll take off. (*Glances furtively toward darkroom*)

VIOLET: I'm still swamped, but I'm going to have to leave everything on my desk and run.

JANICA: Going to a party tonight?

VIOLET: Yes, but somehow I can't seem to work up much enthusiasm for it. (*Takes purse from desk drawer*) Don't stay too long, Janica. (*Starts to exit*) Oh, on second thought, could you stay just long enough to give Jimmy a message for me. I—

JANICA (*Sarcastically*): The thing I like about you, Vi, is that you're so subtle. You've done you're share of good deeds today without working on me. As far as I'm concerned, Jimmy Harper can—(SALLY *and* JIMMY *re-enter from darkroom.*)

SALLY (*To* JIMMY): It's been a wonderful little interlude, Jimmy. (*Looks around room*) Where is everybody? What happened to Clifton?

JANICA: He left quite a while ago.

SALLY (*Angrily*): Left? Just went?

VIOLET (*Airily; putting on her coat*): Just went.

SALLY: Didn't he leave a message for me?

VIOLET: No. Not anything I can recall.

SALLY (*Furious*): And he didn't even bother to help me with these packages.

JANICA: Men aren't always completely—tractable, are they? (SALLY *glares at her.*) Don't forget your purse, Sally. (SALLY *goes back and retrieves purse from chair.*)

SALLY (*To* VIOLET, *in a voice with an edge to it*): I think you'd better put the story on hold, Violet. I may have to teach someone a little lesson. (*Warmly, to* JIMMY) Jimmy, I *might* have some time on my hands, and I'd love some lessons in photography. How about it?

JIMMY: Oh, sure. Any time.

SALLY (*Sweetly*): Jimmy, you've been so terribly nice. (*To* JANICA, *coldly*) I'll have Clifton pick up these parcels. (VIOLET *and* SALLY *exit.* JANICA *starts typing.*)

JIMMY (*Sitting on* VIOLET's *desk*): There goes a woman who should be put in cold storage for about a hundred and fifty years.

JANICA (*Coldly, typing fast*): I don't know. She seems to do pretty well.

JIMMY: I guess so. That seems like quite a nice guy she snagged. (JANICA *pointedly says nothing, typing briskly and keeping her eyes on her copy.*) Now, Janica—you're not that busy.

JANICA: You're probably not the best judge of what it means to be busy.

JIMMY: What do you mean by that?

JANICA: Just that *I* don't have time to entertain friends during working hours.

JIMMY (*Laughing*): Janica, you're jealous.

JANICA (*Furiously*): Jealous? Of her? That's the funniest thing I ever heard. (*Turns her head away*)

JIMMY: All right. You're not jealous. You're just angry because she spent a half hour or so in the darkroom with me. Let me put your troubled little mind at ease. I did not invite her. *She* pursued me. (*Teasing*) She thinks I'm cute.

JANICA (*With sarcasm*): "Oh, Jimmy, you've been so-o nice. Let's have some more lovely little interludes, shall we?" (*Angry*) I certainly don't care whether she comes back or not. I just don't want you to think I'm being taken in by your innocent attitude. (*Pulls paper out of typewriter and rolls in new sheet*)

JIMMY: You're being childish and silly now, and in a few minutes you'll be ashamed.

JANICA: Ashamed! I'm certainly not the one that makes dates with other people's fiancées in darkrooms!

JIMMY (*Throwing hands up*): Oh, what's the use? You know, sometimes I think you just don't like me. I try and I try, but I can't get through to you.

JANICA (*Looking away*): I'm sorry, Jimmy.

JIMMY: It's O.K. (*He walks toward door. JANICA sits with her cheek on her hand, staring at typewriter. Suddenly she turns.*)

JANICA (*Calling*): Jimmy! Wait a minute. (*Looks at him for a moment, then goes on quickly and nervously*) Before you go, would you do something for me? I haven't quite finished my stories. If you'd add this last one to the pile on Bert's desk, it'll just make the deadline.

JIMMY: All right. I have a few minutes. (*He sits in chair near door, as she begins to type. Suddenly she stops, and looks hesitantly around.*)

JANICA: I just can't seem to think of the right words. Isn't that funny—it should be automatic.

JIMMY: You're probably just tired. It's the end of the day. (*Comes over and leans over her shoulder to read*) Let's see what you've got so far. "Janica Reed cordially invites James C. Harper to dine with her tonight at the restaurant of his choice. R.S.V.P." (*He pauses, then smiles at her.*) You're off to a fine start! The rest can go something like this. "James C. Harper can't think of a better idea." (JANICA *rises from chair and kisses him on the cheek.*)

JANICA: Neither can I. (*They embrace. Telephone rings two or three times before* JANICA *disengages herself and answers.*)

JANICA (*Into phone*): Society. Yes, Mrs. Snyder. . . . Yes, I remember. (*Smiles at* JIMMY) I see. . . . Your daughter Lulu has decided to marry Mr. Butler, after all? . . . She's not going to marry Mr. Welthorpe . . . Yes, I think you're perfectly right. It never does any good trying to stand in the way of true love. Goodbye, Mrs. Snyder. (*She hangs up, then turns and smiles radiantly at* JIMMY, *as the curtain closes.*)

THE END

P.R.—Planet Relations

by Earl J. Dias

Outer-space solutions to earthly dilemmas . . .

Characters

COMMANDER SIGGZY
PAUL ADAMS, *16*
MRS. ADAMS, *his mother*
BECKY ADAMS, *his sister, 15*
AUNT GWENDOLYN, *his aunt*
LYDIA GREGG, *16*
ANNE REED, *16*

BEFORE RISE: *Beeping sound, increasing in volume, is heard.*
  COMMANDER SIGGZY *bursts in through curtain. Beeping stops.*
  SIGGZY *wears metallic jumpsuit, silver face makeup.*
SIGGZY: Wow! What a traffic jam! I had to stay in a holding
  pattern for half an hour before I could get into the galaxy. (*Sits
  on stage, dangling feet*) I'm Commander Siggzy. And you're
  right—I do come from another planet. I can't tell you which
  one, though. (*Puts finger on lips*) Top secret. (*Puts hand to ear,*

listens, then "speaks into" other wrist) Yes, I'm getting to that.
(*To audience*) That was Mojar, the public relations director
where I come from. He's been a bit disturbed about the bad
press we're getting here on Earth. (*Hand to ear; speaks into
wrist*) All right, Mojar, I get the message. (*Rises and walks
left*) Mojar wants to tell you about something I saw at one of
your movie theaters the other day. I was never so insulted in
my life! It was a science fiction movie about some creatures
from another planet that took a whole town of Earthlings
hostage. These space creatures were horrible-looking, with
flat heads and webbed hands. Why, you never see a monster
like that any more—even in deep space. (*Shakes head*) No
wonder we're getting bad press. I mean, we're just normal
public-spirited citizens like all of you. We're always willing to
lend a helping hand when we can. (*Suddenly puts hand to ear;
pauses*) Mojar wants me to tell you about my experience with
an Earthling, Paul Adams. Before I show you what happened,
though, you must remember one thing. I'm invisible to Earthlings unless I want to be visible. It's the law. And I can show
myself to only two people in any one Earth household. It's a
sensible law because it conserves our energy. (*Crossing center*)
Well, here's the story. I was flying by the Adams house one day
when I overheard an interesting conversation and decided to
drop in. Here—let me show you. (*Exits as curtain opens*)

* * *

SETTING: *Adams living room.*

AT RISE: PAUL ADAMS *is asleep on sofa.* MRS. ADAMS *enters, goes
to coffee table, center, straightens books and magazines, looks
at* PAUL *and shakes her head.* BECKY *enters, singing a popular
song.*

MRS. ADAMS: Becky! Sh-h! Your brother's asleep.

BECKY: Why can't he do his sleeping at night like everyone else?

MRS. ADAMS (*In stage whisper*): Poor Paul is exhausted. He seems
to be worrying about something these days.

BECKY: What in the world does he have to worry about? His two
girl friends help him with his school work. His only problem is
how to live from one meal to the next!

MRS. ADAMS (*Smiling in spite of herself*): Becky! (BECKY *picks up magazine and sits in chair near couch.*) If you're going to stay here, don't make any noise.

BECKY: O.K., Mom. I won't disturb Sleeping Beauty.

MRS. ADAMS: Good. (*She tiptoes out.* BECKY *begins to flip pages of magazine.* PAUL *opens eyes, yawns, stretches, and sits up.*)

BECKY: Afternoon, Rip Van Winkle. Is something disturbing your beauty sleep?

PAUL (*Rubbing eyes*): No one could sleep through the racket you're making. What's that magazine made out of, anyway? Sandpaper?

BECKY: What's wrong with you, Paul? There's no reason you should be sleeping in the afternoon.

PAUL: I have problems, Becky.

BECKY: Who hasn't? My math grades are terrible, and I know less about American history than anybody else in my class. But at least I don't spend all afternoon snoring!

PAUL (*Swatting at* BECKY, *who ducks*): I was not snoring! (*Stalks over to window upstage. Beeping sound is heard.* SIGGZY *enters, unseen by* PAUL *or* BECKY. *He waves to audience, smiles, and perches on arm of chair.*)

BECKY: What's bugging you, anyway, Paul?

PAUL (*Suddenly turning*): I suppose I ought to tell someone. The prom's in two weeks, and I don't know whether to ask Anne or Lydia.

BECKY (*Incredulously*): A date for a dance? That's what bothering you?

PAUL (*Deadly serious*): It's not a little thing, Becky. I like Anne, and I like Lydia. But if I ask Anne, Lydia will be hurt.

BECKY: Lydia? Hurt? If I know Lydia, *you're* the one who's going to get hurt.

PAUL: You may be right. But if I invite Lydia, Anne will be hurt.

BECKY: Well, at least Anne will suffer in silence. (*She laughs.* PAUL *shakes his head.*) What's the big deal? You must like one of them better than the other.

PAUL: That's the problem. I think they're both great.

BECKY: I know what I'd do if I were you, but I learned long ago to keep my nose out of other people's business. (*Gets up, holding magazine*) I'm going upstairs so I won't have to hear about your love life or Aunt Gwendolyn's soggy sonnets. (*Crosses to doorway*)

PAUL (*Sarcastically*): Thanks a lot! Where is Aunt Gwendolyn, anyway?

BECKY: In her room, I think. She usually writes her poetry about this time of day and tries to con someone into listening to her latest masterpiece. I just don't feel like listening today. So I'm out of here. (BECKY *exits.* PAUL *remains on sofa, looking worried.* SIGGZY *crosses to sofa.*)

SIGGZY: You're right, Paul. You do have a problem. (PAUL *jumps up and stares around room, startled.*)

PAUL: What? Who is that? What's going on here? (*Shakes head*) I must be more upset than I thought! I'm starting to hear voices.

SIGGZY: No, no. You're perfectly normal—for an Earthling, that is.

PAUL: Maybe all this worrying about the prom is giving me a neurosis or something.

SIGGZY: Come on, Paul. Pull yourself together! Wait a minute. (*Speaks into wrist*) Mojar, give me a visibility beam. (*Beeping sound is heard. Suddenly* PAUL *sees* SIGGZY.)

PAUL (*Sinking onto sofa and speaking weakly*): Help! Help!

SIGGZY: Help is what you need, my boy. Look at me. I'm not so unusual, am I?

PAUL (*Slowly*): I wouldn't say that, exactly.

SIGGZY (*Irritated*): Just because I'm from another planet, you think I look peculiar. You Earthlings are prejudiced and intolerant.

PAUL (*Frightened*): Another planet!

SIGGZY: Control yourself! I heard that Earthlings are always stressed, but you're unbelievable. Relax. (*He holds out his hand.*) I'm Commander Siggzy.

PAUL (*Timidly shaking hands*): Nice to meet you—I think.

SIGGZY: That's more like it. After all, I'm here to do you a big favor. I'm going to help you decide which girl to take to the prom.

PAUL: You are?

SIGGZY: Certainly. The whole thing's elementary. Where I come from, a five-year-old could solve your problem. But, of course, we're trained in decision-making at an early age. (*Doorbell rings.* PAUL *goes to window and looks out.*)

PAUL: Oh, no! It's Lydia.

SIGGZY: One of the two girls, eh?

PAUL: Yes. What should I do now?

SIGGZY: Let her in, of course. I'll be able to observe her in action. (PAUL *hesitates. Doorbell rings again.*) Don't worry. She won't be able to see me. (*He sits on arm of chair.* PAUL *opens door, and* LYDIA *enters, carrying book.*)

LYDIA: Hi, Paul. I was in the neighborhood, so I thought I'd return your book. (*Hands him book*)

PAUL: Thanks, Lydia. (*Looks nervously at* SIGGZY)

LYDIA: You look nervous. (*Flirtatiously*) Not used to having women drop in on you? (*She ruffles* PAUL'S *hair, and he backs away.*)

PAUL (*Putting book on table and looking anxiously at* SIGGZY, *who smiles and nods*): Uh—come sit down, Lydia.

LYDIA: Thanks! (*She puts her arm through* PAUL'S *and leads him to sofa.*) Let's get comfortable! (*They sit.*) Isn't this nice? (SIGGZY *chuckles and winks at* PAUL, *who shakes his head at him.*) What's wrong, Paul? Don't you want me around?

PAUL: Of course I do, Lydia. I'm—um, really glad you stopped by.

LYDIA: Good. (*Snuggles up to him*) You know, Paul, I'm a little ashamed of myself. I told you a white lie, just now. Bringing the book back was just an excuse to see you. I hope you don't mind if I put all my cards on the table.

PAUL: Oh, no. I appreciate your honesty.

LYDIA: I'm so glad! (*Takes his hand*) Can you guess why I wanted to see you? No, don't guess. I'll tell you.

SIGGZY: This girl certainly isn't shy!

PAUL (*Starting to answer* SIGGZY): She sure isn't. She's—(*Catches himself*)

LYDIA: What did you say, Paul?

PAUL: Nothing. Just thinking out loud.

LYDIA (*Edging closer to him and putting her head on his shoulder*): Paul, the prom is just two weeks away, isn't it? (SIGGZY *laughs.*)

PAUL (*Nervously*): Yes. That's right. (SIGGZY *walks to sofa and looks down at* PAUL. *Embarrassed,* PAUL *tries to edge away from* LYDIA, *but she keeps her head on his shoulder.*)

LYDIA (*Wistfully*): Jack Holmes is going with Lindsey Reynolds, and Sam Bestor is going with Sue Masters, and Bob Hunt is taking Mandy Norcross, but nobody has asked me yet. (SIGGZY *chuckles and rubs hands together gleefully.*)

PAUL (*Uncomfortably*): Somebody will, Lydia. After all, the prom is two weeks away, and—

LYDIA (*Getting to her feet, angrily*): Paul Adams, you know very well what I'm getting at! Do I have to spell it out for you? (*Hands on hips*) Are you going to ask me to the prom, or not?

PAUL: Well, Lydia, I'd like to take you—

LYDIA (*Brightening*): Great!

PAUL (*Suddenly inspired*): But I might not be here! (SIGGZY *groans and shakes head.*) Um—my family may take a trip that weekend.

LYDIA (*Angrily*): You don't expect me to believe that, do you? After all we've meant to each other—

SIGGZY: That wasn't very good, Paul.

PAUL: Well, Commander, I had to say something.

LYDIA: Commander? What in the world do you mean by that?

PAUL: It's not in the world, Lydia. You see, there's a man here visiting me from another planet. He's standing right in front of you, but he's invisible to you.

LYDIA (*Enraged*): Now I see what you're trying to do. You're trying to make me think you're crazy so you won't have to take me to the prom. Well, let me tell you, Paul Adams, your stupid extraterrestrial story wouldn't fool anyone.

SIGGZY: Now, just one minute! (AUNT GWENDOLYN *enters left, carrying a notebook.* SIGGZY *returns to sit on arm of chair.*)

GWENDOLYN: What's going on in here? Raised voices! A poet can't write with all this noise.

PAUL: I'm sorry, Aunt Gwendolyn. I didn't mean to interfere with your writing.

GWENDOLYN: Hello, Lydia.

LYDIA (*Glumly*): Hello, Gwendolyn.

GWENDOLYN: Has Paul done something to upset you, Lydia? (LYDIA *glares at* PAUL.)

PAUL (*Quickly*): We were just discussing a school matter. Um—it was about math. (SIGGZY *clucks his tongue.*)

GWENDOLYN (*Going to chair left of table and sitting*): Oh, math. I never could see the use of it, anyway. Now, poetry—that's different. (*Holds up notebook*) Let me read you my latest creation. (*Reads with gestures*)

Illumination of the darkest noon
More dazzling than
A thousand weeping
Daffodils.

(SIGGZY *groans and puts his head in his hands.*) Isn't that lovely?

LYDIA: What does it mean?

GWENDOLYN: Don't worry about meaning, Lydia. That's just an old-fashioned idea. We modern poets have gone beyond meaning. It's the sound that's important. (SIGGZY *laughs and shakes chair on which* AUNT GWENDOLYN *is sitting.*) Good heavens! Is there an earthquake or something? (SIGGZY *stops shaking.*) Perhaps I just had a nervous spasm. I think I'd better lie down for a minute. Nice to see you, Lydia. (GWENDOLYN *exits.*)

LYDIA (*Sarcastically*): Now, to get back to this math discussion. Are you taking me to the prom?

PAUL (*Nervously*): I don't know, Lydia. I—

LYDIA: Well, then, I hope I never see you again. (LYDIA *starts for door, and* PAUL *rushes ahead of her, puts his arms across door.*)

PAUL: Wait, Lydia. Don't go. I can explain everything.

LYDIA: It's too late for that. (*Extends her foot, grabs* PAUL's *arm, pulls him forward and trips him. He falls, then slowly sits up, rubbing his arm.*)

PAUL: Wow! How did you do that?

LYDIA: Karate. I've had one lesson. Wait till you see what I can do after I get my black belt! (LYDIA *exits.*)

SIGGZY (*Shaking his head sadly*): You're not much of a diplomat, Paul. (*As* PAUL *slowly gets up*) She's fiery, isn't she?

PAUL: She has spirit, all right. (*Rubs arm*) I guess I had that coming to me. I wonder if she'll ever speak to me again?

SIGGZY: Invite her to the prom and find out.

PAUL: But you haven't met Anne yet. (*Looks at watch*) She'll be here soon. She's coming over to help me with my math. (GWENDOLYN *enters.*)

GWENDOLYN (*Concerned*): Paul, were you talking to yourself just now? You have to take it easy.

PAUL: Aunt Gwendolyn, I'm fine. Really. I might as well tell you. Commander Siggzy here (*Points to* SIGGZY) is from another planet.

GWENDOLYN: Commander Siggzy? Yes, dear, of course. (*Soothingly*) Now, why don't you lie down for a while. (*Feeling his forehead*) There's a lot of flu going around. Maybe that's what's wrong with you. (*Taking his arm*) What you need is some rest. (*Pulls him to sofa;* SIGGZY *grins broadly.*)

SIGGZY: She can't see or hear me, you know.

PAUL (*Desperately*): Well, show yourself to her somehow—and hurry! She thinks I've lost it!

GWENDOLYN (*To* PAUL): Steady now, Paul. Rest quietly, and I'll call Dr. Benson.

SIGGZY (*To* PAUL): The law says we can reveal ourselves to only two people in an Earth household.

PAUL: So, she'll be the second. Please!

SIGGZY: If you insist. (*Speaks into his wrist. Other hand on his ear*) Mojar! Another visibility signal, please! (*Pauses as if listening*) Don't worry. I'm not overdoing it. (*Pauses*) Thank you. (*Beeping sound is heard.* SIGGZY *walks over to* GWEN-DOLYN *and taps her on the arm. She turns, sees him, and shrieks.*) At your service, madam. (SIGGZY *bows.* GWENDOLYN *shrieks again and faints.* SIGGZY *shakes his head.*) Bundle of nerves, that's what these Earthlings are. (MRS. ADAMS *rushes in.*)

MRS. ADAMS: Who screamed? What's the matter?

PAUL: Aunt Gwendolyn has fainted.

MRS. ADAMS: Good heavens! I'll get her a glass of water. (*She rushes out.* SIGGZY *takes flowers from vase on table and dumps water on* GWENDOLYN, *who sputters, sits up, and seeing* SIGGZY *shrieks.* MRS. ADAMS *rushes back in with glass of water.*)

GWENDOLYN: He's still here! (*She faints again.* MRS. ADAMS *lifts* GWENDOLYN *by shoulders and forces water to her lips.*)

MRS. ADAMS: What is she talking about? And where did all this water come from?

PAUL: Commander Siggzy, Mom.

MRS. ADAMS: Paul, this is no time to be funny. Gwen may be seriously ill. (BECKY *enters.*)

BECKY: Oh! What's wrong with Aunt Gwendolyn?

MRS. ADAMS: She fainted.

SIGGZY (*Into wrist*): Cancel that last request, will you, Mojar? (*Beeping is heard.* GWENDOLYN *looks around cautiously, then sighs with relief.*)

GWENDOLYN: Thank heavens he's gone!

BECKY: Who's gone?

GWENDOLYN: That space man. (BECKY *and* MRS. ADAMS *exchange glances, then help* GWENDOLYN *up.*)

MRS. ADAMS: Gwen, why don't you go upstairs and lie down for a while? You've been working too hard on your poetry.

PAUL: But, Mom—

MRS. ADAMS (*Taking one of* GWENDOLYN's *arms*): Becky, let's help Gwendolyn upstairs. (BECKY *takes her other arm.*)

GWENDOLYN: But I tell you, Helen, I did see this man as plainly as I see you now.

BECKY *and* MRS. ADAMS (*Humoring her, ad lib*): Of course, Gwendolyn. We know. (*Etc. They exit.*)

SIGGZY (*Shaking his head*): I don't understand it. The way she carried on, you'd think there was something terrifying about me.

PAUL: You terrified her, all right. (*Doorbell rings.*)

PAUL: Oh, no! That must be Anne. (*Crosses to door*)

SIGGZY: Ah! The other woman.

PAUL (*Opening door*): Hi, Anne. (ANNE REED *enters, carrying book.*)

ANNE: Hello, Paul. (*Going to sofa*) Did you have any trouble with those equations?

PAUL (*Following her to sofa and sitting down*): I sure did.

SIGGZY (*Perching on arm of chair and looking at* ANNE): She seems very intelligent, Paul. Pretty, too.

PAUL: She is. Oops! (*Clasps hand over mouth*)

ANNE: What was that?

PAUL: I just meant the math is hard.

ANNE (*Opening book; taking pencil from pocket*): Let's see, now. This first problem really isn't difficult.

PAUL (*Looking at book*): It isn't? It looks impossible to me!

ANNE: If you'd only concentrate, Paul. Mr. Latimer says that an understanding of math comes suddenly—like a flash of lightning.

PAUL: I wish a bolt would hit me. (*Looks at book*) I can't even see how to begin.

SIGGZY (*Walking over to them*): It's just a question of learning basic principles. (*Looks at book*) Hm-m. (*He whispers into* PAUL's *ear.* ANNE *still stares intently at book.*)

PAUL (*Suddenly excited*): I've got it! (*He takes pencil from* ANNE, *writes rapidly on paper, and hands it to her.*) How's that?

ANNE (*Looking at paper; smiling*): Why, it's perfect, Paul.

PAUL: It's amazing! The whole thing came to me in a flash, just the way Mr. Latimer said. It's a matter of seeing the basic principles.

SIGGZY (*Proudly*): Isn't that what I told you?

ANNE: Congratulations, Paul!

PAUL (*Sheepishly*): To tell you the truth, I had some help.

ANNE: Help? You mean from me?

PAUL: From you, of course, and I'm grateful for it. But—well—I might as well tell you, Anne. I hope you'll believe me. Nobody else does. . . .

ANNE (*Puzzled*): You sound so mysterious, Paul. Of course, I'll believe you. You've never lied to me.

PAUL: Well, here goes. (*Nervously*) There's someone else in this room with us—only you can't see him. (ANNE *looks around.*) He's from another planet—I don't know which one—and his name is Commander Siggzy. He just made me see the light about the math problems.

ANNE: But why can't I see him?

PAUL: He's allowed to show himself to only two people in an Earth household, and he's already shown himself to me—and to Aunt Gwendolyn. She fainted. (*Slight pause*) Do you believe me?

ANNE (*Smiling*): Why shouldn't I believe you? There are some things science can't explain.

SIGGZY: What a delightful Earthling!

PAUL (*Relieved*): You're great, Anne! No one else around here believes me.

SIGGZY (*Suddenly*): I've just thought of something. Our law says I can show myself to only two members of an Earth household. But strictly speaking, this fine young woman is not a member of this particular household, is she?

PAUL: Say, that's right, Commander.

ANNE: Oh, you're talking to him, aren't you?

PAUL: Yes. He's just had a great idea.

SIGGZY: I'll signal Mojar again. (*He speaks into wrist. Other hand at his ear*) Mojar! A visibility signal, please. (*Listens*) Yes, I know, but this person is not a member of the Adams household. . . . Yes, of course I'm sure. (*Beeping sound, then* ANNE *sees* SIGGZY.)

ANNE (*Surprised*): Oh! So this is your man from outer space!

SIGGZY (*Beaming*): How do you do? I'm delighted to meet you.

ANNE: You don't look as unusual as I expected.

SIGGZY: Thank you, my dear. You're a charming Earthling. (BECKY *enters*.)

BECKY: Aunt Gwendolyn is resting quietly. Hi, Anne.

ANNE: Have you met Commander Siggzy, Becky?

SIGGZY: No, she hasn't.

ANNE: Oh, I forgot. (*To* SIGGZY) She can't see you, can she, Commander?

SIGGZY: I'm afraid not. I've used up my energy limit for one visit.

PAUL: Anyway, *we* know you're here, Commander.

BECKY (*Bewildered*): What is the matter with everybody around here?

ANNE: Commander Siggzy is here, Becky—even if you can't see him.

BECKY: Anne, you've been hanging around Paul too long.

PAUL: Can't you just take our word for it?

BECKY: I think you've lost your marbles, Paul! Anne, why don't you come upstairs with me for a while? We ought to have a long talk. (ANNE *looks questioningly at* PAUL.)

PAUL: Go ahead, Anne. We can't convince these skeptics. I'll stay with Commander Siggzy.

ANNE: O.K. It was nice meeting you, Commander.

SIGGZY: The pleasure is all mine. (BECKY *looks on in astonishment.*)

BECKY (*Taking* ANNE's *arm*): Come on, Anne. You'll be O.K.—really. (BECKY *and* ANNE *exit.*)

SIGGZY (*Going to sofa and sitting beside* PAUL): I like Anne very much, Paul.

PAUL: I thought you would. Lydia and Anne are both fantastic in their own way, and I don't want to hurt either of them. I have a real problem.

SIGGZY: I told you I'd help you solve your problem, and I will. I'll give you the simplest solution.

PAUL: Great! I'm ready.

SIGGZY: Where I come from, we are taught how to deal with these matters—particularly matters of male-female relationships—by keeping one simple, sensible question in mind.

PAUL: And what is that?

SIGGZY: Just this: If you were taking a long interplanetary voyage in a spaceship, which girl would you want to take with you?

PAUL (*Disappointed*): Is that the question?

SIGGZY: Yes, and an excellent question it is. Say that this trip took a couple of light years or so. Which girl would be a better companion?

PAUL: I don't know.

SIGGZY: Let's think about Lydia. Bright? Yes. Spirited? Yes, indeed. Can she adapt to new situations? Ah, that's a problem—you saw how she treated me. Is she interested in you or in herself? Another problem. (*Paces about*) Now, about Anne. Intelligent? Unquestionably. Does she have an imagination? Is she interested in herself or you? Paul, the answers are obvious. Note how she acted when we met. Adjusted herself well—

showed plenty of imagination. Note also her enthusiasm when you solved your math problems!

PAUL (*Thoughtfully*): That's right!

SIGGZY: I have a suspicion Lydia can take care of herself. Anne, on the other hand, is more sensitive, quieter perhaps, but more imaginative, and she seems to be a better friend.

PAUL: And on a long space trip those qualities would be important, wouldn't they?

SIGGZY: They sure would.

PAUL (*Rising*): Thanks, Commander. I think I know what to do now.

SIGGZY (*Also rising*): Splendid, Paul, splendid. (*Going toward upstage center door*) Well, I'll be off now.

PAUL: I can't thank you enough, Commander. You don't know what this means to me.

SIGGZY: Think nothing of it. But remember this. Don't believe all you see in the movies about creatures from other planets. Those stories are slanderous!

PAUL: Yes, sir.

SIGGZY: Whenever you get a chance, put in a good word for us. You'll make Mojar and me very happy. Well, goodbye and good luck.

PAUL: Goodbye, Commander Siggzy. (SIGGZY *exits.* PAUL *walks to sofa and lies down.*) Gosh, I feel a lot better with that decision out of the way. (*Yawns*) Funny—I really feel sleepy all of a sudden. (*Closes eyes and curtain closes.* SIGGZY *reenters in front of curtain.*)

SIGGZY (*To audience*): Well, folks, that's what happened on my visit to the Adams household. Paul doesn't know it, but I've fixed it so he'll think he dreamed this all up. But you and I know it really happened. Watch! (*Exits as curtain opens on same scene.* PAUL *is asleep on sofa.* MRS. ADAMS *enters, goes to coffee table, center, straightens books and magazines, looks at* PAUL *and shakes her head.* BECKY *enters singing a popular song.*)

MRS. ADAMS: Becky! Sh-h! Your brother's asleep.

BECKY: Why can't he do his sleeping at night like everyone else?

MRS. ADAMS (*In a stage whisper*): He seems to be worrying about something these days.

BECKY: What in the world does he have to worry about? His two girl friends help him with his school work. His only problem is how to live from one meal to the next!

MRS. ADAMS (*Smiling in spite of herself*): Becky! (BECKY *picks up magazine and sits in chair near couch.*) If you're going to stay here, don't make any noise.

BECKY: O.K., Mom. I won't disturb Sleeping Beauty.

MRS. ADAMS: Good. (*She tiptoes out.* BECKY *begins to flip pages of magazine.* PAUL *opens eyes, yawns, stretches, and sits up slowly.*)

BECKY: Afternoon, Rip Van Winkle.

PAUL: Commander Siggzy? (*Looking around*) I guess he's gone.

BECKY (*Puzzled*): Commander who?

PAUL: Is Aunt Gwendolyn all right? Did Dr. Benson come?

BECKY: What in the world are you talking about? There's nothing wrong with Aunt Gwendolyn. She's in her room—writing poetry, as usual.

PAUL (*Rubbing his eyes*): No, no—she fainted when she saw the man from outer space. Don't you remember? (*Slowly*) Or did I dream it all?

BECKY (*Still looking through magazine*): Dream? No. (*Sarcastically*) I'm sure Aunt Gwendolyn fainted because she saw a space man. (PAUL *picks up math book from coffee table.*)

PAUL: Let's see. Here's the math problem that was giving me trouble. (*Takes paper and pencil from table and writes rapidly*) Wow! I can do it! Commander Siggzy was right!

BECKY (*Looking up*): Paul, what are you talking about?

PAUL (*Ignoring* BECKY): And if he's right about that, he's probably right about my other problem, too. (PAUL *rushes to phone and dials.*) Anne? . . . Guess what. I can do the math! . . . Really! You know the problem about the trains! Well, the whole thing suddenly became clear to me. It's 35 mph. . . . Look, Anne. I was wondering if you'd go to the prom with me. . . . You will? That's great! . . . O.K. See you at school tomorrow. (*Hangs up*)

BECKY: Ah, love—what a beautiful thing! (GWENDOLYN *enters, looking sleepy.*)

GWENDOLYN: I just had the strangest dream! There was a space man—right here in the house.

PAUL: Did he tell you his name?

GWENDOLYN: Yes, I think he did. It was—it was Commander Siggy, Sizzy . . .

BECKY (*Amazed*): Commander Siggzy!

GWENDOLYN: Yes, that was it.

BECKY (*Going left; weakly*): Excuse me. I'm going to go upstairs and lie down. (*Exits*)

GWENDOLYN: Poor child. What's wrong with her?

PAUL: She'll be all right. Say, Aunt Gwendolyn, I've just thought of a couple of lines you can use in a poem. Listen:
Illumination of the darkest noon
More dazzling than
A thousand weeping
Daffodils . . .

GWENDOLYN (*Astonished*): But, Paul—I just wrote those lines before I came down!

PAUL (*Smiling*): Some coincidence, huh?

GWENDOLYN (*Moving left; weakly*): I think I'll take a rest, too. (*She exits.* PAUL *chuckles. Beeping sound is heard.* PAUL *goes to window, looks out, and waves.*)

PAUL: So long, Commander Siggzy! (*Curtain*)

THE END

Miss Cast

by Barbara Brem Heinzen

Famous playwright helps stagestruck teenager come down to earth. . . .

Characters

JUDY JOHNSON
MR. JOHNSON
MRS. JOHNSON
BILL JOHNSON
NANCY JOHNSON
RAY MEAD, *Nancy's boyfriend*
MR. RANDALL
DAVID RANDALL, *his son*

SCENE 1

TIME: *Saturday morning.*
SETTING: *The Johnson living room. Sofa and chairs are center; card table with model airplane parts on it is up right. Telephone is on an end table. Exit outside is right; exit to rooms in house is left. There is an open window in rear wall. Some magazines are scattered on floor.*

AT RISE: MRS. JOHNSON *is knitting.* BILL JOHNSON *is working on model airplane.*

JUDY JOHNSON (*Off left*): Romeo, where art thou, Romeo, my handsome, elusive Romeo?

BILL: Mom, can't you do something about Judy? She's driving me out of my mind!

MRS. JOHNSON: Now, Bill, be patient. You know how worked up Judy is about trying out for the play. (JUDY *continues her recitation.*)

BILL: But she's been going on like this for weeks. (MR. JOHNSON *enters left.*) Hi, Dad.

MR. JOHNSON: Morning, Bill. You won't forget to mow the front yard this morning, will you?

BILL: No, Dad. I'll get to it in a little while. (MR. JOHNSON *kisses* MRS. JOHNSON *on cheek.*)

MR. JOHNSON: I've got to go, or I'll be late. See you later this afternoon. (*Exits.* JUDY *enters left, wearing sunglasses.*)

JUDY (*Dramatically*): Hark! 'Tis Lady Judith entering the drawing room.

BILL: Judy, you have about as much chance of getting the lead in that play as I have of winning the Kentucky Derby with one leg in a cast and the other in a bucket of bread dough.

JUDY: My dear, dear brother, how many times must I tell you . . . my name is Judith!

BILL (*Mocking her*): Of course, fair maiden! But thou must remember to call me Sir William!

JUDY: You just don't understand the theater, do you, little brother? I'm simply trying to sustain a mood!

BILL: Ha!

JUDY: Just wait till I'm discovered. I'll have the last laugh then. Someday I'll be the hottest property in Hollywood!

MRS. JOHNSON: Judy, you know how your father and I feel about Hollywood.

JUDY: But Mother, my innate creativity is like a powerful magnet pulling me to stardom.

BILL (*Disgusted*): Ick!

JUDY: Now, where was I? Ah, yes! (*Reciting*) "Romeo, why dost thou ignore me? Art thou blind to my beauty?"

MRS. JOHNSON: Judy, this would be a good day to clean up your room. I've never seen such a mess in my life. And I'm tired of finding movie magazines all over the house.

JUDY (*Still reciting*): Why art thou so obstinate? Canst thou not see I am the essence of charm and grace?

MRS. JOHNSON: Judy, are you listening?

JUDY: Mother, please! It's *Judith*! Try to remember, or I shall simply perish.

BILL: Is that a promise?

JUDY (*Reciting*): If thou wouldst only speak to me! (*She abruptly drops pose, sits up and looks out window. Now she speaks naturally.*) Gosh, what's the matter with David Randall, anyway? It's been one month since the Randalls moved in, and David hasn't said two words to me.

BILL: Yes, he has—hello and *goodbye!*

MRS. JOHNSON: Mr. Randall tells me David is quite shy.

JUDY (*Excitedly*): You mean you talked to David's father and you didn't tell me? If he looks like David, he must be handsome.

MRS. JOHNSON: They're having a terrible time getting rid of the crabgrass on their front lawn, so I told him about the weed spray we tried on ours last year. (*Pauses*) But I couldn't remember the name of it.

JUDY: Mother, you talked to David Randall's father about *crabgrass?*

MRS. JOHNSON: It is a problem, dear, and it's so unsightly! That reminds me, Judy, you still haven't straightened out your room, and I want it done . . . (JUDY *sighs.* MRS. JOHNSON *goes over to her and speaks loudly*) now!

JUDY: Mother! Must you be violent? (*She slinks left.*) It's simply imperative that my emotional equilibrium is not disturbed! Tryouts start in less than an hour, and I must be at my zenith! (*She exits and is heard off left.*) My absolute zenith!

MRS. JOHNSON (*Sinking onto sofa*): I hope she gets a part in the play; maybe it will cure her once and for all!

BILL: Well, she'd better make a quick recovery. Everyone at school thinks she's crazy! (NANCY JOHNSON *and* RAY MEAD *enter right.* NANCY *carries a script.*)

MRS. JOHNSON: Nancy! Where have you been keeping yourself? Hi, Ray. How are you?

RAY: Fine, Mrs. Johnson.

NANCY: I've been really busy this semester, Aunt Helen. I've had loads of homework and lots of extracurricular stuff.

BILL: What she means, Mom, but is too polite to say, is that she hasn't been around because she can't stand Judy anymore.

NANCY: Oh, Bill, that's not true. Judy is still the same old wonderful Judy. She's just . . . (*Groping for words*) well, she's just going through a phase, that's all.

BILL: Well, I'm beginning to wish she'd phase out altogether!

MRS. JOHNSON (*Warningly*): Bill, you'd better get the lawn mowed before Dad gets home.

BILL (*Grudgingly*): O.K., Mom. (*Exits right*)

NANCY: Is Judy . . . I mean, *Judith* about ready, Aunt Helen? Tryouts start at one.

MRS. JOHNSON: I'll tell her you're here, dear. (*Exits left*)

RAY: Nancy, about tonight. . .

NANCY: What about tonight? I thought it was all set.

RAY (*Squirming*): Well, I think we'd better call off Judy's blind date with David Randall.

NANCY: What do you mean?

RAY: Well, I would have told you before, but . . .

NANCY: But what?

RAY: David's father is famous, Nancy. He's a famous playwright.

NANCY: He is? If he's so famous, how come I've never heard of him before?

RAY: You've never heard of John Anderson Randall?

NANCY: Of course, silly, I've heard of John—(*She stops short.*) Ray, you don't mean David's father is *the* John Anderson Randall, the playwright?

RAY: That's exactly what I mean.

NANCY: What's he doing in Harrisville, of all places?

RAY: Writing a novel. David says he needed a new atmosphere, away from New York. Peace and quiet, you know?

NANCY: Oh, Ray, if Judy finds out about this, she'll be absolutely impossible.

RAY: Nancy, she *is* absolutely impossible. But think of poor Mr. Randall. It would be the end of his peace and quiet. He'd be better off trying to write his novel in the middle of Grand Central Station.

NANCY: And Judy would never leave David alone. (*Dismayed*) What are we going to do?

RAY: First of all, I'm going to tell David the blind date is off.

NANCY: We can't do that! We just won't tell Judy about David's father, that's all.

RAY: She'd find out. It's just not fair to David—he's too nice a guy. You haven't said anything to Judy about the blind date, so she'll never know the difference, right?

NANCY: But I know the difference. Judy doesn't always act like this . . . it's just been lately. (*Coaxing*) David would like her, I know he would, once he got to know her.

RAY: *Know* her? Even *Judy* doesn't know who she is anymore!

NANCY: Please, Ray, would you do this as a favor for me?

RAY (*Relenting after a pause*): Well, O.K.

NANCY (*Hugging him*): Oh, I knew you'd come through for me. Now, don't worry. The four of us will have a great time. (JUDY *enters left.*)

JUDY: Hello-o, darlings! How marvelous to see you again! It seems like eons since I've seen you. Simply eons!

NANCY (*Laughing*): Judy, it was just yesterday.

RAY: Hi, Judy.

JUDY: Ray, it's Judith, remember?

RAY (*Snapping fingers*): Right! Hey, I'm going to give Bill a hand with the lawn. I'll be out in front when you're ready to go, Nancy. (*He starts to exit right.* MRS. JOHNSON *pokes her head in from left.*)

MRS. JOHNSON: I just made some sandwiches, kids. Come on in and help yourselves. (*She exits.* RAY *does an about-face and follows her.*)

JUDY: Food! How on earth could anyone think about food at a moment like this? I'm consumed with tension! My innate creativity is like a powerful magnet pulling me to stardom, pulling . . .

NANCY (*Breaking in*): Oh, come on, Judy, I've heard all about your magnet a hundred times. Forget about it and relax. You'll do a lot better at tryouts if you aren't so keyed up.

JUDY: Oh, if only I could relax, Nancy, but, for a creative person like me it's impossible to relax, to let go.

NANCY: Tryouts aren't the end of the world.

JUDY: Maybe not for you, but for me (*Melodramatically*) it would be the end of the world if I don't get the leading role. I'll die! Simply wither and die.

NANCY (*Matter-of-factly*): I doubt that. Besides, there are loads of good character parts.

JUDY (*Shocked*): I—take a character part? Nancy, darling, surely you jest!

NANCY: Ray is trying out for one of the character parts, and so is David Randall, I understand.

JUDY: David Randall? He is? But, Nancy, he should be trying out for the male lead! He'd be perfect! He's so good-looking, so magnetic . . . yet shy and boyish.

NANCY: Judy, while we're on the subject of good-looking men, would you like a blind date for the drama club party tonight?

JUDY: Blind date? Nancy, dear, really. . . .

NANCY: Judy, say yes. I know you won't be disappointed.

JUDY: Who is he?

NANCY (*Nervously*): Oh, I don't really know him. He's a friend of Ray's.

JUDY: Is he good-looking?

NANCY: Very.

JUDY: He is? (*Considering*) Well, I suppose it would be good for my image. All right, I'll do it!

NANCY: Great. (*Glancing at her watch*) Listen we'd better get going or we'll be late. (*Calls off*) Ray, let's go!

JUDY: By the way, Nancy, darling, what part are you reading for?

NANCY: Gosh, Judy . . . I mean, *Judith* . . . I thought you knew! I'm trying out for the female lead, too! (JUDY *looks stunned. Quick curtain*)

* * * * *

SCENE 2

TIME: *Afternoon.*

SETTING: *Same as Scene 1.*

AT RISE: MRS. JOHNSON *is reading, as* BILL *enters right.*

MRS. JOHNSON: Bill! Where have you been? I've been looking all over for you!

BILL (*Sheepishly*): Well, I tried out for the play, Mom.

MRS. JOHNSON: Why, that's wonderful! What part did you try out for?

BILL: Just about everything except the female lead. (MRS. JOHNSON *laughs.*)

MRS. JOHNSON: Tell me, how did Judy do?

BILL: Just between you and me, Mom, she was awful!

MRS. JOHNSON: Oh, no! Really?

BILL: Yes. She was a one-woman disaster area! (*Shakes his head*) Old Sarah Heartburn really did herself in this afternoon. One thing's for sure, she didn't get the female lead. Nancy walked off with that role, no question about it.

MRS. JOHNSON: Are you sure? I thought Mr. Wilson was going to call everyone tonight to announce the parts.

BILL: Well, I doubt if he'll let Judy pull the curtain, let alone assign her a part.

MRS. JOHNSON: Oh, dear! If only she'd realize . . . (*She shakes her head despairingly.*)

BILL: It's too late now, Mom. She really blew it. (*Doorbell rings.*) I'll see who that is. (*He opens door and* MR. RANDALL *enters.*) Oh, hi, Mr. Randall.

MR. RANDALL: Hi, Bill, (*To* MRS. JOHNSON) Helen. Is Phil home?

MRS. JOHNSON: Yes, he's in the study. (*To* BILL) Would you call him, dear?

BILL: Sure. (*Exits left*)

MRS. JOHNSON: Have a seat, John. (MR. RANDALL *sits.*) Isn't the weather nice for this time of year?

MR. RANDALL: Yes, especially for working in the yard! (*They laugh.*) I hope Phil remembers the name of the weed killer you mentioned; the weeds are taking over our lawn. (MR. JOHNSON *and* BILL *enter.*)

MR. JOHNSON: Hello there, John. (JUDY *bursts through front door.*)

JUDY: Hello, darlings! I'm home!

MR. JOHNSON (*To* JUDY): How were the tryouts, honey?

JUDY (*Sweeping around room*): Sensational! Simply sensational! I am the toast of the town! (*She twirls around giddily and bumps into a piece of furniture.*)

BILL: Judy, were you and I at the same tryouts?

JUDY: Bill, can you sit there and deny that I held everyone spellbound this afternoon? Mr. Wilson was awed by my brilliant performance. Simply awed!

BILL: Stunned is more like it.

JUDY (*Ignoring him*): And Nancy! Dear, sweet Nancy! When I read that last scene, it actually brought tears to her eyes.

BILL: You can say that again! She was crying because she felt so sorry for you.

JUDY (*Wounded*): How can you say such a thing, Bill?

BILL: Because it's the truth.

JUDY: The truth is, you're jealous! At least my friends appreciate me.

BILL: The truth is, you don't have any friends left! Half the kids in school think you're a big phony, and the rest can't stand the sight of you.

MRS. JOHNSON: Bill, that's enough.

MR. JOHNSON: Bill, why don't you run out to the garage and look for that weed killer.

JUDY: Mother, you're simply going to have to speak to Bill about his boorish behavior! (*Almost in tears*) He is so rude! (*She starts left.*)

MRS. JOHNSON: Judy, you haven't met . . .

JUDY (*Over her shoulder*): Mother, I simply haven't time for trivia. (*She sniffs.*) I must get ready for the party. I can't disappoint my fans, you know. (*Exits*)

MRS. JOHNSON: John, I'm sorry. I think we all have a touch of the jitters since the tryouts this afternoon.

MR. RANDALL: There's no need to apologize. I understand perfectly. Tryouts can bring out the best or the worst in almost anybody.

MR. JOHNSON: And you should know, John.

MRS. JOHNSON (*Innocently; to* MR. RANDALL): Oh, are you interested in the theater?

MR. JOHNSON: Helen, do you know who John is?

MRS. JOHNSON (*Baffled*): Well, of course, dear, he's our new neighbor.

MR. JOHNSON: Remember the show we saw in New York—*Buffalo Blues*?

MRS. JOHNSON: Remember it! It was one of my favorite shows of all time!

MR. JOHNSON (*Pointing to* MR. RANDALL): Well, this is John Anderson Randall, the playwright!

MRS. JOHNSON (*Surprised*): Oh, my goodness! I had no idea! (*Phone rings.*) Excuse me a moment. (*Answers phone*) Hello. . . . Yes, she is, Nancy. Hold on a second. (*Calls off*) Judy! Phone!

JUDY (*Off left*): Coming. (MRS. JOHNSON *ad libs surprised conversation with* MR. RANDALL. JUDY *enters and takes phone.*) Hello. . . . Nancy, darling! . . . I'm exhilarated, simply exhilarated. . . . Oh, no, poor Ray! Tryouts must have been too much for him. . . . O.K., if you aren't here by eight, I'll go on to the party by myself. Thanks for calling. (*Hangs up; bleakly*) I won't have to go on a blind date tonight, after all.

MRS. JOHNSON: Why not, dear?

JUDY: Ray's really sick. (*Shrugs*) If he doesn't get better by tonight, he and Nancy won't be going to the party.

MRS. JOHNSON: That's too bad.

JUDY (*With a brave front*): Frankly, I'm relieved. (*Starts to exit*)

MRS. JOHNSON: Wait a minute, Judy. (JUDY *turns slowly, listlessly.*) I thought you might like to meet our new neighbor, John Anderson Randall, the playwright.

MR. RANDALL: Hello, Judy, I'm glad to meet you. (*For a moment,* JUDY *is stunned, then she assumes her theatrical style.*)

JUDY (*Gushing*): Oh, I can't believe this is happening! Imagine, the divine John Anderson Randall, in our humble little home!

BILL (*Entering*): Dad, I can't find that weed spray anywhere.

MR. JOHNSON: Let me see if I can find it. Be right back, John. (*Exits with* BILL)

MRS. JOHNSON: I left something on the stove. (*To* JUDY) Judy, would you entertain Mr. Randall for a few minutes? (*She exits left.*)

JUDY (*Affectedly*): I suppose Harrisville must seem deadly dull to you, Mr. Randall.

MR. RANDALL: Well, no it doesn't. We like Harrisville . . . crabgrass and all!

JUDY (*With a forced laugh*): You are so terribly witty, Mr. Randall. Simply terrible! (*Flustered*) What I mean is, you are so terribly simple! Oh, you must forgive me, Mr. Randall, you really must! I've had an exhausting day. Tryouts for the school play were this afternoon, you know.

MR. RANDALL: Yes, I know.

JUDY: Then you know what *enormous* pressure I've been under.

MR. RANDALL: You must take acting very seriously.

JUDY: Oh, I do! My innate creativity is like a powerful magnet pulling me to stardom . . . pulling . . . pulling! Frankly, I can't resist it. I'm desperate!

MR. RANDALL (*Going along with her*): Like a compulsion, is that it?

JUDY: Compulsion? Yes! Yes, a compulsion! That's it, exactly. A compulsive force, throbbing, taunting, whispering in my ear . . . you must go to Hollywood! You must be on Broadway. You must! You must!

MR. RANDALL (*Trying to hide a smile*): I think I get the idea.

JUDY: I'm leaving Harrisville the second I graduate.

MR. RANDALL (*Shaking his head*): Every year hundreds of young girls flock to Hollywood. Inexperienced and immature, most of them, with more hope than talent.

JUDY: I'm not worried. My wagon is hitched to a star, and I'm going wherever it takes me.

MR. RANDALL: Hollywood is a long way from Harrisville, Judy, in more ways than one.

JUDY: Please call me Judith. That's my stage name.

MR. RANDALL: I think you'll have to change more than your name if you want to become an actress.

JUDY (*Enthusiastically*): Well, you're the expert. Where do I start?

MR. RANDALL: You could start by being yourself.

JUDY (*Taken aback*): But I *am* myself!

MR. RANDALL (*Calmly*): Are you?

JUDY: Of course! I simply have a dramatic flair, that's all. (*Flustered*) My innate magnet is forcing me . . . I mean, my creative magnet is . . . I mean, I'm pulling my magnet. (*She throws up her hands in frustration.*) Oh, I don't know what I mean! (*Pauses*) Except that I'm going to become an actress, and a good one.

MR. RANDALL: Well, Judy, right now, I'd say you lack the experience that a professional actress needs. In fact, the best thing you could do for your career is plan to go on to college after you graduate.

JUDY: College? You're not serious!

MR. RANDALL: I couldn't be more serious.

JUDY: But, Mr. Randall—

MR. RANDALL: Believe me, Judy, I've been in show business long enough to know that being an actress takes more than a pair of dark glasses. It takes discipline and hard work as well as talent. (MR. JOHNSON *enters, carrying a bottle of weed killer.* MR. RANDALL *stands up.*)

MR. JOHNSON (*Handing bottle to* MR. RANDALL): Here you go, John. If this doesn't kill your weeds, nothing will. Want some help with your lawn?

MR. RANDALL: That would be great. Goodbye, Judy. Think about what I've said, won't you? (JUDY *doesn't reply. She crosses to look out window, her back to the others.* MR. RANDALL *exits with* MR. JOHNSON. MRS. JOHNSON *enters.* JUDY *wipes away tears under her sunglasses.*)

MRS. JOHNSON: Judy, dear, do you have something in your eye?

JUDY (*Almost sobbing*): Just a little stardust, Mom. (*She turns and removes sunglasses.*) I've been such a fool! (*She runs off left.*)

MRS. JOHNSON: Oh, Judy! (BILL *enters right.*)

BILL: Mom, I'll be leaving in a few minutes for the party.

MRS. JOHNSON: Is it that late already? I guess Nancy isn't coming by for Judy.

BILL: No blind date, huh? (*Shrugs*) Well, I can't blame them for backing out. Who could stand Judy for a whole evening?

MRS. JOHNSON: Bill, I think you should be a little more understanding! Besides, that isn't the reason Nancy isn't coming. Ray isn't feeling well. (*Doorbell rings.* BILL *opens door to* NANCY, RAY, *and* DAVID RANDALL.)

BILL (*Surprised*): Well, look who's here! Ray, it seems you've made a remarkable recovery.

RAY (*Sheepishly*): I feel much better, thanks.

NANCY: Bill, you were wonderful this afternoon. I had no idea I had such a talented cousin.

BILL: Neither did I. I think we should be billed as the Johnson Family Thespi-hams. (*Puts his arm around* NANCY's *shoulder, and they strike a pose. Everyone laughs.*) By the way, Mom, have you met David Randall?

MRS. JOHNSON: No, we haven't met, though I've heard a lot about you, David. It's nice to meet you.

DAVID: And I'm glad to meet you, Mrs. Johnson.

NANCY: I hope Judy hasn't given up on us, Aunt Helen.

MRS. JOHNSON: Of course not. I'll go tell her you're here. (*Exits left*)

RAY: Nancy, I wish I'd stayed home, and so does David.

NANCY: Will you stop fuming, Ray? Everything is going to work out.

RAY: For David's sake, I hope so. You almost died this afternoon when I told you who your blind date was, didn't you, David?

DAVID (*Embarrassed*): I was just surprised, that's all. I'm sure we'll have a good time.

NANCY (*Relieved*): Oh, David, you will. Once you get to know Judy, you'll really like her. And I'm not saying that just because she's my cousin. Judy really is a wonderful person, friendly and full of fun.

RAY (*Dryly*): Right. She's just a barrel of laughs. (NANCY *glares at him.* MR. JOHNSON *enters.*)

MR. JOHNSON: Nancy, I heard you brought down the house at tryouts.

BILL: In fact, Nancy, if I were Mr. Wilson, you'd get the lead. (*Unnoticed,* JUDY *enters with* MRS. JOHNSON. *She is without sunglasses, and wears simple dress.*)

NANCY (*Modestly*): Thanks, Bill, but I doubt it.

JUDY: Well, I don't doubt it, Nancy. You were terrific this afternoon. (*Everyone looks at* JUDY, *amazed.*)

NANCY: Judy! Well, I thought you were . . . well . . .

BILL: Ghastly!

MRS. JOHNSON: Bill!

JUDY: Bill's right, Mom. It's about time I faced up to the truth.

MRS. JOHNSON: Oh, I'm sure you'll get a role of some kind, Judy.

JUDY: It's O.K. if I don't, Mom, really it is. Of course I'd like to be in the play, but if I don't get a part, it won't be the end of the world.

MRS. JOHNSON: Why, Judy, what's come over you? This play has consumed you for the past several weeks.

JUDY: It took me a while to get this through my head, but I realize I've been a real phony lately, and that I haven't been much fun to be around. I want to apologize to all of you.

BILL (*Dramatically*): Friends, be sure to tune in next week, at the same time, for another thrilling chapter in the life of plain old Judy Johnson and her search for happiness! (*Everyone laughs.*)

JUDY (*Playfully hitting* BILL): Everyone needs a little brother to set them straight. (*To* DAVID) And David, well, now that I have my feet on the ground, maybe we . . .

BILL: What she means is, now she's back down to earth, she'd be glad to help you pick the crabgrass out of your front lawn! (*All laugh.*)

DAVID: Gee, Judith, I can't believe—

JUDY: Call me Judy, O.K.?

DAVID: Judy, this is the first time I've ever seen you without your sunglasses, and . . . (*Phone rings.* MRS. JOHNSON *answers it.*)

MRS. JOHNSON (*On phone*): Hello. . . . Oh, hi, Mr. Wilson. . . . Yes, they're all here. I'll let Judy take the message. (*To* JUDY) Judy, it's Mr. Wilson. (JUDY *takes the phone.*)

JUDY (*On phone*): Hi, Mr. Wilson . . . Yes, of course, I'd be glad to tell them. . . . Great! . . .Oh, that's wonderful! . . . Thank you,

Mr. Wilson! . . . Yes, I'm sure we'll have a great time tonight . . . O.K., see you on Monday. Goodbye. (*Hangs up, then spins around, delighted*) Guess what? Nancy got the female lead, and Ray got the male lead! (*Everyone congratulates them.*) And Bill and David both play disk jockeys. (*They receive congratulations.*) Oh, and I got a part, too!

BILL: Great! Which one?

JUDY (*Laughing*): Well, he said the part was perfect (*Mimicking herself*), simply perfect for me.

MR. JOHNSON: Well, don't keep us in suspense!

JUDY: I play the part of a kooky teen-age actress! (*All laugh and groan. Quick curtain*)

THE END

Middle Grades

Buffalo Bill's Wild West Show

by Craig Sodaro

Stagecoaches, outlaws, and shootouts come to life in this rousing tale of pioneer days. . . .

Characters

BUFFALO BILL CODY, *great scout and entrepreneur*
ANNIE OAKLEY, *sharpshooting queen*
VILLAIN
RAILROAD QUARTET
DINAH, *Quartet's cook*
BANJO PLAYER
SPIKE ⎫
DOGGIE ⎭ *cowboys*
CALAMITY JANE, *lady muleskinner*
LILLY ⎫
MILLY ⎭ *dance hall girls*
CATTLE CORRIE, *outlaw*
LI'L BRITCHES, *her sidekick*
DAISY, *schoolmarm*

113

MRS. BLUNTPOUND, *forceful woman*
MR. BLUNTPOUND, *her husband*
STAGECOACH DRIVER
FOUR HORSES

TIME: *Turn of the century.*
SETTING: *Bare stage. It may be decorated with a Western mural or several large cacti.*
AT RISE: BUFFALO BILL *enters.*

BUFFALO BILL: Ladies and gentlemen! Children of all ages! Welcome to the Wild West Show, in which you will witness the exciting spectacle of the settling of the American West! The thrilling sights and sounds of that bygone era will come to life before your very eyes, or my name isn't Buffalo Bill Cody! To begin our extravaganza, we have a useful lesson in the art of sharpshooting. And who better to teach us how to protect ourselves from the perils of the plains than the one, the only little Darling of the Plains herself, Miss Annie Oakley! (AN-NIE OAKLEY, *wearing holster with gun, runs on right, while* BUFFALO BILL *leads audience in applause. She blows him a kiss. He exits.*)

ANNIE (*Flamboyantly*): Howdy, folks! Colonel Cody asked me to present a short demonstration of the lively art of self-defense as needed by a lady traveling through the Wild West—where dangers lurk around every bend in the road, under every rock, and behind every waxed moustache.

The first danger that might be faced is starvation. The sparse lunch packed in Cheyenne might run out quickly if bad weather overtakes the lone traveler. If this happens to you, the first rule is, *Do not panic!* (*Demonstrates*) Simply take out your six-shooter, load with fresh cartridges, and then stalk game! (*Draws gun, then scans audience*) In stalking game, keep your eyes open for anything that moves. Shoot only at furry things, and try not to shoot anything that is too heavy to carry. An ideal subject is a bird. Light, easy to hit, and nutritious. (ANNIE *pretends to spot bird in flight.*) Aha! A fine specimen now overhead! (*She fires gun. A bucket of fried chicken falls from above stage or can be thrown onto stage from wing.* ANNIE *returns gun to holster.*)

The second danger—the deadly diamondback—lurks under rocks. Should you be treading upon an untrod path and hear the sinister rattle, rattle, rattle of a rattler, *freeze!* (ANNIE *does so.*) This fools the snake into thinking you are a rock. Second, with a slow, steady hand, withdraw your pistol. (*Draws pistol from holster*) Third, take careful aim. (*Aims*) Finally, *fire!* You could come up with a fine snakeskin belt! (*Belt is thrown onto stage.*)

The final danger is the worst of all. A lady traveling alone can easily find herself at the mercy of a villain who might try to take advantage of her. (VILLAIN, *in moustache, cape, and top hat, slinks on left. He has cigar in mouth. Recorded "villain music" may be played.*) Should you face this formidable foe, the old mirror trick is very good for stopping him in his tracks. (ANNIE *takes mirror from pocket, and aims gun by looking into it. She fires. Cigar flies out of villain's mouth. To audience*) If this does not work, it may be necessary to execute a different defensive maneuver, such as the old "one, two!" (VILLAIN *sneaks up on* ANNIE. *She turns suddenly and fells him with karate chop.*) If, however, the villain still persists . . . (VILLAIN *rises.*) a third suggestion is in order! *Run!* (ANNIE *runs off right, followed by* VILLAIN. BUFFALO BILL *enters left, leading audience in applause.*)

BUFFALO BILL: Isn't that little lady something! . . . Now, ladies and gentlemen, one of the most important factors in the winning of the West was the building of the Transcontinental Railroad, which was finally completed May 10, 1869, at Promontory Point, Utah. A tribute now to the gallant men who toiled over thousands of miles of rugged terrain to link East to West! (*Stands off to one side as* RAILROAD QUARTET *enters and sings, "I've Been Working on the Railroad," pantomiming driving spikes, laying tracks.* DINAH, *in apron and chef's hat, enters, followed by* BANJO PLAYER, *who strums on an imaginary banjo. During song,* RAILROAD QUARTET *pleads with* DINAH *on lines, "Dinah won't you blow your horn," but she ignores them as she moons over* BANJO PLAYER. *At end of song,*

QUARTET, DINAH, *and* BANJO PLAYER *exit.* BUFFALO BILL *crosses to center.*) With the railroad came the cattle trails, for the train provided a way to sell cattle back East. Cattle were driven north from Texas and south from Montana to cow towns at the end of the trail. Along the way, drovers stopped at any watering hole for a little relaxation and possibly some excitement! (SPIKE *and* DOGGIE *enter, carrying three stools and small table. They sit center.* MILLY *and* LILLY *enter right and do a few dance steps, as* BUFFALO BILL *exits.*)

SPIKE (*Clapping*): Why, Lilly and Milly, that dance was a dilly!

DOGGIE: You two are just the sweetest heifers this side of Austin!

LILLY: You're just saying that 'cause you're so lonesome after punching all those cows.

SPIKE: We're lonesome, all right, but we've been waiting just for you two.

MILLY (*Flattered*): Gosh, boys, how long are you in town?

DOGGIE: Trail boss said we'll be heading north again tomorrow.

LILLY (*Happily*): Why, that'll be just perfect! You can invite us to the big dance tonight! (CLEM *runs on right.*)

CLEM: Hey, fellers, did you hear the news? Calamity Jane's in town!

LILLY (*Distastefully*): That old muleskinner?

MILLY (*Venomously*): She's a disgrace to all women.

CLEM: Maybe, but you know what?

SPIKE (*Intrigued*): What?

CLEM: Calamity's struck it rich! Said she found the map to the old Lucky Seven Mine near Buffalo.

MILLY: The place where those seven prospectors pulled out seven thousand dollars worth of gold dust—

LILLY: Then disappeared into thin air?

CLEM: That's it! Anybody who finds *that* mine will be one rich feller! (*Exits*)

DOGGIE (*Scratching his head*): Gosh—I could give up cow punching.

SPIKE: Yeah—no more saddle sores! (CALAMITY JANE *enters right.*)

CALAMITY: Howdy, y'all! (*To* LILLY) How about a glass of goat's milk, Lilly? It's great for my complexion! (LILLY *exits.*)

DOGGIE (*Rising, gallantly*): Sit down, Calamity.

SPIKE (*Rising*): No, sit over here.

CALAMITY: Why don't I sit between the two of you? (*Sits*)

DOGGIE: Gosh, you sure look pretty today!

CALAMITY (*Fluttering her eyelids*): Do I?

SPIKE (*Romantically*): Like dewdrops on a cactus.

CALAMITY (*Primping*): Must be my hair. I washed it last month.

DOGGIE: You smell like a rosebud to me.

CALAMITY (*Sweetly*): You two are about the sweetest drovers I ever met! (LILLY *enters left, with glass of milk. She hands it to* CALAMITY, *who drinks it in one gulp, then wipes her mouth on her sleeve.*)

LILLY: Tell me, Calamity. What've you been doing since you crawled in here the last time? (SPIKE *goes over to* MILLY *and whispers in her ear.* MILLY *exits left.* SPIKE *returns to seat.*)

CALAMITY: Well, I hitched on at Ft. Laramie, and that went fine till they found out I was a gal. Then I headed north to play cards with Wild Bill. Got tired of that and went to live with the Sioux for a couple of months. That's how I found this map. (*She takes map from pocket, lays it on table.* SPIKE *and* DOGGIE *eye it carefully.* MILLY *reenters left.*)

MILLY: Doggie, there's somebody outside to see you.

DOGGIE (*Annoyed*): Now, who could be looking for me? (*Sighs heavily*) I'll be right back. (*He exits left.*)

SPIKE: Sounds really exciting, Calamity. Especially the map. Say, did you hear about the big dance tonight?

CALAMITY: Dance? Who's going on the warpath?

SPIKE: It's just a friendly dance, Calamity, not a war dance.

CALAMITY: Doesn't sound like much fun to me.

SPIKE: I'd be mighty obliged if you'd go with me. (DOGGIE *reenters left.*)

DOGGIE (*To* SPIKE, *angrily*): Hold on there, you snake in the grass!

CALAMITY (*Furiously*): Don't you call me a snake, Jake!

DOGGIE: Not you, Calamity. (*Turns*) You, Spike! There wasn't anyone out there. You got rid of me so you could ask Calamity to the dance, right?

CALAMITY (*Beaming at* SPIKE): He sure did!

DOGGIE: Well, that's a fine kettle of fish!

CALAMITY (*Coyly*): I haven't said yes, yet, cowboy.

DOGGIE: You haven't? Then, how about going with me?

CALAMITY: Well, now, this hasn't ever happened before!

MILLY (*Sarcastically*): Not surprising!

SPIKE: You clear out of here, Doggie! (*Angrily*) I asked Calamity first! She's going with *me*!

DOGGIE (*Fuming*): She'd rather go with me!

SPIKE: You smell like a barn floor!

DOGGIE: Is that so? Well, half your teeth are missing!

SPIKE (*Rising and drawing his gun*): At least I've still got my six-shooter!

CALAMITY (*Rising, nervously*): Now hold on there, boys. (MILLY *and* LILLY *cower.*)

SPIKE: I'll give you to the count of three, Doggie.

CALAMITY: Are you sure this isn't some kind of war dance?

DOGGIE (*Rising, drawing gun and backing away from table*): Stay clear, Calamity!

SPIKE (*Circling around*): This could get messy for some crazy cowhound.

CALAMITY: I'm not worth fighting for—(*Hopefully*) am I?

LILLY: Don't press your luck!

SPIKE: All right, you varmint! On the count of three! (SPIKE *and* DOGGIE *stand facing each other.*) One . . . two . . . three! (SPIKE *and* DOGGIE *fire wildly, then terrified, duck for cover under table.*)

CALAMITY (*Angrily*): Boys, you're the worst shots I've ever seen! I'm not going to the dance with any cowpokes who shoot up my map of the Lucky Seven Mine! (*She holds up map, which is full of holes.*) Why, if I ever see you two again, I'll make a pair of boots out of each of you! Now, get back to your herd where you belong! (SPIKE *and* DOGGIE, *grabbing table and stools, race off right.*)

CLEM (*Running in left*): Hey, what's all the shootin' about? (*Looks around*) Where are Spike and Doggie?

LILLY: Calamity scared 'em away.

MILLY: Calamity, was that really a map of the Lucky Seven Mine?

The Mystery of the Gumdrop Dragon

by Gerry Lynn Burtle

An unusual reward is offered for the return of a royal favorite. . . .

Characters

TWO GUARDS
PRINCESS
LADY CANDY FLOSS
LADY LEMON DROP
LADY DIVINITY
PAGE
COURT SCRIBE
TOWN CRIER
THREE CLOWNS
WIZARD
GATEKEEPER
PRINCE PEPPERMINT STICK
SIR SOURBALL
GUMDROP DRAGON

Scene 1

SETTING: *Throne room in the Kingdom of Candyland.*

AT RISE: TWO GUARDS *stand at attention at either side of stage.* PRINCESS *enters, weeping, followed by* LADY CANDY FLOSS, LADY LEMON DROP, *and* LADY DIVINITY, *who are wringing their hands and whispering to one another.* PRINCESS *takes her seat on the throne, center, and ladies sit in chairs on either side of her.*

PRINCESS: Alas, what woe has fallen on our Candyland Kingdom today!

LADY CANDY FLOSS: Yes, my Princess. The Gumdrop Dragon, your favorite pet, has been stolen.

PRINCESS: Who could have taken him?

LADY LEMON DROP: If you ask me, my Princess, I'd say it was the Keeper of the Town Museum. He always did think the Gumdrop Dragon would look lovely stuffed and mounted. (PRINCESS *begins to wail.*)

LADY DIVINITY: Now, now, Princess, I'm sure the Museum Keeper would never take your pet. He knows how much you love the Gumdrop Dragon.

PRINCESS: That is probably true, Lady Divinity, but we still don't know who *did* steal the Gumdrop Dragon.

LADY CANDY FLOSS: Princess, I have an idea!

PRINCESS: What is your idea, Lady Candy Floss?

LADY CANDY FLOSS: I thought you might send the Town Crier throughout Candyland, with a proclamation offering a reward to the person who finds the Gumdrop Dragon.

PRINCESS: Why, that's a wonderful idea!

LADY LEMON DROP (*Tartly*): Just what would you offer as a reward?

PRINCESS (*Slowly*): Why, I hadn't thought about that. I don't know.

LADY LEMON DROP (*Crossly*): I thought not. Then I'd say it isn't a very good idea.

LADY DIVINITY: I disagree. The idea is a very good one, and I know it can work.

PRINCESS: How, Lady Divinity?

LADY DIVINITY: Simply put into your proclamation that whoever finds the Gumdrop Dragon may choose his own reward.

PRINCESS (*Excited*): Of course! The very thing! How does one go about sending a proclamation? I've never done it before.

LADY DIVINITY: Call in the Court Scribe. He will write the proclamation on a scroll, and the Town Crier will read it throughout the land. (PRINCESS *claps her hands, and* PAGE *enters and bows.*)

PRINCESS: Send the Court Scribe to me at once, please.

PAGE: Yes, Your Highness. At once! (*Exits*)

PRINCESS: I do hope this will work.

LADY DIVINITY: I'm sure the Dragon will be found.

PAGE (*Re-entering and bowing*): The Court Scribe! (SCRIBE *enters and bows as* PAGE *exits.*)

SCRIBE: At your service, Your Highness. What will it be—a poem, a story of magic?

PRINCESS: Neither of those. Today the task I place before you is not a happy one.

SCRIBE: In that case, if you'll excuse me, Your Highness, I'll get my handkerchief ready. I always cry when I write sad things. (*He pulls handkerchief from sleeve, and holds it ready at his nose.*) Now, then, Princess, if you will, proceed.

PRINCESS: My pet Gumdrop Dragon was stolen from his cage in the courtyard. No trace of him can be found. (SCRIBE *begins to sniffle.*) I would like you to write a proclamation to send throughout the kingdom, offering a reward for his return.

SCRIBE (*Sobbing into handkerchief*): Your every word is my command, Princess. (*He takes roll of paper and feather pen from under his cap.* LADY DIVINITY *brings him an ink well; he dips his pen into it, then goes toward* 1ST GUARD, *holding pen and paper.* 1ST GUARD *bends over, and* SCRIBE *places paper on his back.*) Begin, Princess.

PRINCESS: I should like to address this proclamation to all the people of the kingdom.

SCRIBE: Uh-h-h, how about something like this: "Hear ye! Hear ye! All ye good people of the kingdom!"

PRINCESS: The very thing! Perfect.

SCRIBE (*Writing*): Always willing to help, Your Highness.

PRINCESS: Now I suppose I'd better tell who's sending the proclamation.

SCRIBE: That's simple. "This is a proclamation from the Princess of Candyland."

PRINCESS: Exactly. Now say something about the reward for bringing back my Gumdrop Dragon.

SCRIBE: What is the reward, Princess?

PRINCESS: They may choose anything they want.

SCRIBE: Very handsome of you, Princess. It will go this way, then: (*Reading*) "The Princess of Candyland offers a reward to anyone who finds her missing pet, the Gumdrop Dragon, and the villain who stole him away. The person returning both to her may choose anything he desires for a reward."

PRINCESS (*Clapping her hands*): It's very well worded. Now it must have an ending.

SCRIBE: We will end with: "Hear ye! Hear ye!" (*He writes busily.*) There. Is that all, Princess? (SCRIBE *rolls up paper, hands it to* PRINCESS.)

PRINCESS: Yes, thank you. I'm very grateful to you.

SCRIBE: Thank you, Princess. (*Bows and exits.* PRINCESS *claps her hands and* PAGE *enters.*)

PAGE: Yes, Your Highness.

PRINCESS: Bring the Town Crier to the throne room, please. Immediately.

PAGE: Yes, Your Highness. Immediately! (*Exits*)

PRINCESS (*Holding up paper*): And now to send my proclamation throughout the kingdom for all to hear.

PAGE (*Re-entering and bowing*): The Town Crier, Your Highness. (TOWN CRIER *enters, bows, clears his throat importantly and speaks.*)

TOWN CRIER: I hope you can make this brief, Your Highness. I'm about to begin my morning rounds with the news, and I can't be late.

PRINCESS: I shall take only a minute of your time, Town Crier. I want you to take this proclamation throughout the kingdom for me, and read it to all my people. (*Hands proclamation to him*)

TOWN CRIER: Glad to do it, Princess. (*He unfolds proclamation.*) Would you like to hear me read it now? I've a very good voice, you know.

PRINCESS: I should like that very much, thank you. But won't you be late with the news if you take the time?

TOWN CRIER: Well, just a little late. After all, a proclamation is very important business!

PRINCESS: Yes, of course. (TOWN CRIER *takes a deep breath, clears his throat.*)

TOWN CRIER (*Reading; loudly*): "Hear ye! Hear ye! All good people of the kingdom! This is a proclamation from the Princess of Candyland . . ."

LADY DIVINITY: My, such a nice strong voice!

TOWN CRIER (*Looking up from paper*): Thank you, Lady Divinity, but please, no interruptions. I cannot work with interruptions. It is one of the rules.

PRINCESS: Please continue, Town Crier. No one will interrupt again.

TOWN CRIER: Thank you, Princess. Now, let me see. Where was I? (*Reading*) "The Princess of Candyland offers a reward to anyone who finds her missing pet, the Gumdrop Dragon, and the villain who stole him away. The person returning both to her may choose anything he desires for a reward. Hear ye! Hear ye!" (*He looks to* PRINCESS *for approval.*)

PRINCESS: The reading was beautifully done. I shall depend on you to read it throughout the kingdom, and to see that every one of my subjects hears it.

TOWN CRIER: You can depend on me, Your Highness. I will not fail you. (*Clicks heels together, bows low and exits*)

PRINCESS: And now I must hope with all my heart that the Dragon will be found. Perhaps because I believe it will be so, my Gumdrop Dragon will be returned to me. (*Curtain*)

* * * * *

SCENE 2

TIME: *One week later.*
SETTING: *Same as Scene 1.*

AT RISE: PRINCESS *is on her throne, surrounded by ladies-in-waiting, who appear dejected.* GUARDS *stand at right and left.*

LADY CANDY FLOSS: Princess, the sun is shining this morning, and the birds are singing. Won't you try to smile?

PRINCESS (*Sighing deeply*): I will never smile again. A week has passed, and no one has found my beloved Gumdrop Dragon.

LADY DIVINITY: I fear the Gumdrop Dragon is gone for good. You must learn to live without him, Princess.

LADY LEMON DROP (*Sharply*): I never did think we'd find that Dragon. (PRINCESS *sobs softly.*)

LADY DIVINITY: Princess, do try to be cheerful. When you are sad, the whole Kingdom of Candyland is sad.

PRINCESS: How can I be happy, when my heart is broken?

LADY CANDY FLOSS: Perhaps we can mend it for you.

PRINCESS: You may try, but I am sure nothing will ever make me smile again, unless my Gumdrop Dragon is found.

LADY DIVINITY: Nevertheless, may I have your permission, Princess, to call the Clowns?

PRINCESS: You may call them. (LADY DIVINITY *claps her hands.* PAGE *enters.*)

LADY DIVINITY: Send the Clowns to the throne room, please.

PAGE: Yes, Lady Divinity. At once. (*Exits*)

PRINCESS: I do not think the Clowns will seem funny to me today.

LADY DIVINITY: But, on the other hand, perhaps they will.

PAGE (*Entering*): The Clowns! (CLOWNS *enter, tumbling over each other. All but* PRINCESS *laugh.* CLOWNS *bow.* PAGE *exits.*)

1ST CLOWN: Good evening. We're here as you can see . . . somewhere. (*He looks around to see where, and all but* PRINCESS *laugh again.*)

LADY CANDY FLOSS: It's not evening. It's morning.

1ST CLOWN: Oh, is it? Well, morning or evening, we're at your service. What would you like? A song, perhaps? Come, Clowns.

CLOWNS (*Reciting together; merrily*):
Hurray, hurray, today's the day,
Today's the day, we've chosen to play.
Of course today could be any day,
'Cause any day is the day that we play.

(*They do somersaults and pretend to hide from one another behind throne. All laugh but* PRINCESS; *she lowers head and weeps.*)

LADY DIVINITY: Enough, enough. You have done your best, but it does not make the Princess happy. You may go now, and thank you for trying. (CLOWNS *exit.*)

LADY CANDY FLOSS: Well, let's not give up. Try the Wizard. He's a master of magic. Perhaps he can cheer the Princess. (LADY DIVINITY *claps her hands again.* PAGE *enters.*)

PAGE: You called me, Lady Divinity?

LADY DIVINITY: Bring the Chocolate Wizard here at once.

PAGE: Yes, Your Highness. At once. (*Exits*)

LADY CANDY FLOSS: My Princess, if you will observe the Wizard carefully, his tricks will fascinate you, and you will soon forget all about the Gumdrop Dragon.

PRINCESS: I will never forget the Gumdrop Dragon.

PAGE (*Entering*): The Chocolate Wizard! (*Exits as* WIZARD *enters, removes his hat, and bows*)

WIZARD: Good day. And what would the good people of the court like to see this morning? Perhaps a white rabbit. (*Pulls toy rabbit from his hat*)

PRINCESS: You are a wizard, and wizards are supposed to be very wise. Can you read the future?

WIZARD: Alas, my Princess, I cannot. Actually, though I hate to admit it, I am nothing but an overglorified magician.

PRINCESS: Oh, I am so sorry. I know how you must feel. I, too, am unhappy.

LADY LEMON DROP: Here, here, that will do, Wizard. You've done enough damage. Begone!

WIZARD: Alas, I have failed again.

PRINCESS: That's not so. It's not your fault that you failed to cheer me. It just can't be done, that's all.

WIZARD: Thank you for your kindness, Princess. I hope you recover your happiness soon. (*Bows and exits*)

PRINCESS: It is not fair for me to be happy, when my poor Gumdrop Dragon may be lonely somewhere, and a prisoner of the terrible villain who took him from me. (*Wails*) Oh, what a dreadful thought—my Gumdrop Dragon may be a prisoner! (*Weeps. Ladies gather around her and console her as curtain closes.*)

* * * * *

Scene 3

TIME: *That afternoon.*
SETTING: *Same.*
AT RISE: *Court is assembled as in Scene 2.* PAGE *stands before throne.*
PAGE: Your Highness, I came as fast as I could. The Gatekeeper begs an audience with you. He says he has important news.
PRINCESS: Do you think it's about my Gumdrop Dragon? A week and a day have passed since he disappeared.
PAGE: He wouldn't say, Princess. He will talk only to you. Will you see him?
PRINCESS: Of course! At once! Please send him in.
PAGE: Yes, Your Highness. (*He exits.*)
PRINCESS: Perhaps my Gumdrop Dragon has been found at last!
LADY DIVINITY: We shall soon know.
PAGE (*Entering*): The Keeper of the Gates! (*Exits, as* GATEKEEPER *enters, bows, and approaches* PRINCESS)
GATEKEEPER (*Excitedly*): Your Highness! Your Highness! A strange thing! Yes, indeed, a very strange thing.
LADY LEMON DROP: Speak up, and stop sputtering. The Princess is waiting.
GATEKEEPER: Yes, my lady. Yes, yes indeed. Right away.
PRINCESS: What have you to tell me, Gatekeeper?
GATEKEEPER: I'm sorry, Princess, but I am out of breath. I ran all the way from the gate to tell you what I've seen.
PRINCESS: And what have you seen?
GATEKEEPER: This morning from my tower in the gatehouse, I saw a strange procession winding its way toward the town.
PRINCESS: Is that so?
GATEKEEPER: I could not see at first what it was, but as it came

nearer, I began to make out certain figures. First came a young man, a very handsome young man. And next—

PRINCESS (*Excitedly*): Next?

GATEKEEPER: Next, Your Highness, came the Gumdrop Dragon!

PRINCESS (*Overjoyed*): The Gumdrop Dragon! Are you sure?

GATEKEEPER: Yes, Your Highness. They have already passed through my gates, and are even now on their way to the castle.

PRINCESS: At last! My Gumdrop Dragon is found. Prepare a feast. Let there be laughing and rejoicing! We must celebrate the return of my Gumdrop Dragon!

GATEKEEPER (*Hesitantly*): Your Highness, there were others in the procession, too.

PRINCESS: Let them come. They shall all be made welcome.

GATEKEEPER (*Slowly*): Even the villain who stole the Dragon?

PRINCESS (*Agitated*): Is the villain also in the procession?

GATEKEEPER: Yes, my Princess. He comes, slowly, at the end of the line. He is in chains.

PRINCESS: Ah, then he, too, knows what it is like to be a prisoner, as my Gumdrop Dragon was. Thank you for your joyful news.

GATEKEEPER: You're welcome, Princess. (*Bows and exits, as* PAGE *enters*)

PAGE: Your Highness, the victor and his prisoner are here, and your subjects are greeting the Gumdrop Dragon.

PRINCESS: Who is the victor, Page?

PAGE: A very handsome young prince.

LADY CANDY FLOSS: A prince! Oh, my!

PRINCESS: A prince! Bring him to me at once. I must welcome him royally.

PAGE: With pleasure, Your Highness. (*Exits*)

LADY CANDY FLOSS: A prince. A handsome prince! Do I look all right?

LADY LEMON DROP (*Scornfully*): What does it matter how *you* look?

LADY DIVINITY: He must be a very brave prince to have found the Gumdrop Dragon and captured the thief who took him.

PRINCESS: Oh, I am sure he is brave and good.

PAGE (*Entering*): Prince Peppermint Stick! (PRINCE PEPPERMINT

STICK *enters, wearing crown. He removes crown and bows low to* PRINCESS. PAGE *exits.*)

PRINCE: Princess of Candyland, at last we meet. For many years, I have heard tell of your beauty. Now I see for myself that you are far more beautiful than could ever be told.

PRINCESS: You are very kind, noble sir. Is it true you have found my beloved Gumdrop Dragon?

PRINCE: Yes, Princess, it is true. I have found the Gumdrop Dragon and the thief who took him. Both I return to you.

PRINCESS: Again my thanks to you, sir. May I ask you whence you come?

PRINCE: I come from the neighboring kingdom of Peppermint Green, Princess. I was traveling through your kingdom when I heard the proclamation. I immediately joined the search.

PRINCESS: And luck was with you!

PRINCE: Indeed, for I was fortunate enough to stumble upon the entrance of a tiny cave hidden away in the Marshmallow Mountains. I stopped to investigate, and found your Gumdrop Dragon tied up inside.

PRINCESS: How cruel! But what of the villain?

PRINCE: The villain was not to be seen, so I settled myself at the mouth of the cave to await his return.

PRINCESS: How brave of you!

LADY CANDY FLOSS: Please, tell us what happened then.

PRINCE: I had not long to wait. Just as night was falling, the villain sneaked back to the cave, with food for the Gumdrop Dragon.

PRINCESS: What did you do?

PRINCE: I challenged him with my sword, but he was a coward, and surrendered immediately without a fight.

PRINCESS: You are very brave, my Prince, and you shall have your reward. But first . . . (*Claps hands;* PAGE *enters.*)

PAGE: Yes, Your Highness.

PRINCESS: Bring here the villain who stole my Gumdrop Dragon.

PAGE (*Frightened*): Y-yes, Your Highness. (*Exits*)

LADY CANDY FLOSS: The villain!

PRINCESS: Never fear. He will harm no one, for he is in chains.

Even if he were not, we are well protected by the brave Prince, and the soldiers who guard the throne room.

PAGE (*Entering*): The villain! (*He runs out.* SIR SOURBALL *enters in chains and stands before* PRINCESS *without bowing.*)

PRINCESS: You are now in the presence of a princess, villain. You will please bow. (SIR SOURBALL *bows.*)

SIR SOURBALL: Excuse me, Your Highness, but I've never been in the presence of a princess before. I didn't know I had to bow.

PRINCESS (*Coldly*): Now, villain, what is your name?

SIR SOURBALL: My name is Sir Sourball.

PRINCESS: You stole my dragon. That was a very bad thing to do.

SIR SOURBALL (*Sadly*): Yes, I know.

PRINCESS: Then why did you do it?

SIR SOURBALL: I will tell you, Princess. The people of Candyland are all happy, except me. I'm terribly unhappy. So one day, I decided to do something about it. First of all, I looked around to see what was making the people of Candyland happy. And I discovered what was making them happy was you, Princess.

PRINCESS: Me!

SIR SOURBALL: Yes. And I discovered that you were happy because you had the Gumdrop Dragon. So I thought he'd make me happy, too. Only it didn't work. I was still unhappy. Not only that, but I made you unhappy, and all the people of Candyland, too.

PRINCESS (*Kindly*): Oh, poor Sir Sourball. You aren't a wicked villain at all. You're just an unhappy one.

SIR SOURBALL (*Sobbing*): I wish I'd never taken the Gumdrop Dragon.

PRINCESS: Listen to me, Sir Sourball. To be happy, what you need are friends.

SIR SOURBALL: But where am I going to find any friends?

PRINCESS: We're all your friends here. Aren't we, Court of Candyland?

ALL (*Together; ad lib*): Yes! Of course! Certainly! (*Etc.*)

SIR SOURBALL: They are? Oh, I'm so happy! I'm so happy!

PRINCESS: Now you can help us celebrate the return of my Gumdrop Dragon. Guards! Remove Sir Sourball's chains. He is no longer a villain. (*While* GUARDS *remove chains,* PRINCESS *claps hands.* PAGE *enters.*) Page, bring in the Clowns, the Wizard, the Court Scribe, the Town Crier, the Gatekeeper— everyone who tried to cheer me up and help me find the Gumdrop Dragon.

PAGE: Yes, Your Highness!

SIR SOURBALL: I think I'd better go now.

PRINCESS: No! Please stay. You're sorry you took my Gumdrop Dragon, and that's all that matters.

SIR SOURBALL: Thank you, Princess. You are very kind. (PAGE *re-enters, followed by* CLOWNS, WIZARD, SCRIBE, TOWN CRIER, *and* GATEKEEPER.)

PRINCESS: Welcome! Let us begin the celebration and welcome the Gumdrop Dragon home.

ALL: Hurray! (GUMDROP DRAGON *runs in and trots to* PRINCESS, *who hugs him.*)

PRINCESS: Oh, my darling Gumdrop Dragon! You're home! You're home, thanks to Prince Peppermint Stick!

PRINCE: I was only too happy to be of service, Princess.

PRINCESS: And now, Prince Peppermint Stick, you must choose your reward. As you know, my proclamation said that the person who found my Gumdrop Dragon could choose anything he might desire for a reward.

PRINCE: There is only one thing I want more than anything else in the world.

PRINCESS: And that is?

PRINCE: To have you for my bride. (*Kneels before* PRINCESS) Princess, will you do me the honor of becoming my wife?

PRINCESS (*Shyly*): Why, I never dared hope for this.

LADY LEMON DROP: He couldn't have made a better choice, if you ask me.

LADY DIVINITY: And neither could she.

PRINCE: Will you grant me my reward, Princess? Will you be my wife?

PRINCESS (*Softly*): Yes, my Prince. (PRINCE *takes her hand, and they stand together with* GUMDROP DRAGON, *as all cheer.*)

ALL (*Together*):
    Hurray for the Gumdrop Dragon!
    Hurray for our Princess fair!
    Hurray for the Prince who claims her!
    And the villain who gave us a scare!
    (*Curtain*)

THE END

Not Fit for Man or Beast

by *Mildred Hark and Noel McQueen*

A melodrama of the Old West . . .

Characters

LITTLE NELL, *beauteous daughter*
MAW, *dear old mother*
GUY FORSYTHE, *villain*
BABY FACE, *Forsythe's accomplice*
WIDDER CLANCY, *neighbor*
HANDSOME HAL HERBERT, *hero*
PAW, *honest Bill Baxter*

SETTING: *The interior of a shack in the Old West.*
AT RISE: MAW *is huddled up in chair left.* LITTLE NELL *is at window looking out: Flashes of lightning can be seen through window, and sounds of thunder and rain are heard off. These storm sounds continue throughout play and are louder whenever door is opened.*
NELL (*Turning*): Not fit for man or beast.
MAW: What's not fit, Little Nell?
NELL: The night, Maw. Can't you hear the storm?

154

MAW: Reckon I can, now you mention it. Think of your poor paw out on a night like this.

NELL: How do you know he's out?

MAW: Well, he went out five years ago, and he hasn't come back in, has he?

NELL: No, and he's never comin' back.

MAW: What makes you talk that-a-way, daughter?

NELL: I feel it in my bones. When Paw got bit by the Klondike bug, he got bit good. And if he *should* find gold, why should he come back to this shack?

MAW: Because he said he would, that's why. Honest Bill Baxter they call your paw, and if he said he'd be back, then he'll be back. And what's more he said when he got back we'd have steak and onions.

NELL: Steak and onions? What's that?

MAW: You wouldn't remember, Nell. You were too young last time we had 'em, but they're mighty fine vittles. (*Sound of horses' hoofs offstage is heard.*)

NELL: Hist, Maw, someone comes on horseback. (*Sound of hoofs becomes louder, then stops.*)

MAW: Maybe it's your paw. (*Loud knock on door is heard.*)

NELL: If it is, he forgot his key. Shall I open the door?

MAW: Why not? It's not a fit night for man or beast. (NELL *goes to door and opens it.* GUY FORSYTHE *and* BABY FACE *rush in.* NELL *leans heavily on door and closes it against storm.* BABY FACE *carries large sack, which he puts near wall left of door. He sits on it, panting.*)

NELL (*Backing down right*): Oh, it's you, Mr. Guy Forsythe. Think of your paying us poor folks a visit on a night like this.

FORSYTHE (*Bowing low*): Ah, ha, my pretty one, so you still remember me. It's been a long time since you came to the bank with your father, and he signed his name to this mortgage. (*Takes paper from his inside pocket, then strokes his long moustache*)

NELL: Yes, it's five years. Five years ago today.

FORSYTHE: That is right, and today the money is due. Haw, haw, haw. (*He leers at* NELL.)

NELL: Oh, Maw, you heard what the man said. The money is due.

MAW: Yes, I heard. I reckon I'm not deaf. So your paw put the house in hock, did he? No wonder he was in such a rush to be off to the Klondike.

NELL: Of course, Maw. To get gold to pay the mortgage.

MAW: And don't forget the steak and onions. Well, if Mr. Forsythe wants our house, it looks as if we'll have to move out and live on the desert with the cactuses.

NELL: Cacti, Maw.

MAW: All right, cacti, then. You and your book learnin'. We'll have to live with the cacti.

FORSYTHE (*Turning to* MAW *and bowing low*): Excuse me, madam, but it isn't as simple as all that. I want my money.

MAW: Money! Look, mister, if I had money I wouldn't be livin' in a place like this. It's not fit for man or beast.

FORSYTHE: Be that as it may, madam, I must have my money or else—

MAW: Or else what?

FORSYTHE: Or else (*Leers at* NELL) your beauteous daughter must marry me.

NELL: No, no, no, a thousand times no!

FORSYTHE: Ah, ha, my proud beauty. (*Puts mortgage back in pocket and goes toward* NELL) You have spirit. But little do you know what is in store for you. We shall live in my villa in Mexico.

NELL: Mexico? But what about the bank?

FORSYTHE: The bank is closed. The ranchers are all moving away because the country isn't fit for man or beast. I have all the gold from the bank in that sack, have I not, Baby Face?

BABY FACE (*Speaking with a Brooklyn accent*): That's right, boss.

NELL: Did you say all the ranchers were moving?

FORSYTHE: All except Handsome Hal Herbert. He says he won't leave his home on the range.

NELL (*Sighing*): Oh, Handsome Hal Herbert—he's wonderful, and he is the sheriff, and he's brave, and he catches robbers. (*With hand over heart*) Be still, my beating heart.

FORSYTHE: So you know this Handsome Hal. (*Strokes his moustache angrily*) Bah, and again bah. All he will have to catch will be himself after we leave for Mexico. And let us not dillydally. My patience will not last longer.

NELL (*Running up to* BABY FACE): Oh, Baby Face, are *you* going to Mexico?

BABY FACE: That's what the boss says.

NELL: But will you like it there?

BABY FACE: Me? Naw. I don't go for this south of the border stuff. I'd rather go to New York.

FORSYTHE (*Angrily*): Baby Face, you'll do as you're told.

BABY FACE: Sure, boss, sure, anything you say. It's just that I'd like to sleep on the sidewalks of New York. (*Knock on door*)

NELL: Hist, someone at the door.

MAW: Maybe it's your paw, Nell.

BABY FACE (*Rising and picking up bag. Aside to* FORSYTHE): What'll we do, boss?

FORSYTHE (*Aside*): Someone must have followed us here. We must hide the gold and make it appear that these people have stolen it. Do you understand?

BABY FACE (*Aside*): Natch. But where?

FORSYTHE (*Aside*): In the woodbox. We shall have to look for an opportunity.

NELL: Shall I open the door, Maw?

MAW: Natch. (*As* NELL *goes to door,* FORSYTHE *and* BABY FACE *move right with bag.* NELL *opens door, and* WIDDER CLANCY *enters.* MAW *rises and goes toward* WIDDER CLANCY) Well, if it is not the Widder Clancy. Mighty nice of you to come callin' on a night like this.

WIDDER: Yes, dear, it's not much of a night for walking, but I just had to talk to someone.

NELL: 'Spect you must get mighty lonely, Widder Clancy, livin' all by yourself.

WIDDER: You're telling me. I thought I'd like it out here in the wide open spaces, but now I'd give anything to be back in little old New York. (*During above,* FORSYTHE *motions toward woodbox, and* BABY FACE *goes quickly downstage and puts bag out of sight in woodbox. He steps upstage again in time to hear "little old New York."*)

BABY FACE (*All smiles*): Say, who said New York?

WIDDER (*Turning*): Why, I did, dear. (*Then to* MAW) Oh, you have company already. Excuse me, but I don't believe I've met the gentlemen.

MAW: Gents, meet the Widder Clancy. Widder, the one with the handlebars is Guy Forsythe, the banker, and the one with the baby face, that's Baby Face. (*She goes back to chair and sits.*)

WIDDER (*Smiling at* BABY FACE): Hm-m-m, kind of cute. (*She sits in chair right.*)

BABY FACE (*Smiling and straightening his tie*): Say, you sound like Broadway. Listen, Widder, how would you like to go to Mexico?

FORSYTHE: Quiet, Baby Face. (*He bows deeply to* WIDDER.) This is indeed a pleasure, Widow Clancy. You may not know me, but I have heard a great deal about you.

WIDDER: Who hasn't, dear? I was on the radio for years. And that reminds me, have you heard the news? Your bank was robbed last night.

BABY FACE: That's no news. We were the ones who—

FORSYTHE: Quiet, Baby Face. (*To* WIDDER) So my bank was robbed? Tell us more, fair one.

WIDDER: What do you mean, *fair* one? I always got *top* billing, dear. They say a stranger rode into town yesterday from the Klondike.

FORSYTHE: Ah, ha!

NELL: Oh, Maw!

MAW: Maybe it's Paw.

FORSYTHE: Go on, Widow Clancy. Your tale is most interesting. It is true a stranger came to town yesterday and deposited a large bag of gold in the bank. I put it in the safe myself.

WIDDER: Well, you'd better get yourself a new safe, dear, because someone made a withdrawal, and a posse is out looking for him right now.

FORSYTHE (*Aside*): Curses! A posse.

BABY FACE (*Aside*): I'm getting out of here.

FORSYTHE (*Aside*): Ah, ha. Wait, I have an idea. (*To* WIDDER) A posse, you say. Which way did they go?

WIDDER: How should I know? All I know is what I read in the papers.

NELL: But, Mr. Forsythe, how could anyone steal from your bank? You said the bank was closed.

FORSYTHE (*Going to* NELL): Ah, ha, my pretty one, so I did. I meant closed for the night. And now someone has broken in and stolen the stranger's gold. But fear not, my pretty one, we shall apprehend the culprit.

BABY FACE: Sure thing. Don't you worry, Nell, why I could practically put my finger—

FORSYTHE: Quiet, Baby Face.

MAW: Well, if your bank was just closed for the night, why are you totin' that bag of gold to Mexico?

FORSYTHE (*All smiles*): But, madam, I'm afraid I don't understand. What bag of gold?

MAW (*Pointing upstage*): That bag that Baby Face was a-sittin' on by the wall.

FORSYTHE (*Spreading his arms and looking about*): I see no bag of gold. Widow Clancy, do you see a bag of gold?

WIDDER: No, I don't. But I don't see the Brooklyn Bridge either, and it wouldn't surprise me if you had *that* up your sleeve.

BABY FACE (*Laughing*): Smart gal.

MAW: Well, Nell, what do you make of it? You saw the bag, didn't you?

NELL: I thought so, Maw.

MAW: What do ye mean, you thought so?

NELL: Well, gee, Maw, maybe it was an hallucination.

BABY FACE (*All smiles*): Yeah, that's right.

MAW (*Shaking her head*): Book learnin'. I tell you it'll be the ruination of us.

WIDDER: If you ask me, there's something awfully fishy about all this.

FORSYTHE (*Scowling*): Widow Clancy, I give you fair warning. Mind your own business.

WIDDER: Listen, big boy, you can't talk to me like that. You have nothing on me.

FORSYTHE: Oh, yes, I have. You came out to this country masquerading as a widow, and you're not a widow at all. You've never even been married.

BABY FACE: Weren't you ever married, Widder?

WIDDER: No, Baby Face, I've never been married. It's just that I was the Widder Clancy on that radio program so long that everyone started calling me Widder Clancy.

NELL: What kind of program was it?

WIDDER: A soap opera.

MAW: Soap opry. What kind of soap is that, Widder?

WIDDER: Soft soap, mostly. I had to start getting sick on Monday and almost die every Friday so the folks would come back to hear more about soap the next Monday.

MAW: Hm-m-m, doesn't sound fit for man or beast.

WIDDER: That's what I thought, dear. That's why I came out here. But now all I dream about is a ride in a subway. (BABY FACE *sniffs loudly once or twice, takes out large red handkerchief and dabs at eyes.*)

FORSYTHE: What's the matter with you, Baby Face?

BABY FACE (*Sniffling and blinking*): Nostalgia.

FORSYTHE: Well, stop sniffling.

BABY FACE: I can't help it, boss. I want to ride in a subway, too.

FORSYTHE: Quiet.

BABY FACE (*Suddenly angry*): I don't want to be quiet. I'm tired of being quiet. (*Reaches for his gun*)

FORSYTHE (*Pulling gun at same time*): Ah, ha, we have a mutiny. I'll show you who's in charge here.

BABY FACE (*As they start to circle table*): You show me, and I'll show you, boss.

FORSYTHE: I'm going to count ten, Baby Face, and if you don't drop that gun and reach for the roof, I'll shoot.

BABY FACE: I can count, too, boss.

BABY FACE *and* FORSYTHE (*Counting slowly as they circle table several times*): One—two—three—four—five—six—seven—eight—

BABY FACE: Gee, I'm gettin' dizzy, boss.

FORSYTHE: Yes, I can see this isn't getting us anywhere. (FORSYTHE *and* BABY FACE *stop at opposite ends of table. They lower their guns a little.*)

BABY FACE: I have an idea, boss.

FORSYTHE: You've never had an idea in your life.

BABY FACE: Maybe I need only one.

FORSYTHE: All right, what is it?

BABY FACE: Look, boss, I don't want to go to Mexico, see? I want to go to New York. (*Pulls deck of cards from coat pocket and places it face down on table*) I'll play with you, boss. If I win, then I go East.

FORSYTHE (*Aside*): Haw, haw, haw, little does he know he is up against the greatest card player in the West. (*To* BABY FACE) Very well, I agree. What is your game?

BABY FACE: It's easy, boss. I'll give you a break. All I have to do is cut an ace, and I win. (*Shuffles cards and puts them down again*) Now, are you ready?

FORSYTHE: Oh, no, you don't, my fine fellow. I don't trust you. *I'll* cut the cards and, *then,* if it's an ace you win. (*Steps across and takes deck, goes back to his end of table and places cards on table in front of him. As he does this,* BABY FACE *motions* WIDDER *toward door with his gun, and she moves near to door.*)

BABY FACE: O.K., boss, have it your own way.

FORSYTHE: Haw, haw, haw. (*Cuts deck and shows ace*) Curses! An ace!

BABY FACE: Nice going, boss. So long, everybody. (*Rushes to door and opens it.* WIDDER, *smiling, rushes out, and he follows.* WIDDER *slams door shut. Sound of horses' hoofs is heard, gradually fading into distance.* FORSYTHE *strokes his moustache, picks up cards, looks at them, then throws them down on table.*)

FORSYTHE (*Angrily*): All aces! I've been tricked (*Rushes to door, opens it, and looks out*) And they've taken both horses! (*Slams door, then stamps back and forth upstage, pulling at his moustache and muttering*) Ah, the irony of it all. Revenge— revenge! (*Pause*)

MAW (*Brightly*): As long as the party is breakin' up, isn't it about time you were goin', too, Mr. Forsythe? It's past my bedtime.

FORSYTHE: Ah, madam, you want me to go. Very well, then, I shall go. (*Takes mortgage from pocket again*) But first we have some business to transact. This little matter of the mortgage.

MAW: That's right, mister. I'd plumb forgot about the mortgage.

NELL (*Wringing her hands*): Oh, Mother, what shall we do? There is no money.

FORSYTHE: Money is not everything, my pretty Nell. (*He goes to* NELL *and holds up paper as though to tear it.*) Look, I will tear up this paper if you will marry me.

NELL: But, Mr. Forsythe, I cannot marry you.

FORSYTHE: And why not?

NELL: Because I do not love you.

FORSYTHE: Ah, but you could learn to love me.

NELL: But I love another. I love Handsome Hal Herbert.

FORSYTHE: So! (*Angrily stuffing mortgage into pocket*) He is the snake in the grass. Well, he shall not stand between us. (*Grabs* NELL *by the wrist and drags her toward woodbox*)

NELL: Unhand me, villain!

FORSYTHE: Oh, no, my proud beauty! (*Reaches into woodbox with free hand and lifts out bag*)

NELL: Oh, Maw, look, the bag of gold.

MAW: Maybe it's a "hullucination."

FORSYTHE: Oh, no, madam, this is no hallucination. It's gold, all gold. And now, Little Nell, you will come with me to Mexico and marry me and live in my villa! (*Shoves her toward door. Sound of mooing offstage is heard. They stop stage center.* FORSYTHE *still has hold of* NELL's *wrist.*)

NELL: Hist, a cow.

FORSYTHE: Curses! And where there are cows, there are cowboys.

MAW: You'd think the critter'd have more sense than to be out on a night like this. It's not fit for man or beast. (*Sound of horses' hoofs offstage.*)

HAL (*Offstage*): Yippee—yippee!

FORSYTHE (*Backing up right, still holding* NELL *and bag*): Aha, what did I tell you? (HANDSOME HAL HERBERT *throws open door and stands in doorway with two guns drawn.*)

HAL: Nobody move. In the name of the law! (*Steps in and kicks door shut behind him*)

NELL: Oh, it's the sheriff, Handsome Hal Herbert.

HAL: Evenin', Miss Nell. (*Nodding to* MAW) Evening, ma'am.

MAW: Evenin', yourself. What are you doin' out chasin' cows on a night like this?

HAL: Well, ma'am, the bank was robbed last night, and I'm out lookin' for the hombre who did it.

MAW: We heard a posse was out lookin'.

HAL: That's right, and I'm the posse, ma'am. And I figured that as long as I was ridin' I might just as well have a roundup at the same time.

MAW: A roundup, ye say?

HAL: Yes, ma'am—the last roundup, on account there's only one cow left. The rest have all moved away.

MAW: Humph. I don't blame 'em. This country isn't fit for man or beast. (*Nodding toward* FORSYTHE *and* NELL) Those two are on their way to Mexico.

NELL: Oh, no, Maw, no! Save me, Handsome Hal Herbert, save me!

HAL: I was about to tend to that, Miss Nell. I've caught you red-handed this time, Guy Forsythe. Robbin' your own bank, and tryin' to leave the country, and annoyin' a lady besides. Reach for the sky, Forsythe, before I get angry and fill you full of lead. (FORSYTHE *drops bag, then draws his gun, puts his arm around* NELL'S *waist, and pulls her in front of him*)

FORSYTHE: Not so fast, Mr. Handsome Hal Herbert. So fair a prize as Little Nell is not so easily won. Drop those guns!

NELL (*As* HANDSOME HAL *hesitates*): Oh, Handsome Hal, do not listen to him. Death would be better than life with this diabolical brute.

MAW: Never mind your book learnin', Nell. There's no use makin' him more riled up than he is. Better do as the man says.

HAL: Reckon you're right, ma'am. (*Drops guns to floor*)

FORSYTHE: That's better. (*Motioning to chair right*) Sit down! (HAL *does.*) Now, my proud beauty, you shall play your part. (*Pushes her toward* HAL) With his own rope you shall tie him hand and foot.

NELL: Oh, that I should come to this. (*Takes* HAL'S *lasso and winds it round and round him and the chair, pinning down his arms*)

FORSYTHE (*Stroking his moustache*): Aha, very pretty, very pretty. (*Laughs villainously, goes quickly to* MAW, *rips off her shawl and ties her to chair with it.*)

MAW (*To audience*): If he isn't the orneriest cuss!

FORSYTHE: And now for the finishing touch. (*To* NELL) Fetch me a few sticks of kindling from the woodbox.

NELL: Oh, Mr. Forsythe, what are you going to do?

FORSYTHE: Aha, you shall see.

NELL: But, Mr. Forsythe, we need no fire.

FORSYTHE: Do as I say. (NELL *goes to woodbox and takes out several small pieces of kindling.*) Put them near the wall. (*She puts them on floor near wall up right and then stands watching* FORSYTHE. *He strikes match and throws it into kindling. To give burning effect, light behind red paper on wall may be turned on.*)

NELL (*Looking piteously at* MAW *and* HAL): Oh, Mr. Forsythe, you will burn the house down around their heads.

FORSYTHE: Haw, haw, haw. Yes, my sweet one, take a last look at your Handsome Hal Herbert because now—now you are coming with me to Mexico, and you will marry me and live in my villa! (*He grabs bag with one hand and* NELL *with the other and starts for door. Door opens, revealing* PAW *standing in doorway.*)

PAW: Are you goin' somewhere, partner?

FORSYTHE (*Backing down right with* NELL): Curses. (*Aside*) The stranger from the Klondike.

MAW: Well, if it's not Santa Claus, and just in time.

NELL: Oh, stranger, help me, help me.

PAW: Reckon I can do that all right. (*Keeping his head erect, he stoops and picks up* HAL's *guns.* FORSYTHE *drops bag and pulls his gun.*) Get rid of that shootin' iron, mister, and unhand the lady. (FORSYTHE *drops gun and raises hands. Still pointing gun at* FORSYTHE, PAW *steps to "fire," tilts his head forward and splashes water from brim of ten-gallon hat. The light immediately goes off. To audience*) I knew this ten-gallon hat would come in handy sometime. (*To* NELL) Better untie your maw, miss, while I let loose the sheriff. (NELL *quickly unties shawl, and with one or two pulls,* PAW *gets ropes off* HAL.)

HAL (*Rising*): Thank you, stranger. Are you the man from the Klondike?

PAW: That I am. And (*Pointing to bag*) that is my bag. I left it in the bank yesterday with that worthless varmint. (*Pointing to* FORSYTHE) Reckon you'd better arrest him. (*Hands* HAL *his guns.* HAL *puts one in holster, covers* FORSYTHE *with other, and then takes paper from pocket.*)

HAL: You're dead right, stranger. Here's the warrant. (*Reads*) "Wanted for stealin' bag of gold." Guy Forsythe, you're under arrest. Better stand up in the corner till we decide what to do with you. (FORSYTHE *scowls and stands in corner facing wall up right.*)

NELL: Oh, stranger, I don't know how to thank you. You have saved all our lives. You must have been sent from heaven.

MAW (*Going downstage to* HAL): He doesn't look as if he came from heaven to me, daughter. (*Lifts* PAW's *beard and shows collar button in collar band*) Just as I thought, Nell. It's your paw. I can tell by the gold collar button I gave him before we were married.

NELL (*Rushing to* PAW): Oh, Paw, Paw, it *is* you. You did come back just as Maw said you would.

PAW: Yep, I came back all right.

MAW: You're back, and you're still Honest Bill Baxter. What's the idea of the disguise? (*Gives a jerk at* PAW's *beard*)

PAW (*Sadly*): I didn't want you to know me, Maw, 'cause I'm not Honest Bill Baxter any longer.

NELL: Oh, Paw.

MAW: You're not Honest Bill Baxter any longer? Why not?

PAW: Because I broke my word, Maw. I said I'd bring you steak and onions. Remember?

MAW: I haven't thought of anythin' else for five years.

PAW: Well, I have only the onions.

MAW: How come, Paw? You were gone long enough.

PAW: I know, Maw. I staked a claim, and I mined gold from morn till night. But the Klondike isn't what it used to be. When I got all done, I had just ten cents. So I bought a pack of onion seeds and raised a patch and brought 'em along home.

MAW: Where be they, Paw? I could eat *raw* onions—I'm that hungry.

PAW: I put 'em in the bank for safekeepin' while I went huntin' for a steak to go with 'em. They're in that bag. (*Pointing to bag*)

NELL: Oh, Paw, we can eat. (*Starts toward bag*)

FORSYTHE (*Turning*): Ah, ha, not so fast, my pretty one. So, my friends, you think I'm under arrest, do you?

PAW: You are. The sheriff's got the warrant.

FORSYTHE: That warrant says I'm wanted for stealing a bag of gold, not onions. Haw, haw, haw.

PAW: I don't see anythin' to laugh at. What do you think, sheriff?

HAL: Reckon maybe the hombre is right. (*To* FORSYTHE) You're a free man, Forsythe.

FORSYTHE: A free man. (*Bows deeply to* HAL) Thank you, Handsome Hal Herbert. And I am more than a free man. I have you all in my power. (*Pulls mortgage from pocket*) I still hold the mortgage to this house. Unless it is paid, I shall take Little Nell to Mexico, and she shall marry me and live in my villa. Haw, haw, haw!

NELL (*Rushing to* HAL, *who puts his arm around her*): Oh, Handsome Hal, save me.

MAW: Well, Paw, if you don't have any gold, it looks as if we'll be kissin' goodbye to Little Nell.

PAW: I guess so, unless he'll take the bag of onions.

FORSYTHE: Onions! Bah!

HAL: Wait—I have it.

MAW: You mean you have gold, Handsome Hal?

HAL: No, Maw, but I have my home on the range.

PAW: What are you gettin' at, partner?

HAL: Just this. You have the onions. I have the steak tied outside. (*Sound of moo offstage*) We can all go live in my home on the range and leave the varmint here with the shack and his mortgage.

FORSYTHE (*Cowering*): No, no, you can't do this to me.

NELL: Oh, Mr. Hal Herbert, it would be wonderful to live in your home on the range.

PAW: And have steak and onions. What do you say, Maw?

MAW: What are we waitin' for? (PAW *picks up bag.*) This place isn't fit for man or beast. (*All exit except* FORSYTHE, *who throws his arms up in despair. Quick curtain.*)

THE END

The Gala Garage Sale

by John Murray

An expected inheritance may be going, going, gone! . . .

Characters

MRS. FLETCHER
MRS. ADAMS
BILL DENNY
MARY DENNY
TOM PARKER
SUE PARKER
ALICE LACEY
JOE LACEY
JANE GRIFFIN
PROFESSOR GRIBBLE
EXTRAS, *garage sale shoppers*

TIME: *Morning, the present.*
SETTING: *The interior of a garage. Table down center holds coffee mill, vase, unstrung tennis racket, woman's hat with wide brim, money box, and metronome; table left holds garage sale items: dishes, jewelry, books, kitchen utensils, etc. Empty table*

is down right. Sign up center reads, A WHALE OF A GARAGE
SALE!

AT RISE: MRS. FLETCHER *and* MRS. ADAMS *stand behind table
down center.* EXTRAS *mill about, examining wares, talking in
pantomime, entering and exiting throughout play.*

MRS. FLETCHER: Oh, Grace, I'm so excited. Our first garage sale!

MRS. ADAMS: And we have such useful items, too. (*Picks up
pillow*) This pillow would make a perfect gift.

MRS. FLETCHER (*Wryly*): Oh, yes. No home should be without a
pillow that reads, "Lake Winnebago, 1975"! (*They chuckle.*
BILL DENNY *enters right, carrying ugly umbrella stand, which
he places near table.*) Oh, Mr. Denny, how nice! Are you donating this lovely . . . charming (*Puzzled*) what is it, anyway?

BILL: It's an umbrella stand, Mrs. Fletcher. A wedding present
from my wife's aunt. It's been in our front hall for years, but I
can't stand the sight of it.

MRS. FLETCHER: I'm sure someone will pay ten dollars for it.

BILL: Please don't let my wife know that I donated it.

MRS. ADAMS: Won't she notice it's missing?

BILL: Sure, but I'll worry about that later. I can't stand it another
minute. (*He glances right.*) Oh, no! Here comes Mary now. I
have to hide this thing. (BILL, MRS. ADAMS, *and* MRS.
FLETCHER *stand in front of stand.* MARY DENNY *enters right.*)
Hi, honey!

MARY (*Surprised*): Bill! I thought you were going to the supermarket. (*Suddenly sees umbrella stand; brightly*) That umbrella stand!

BILL: I can explain, Mary. . . .

MARY (*Happily*): I know . . . you saw it and thought it would be
just right for the other corner in the hall. (*To* MRS. ADAMS *and*
MRS. FLETCHER) We have a stand exactly like this.

MRS. FLETCHER: Do you? (*Exchanges glance with* BILL) What a
coincidence!

BILL (*Weakly; to* MRS. ADAMS): You said the umbrella stand
would bring ten dollars. (*Takes out bill, hands it to* MRS.
ADAMS)

MARY (*Happily*): I never dreamed we'd find another one like it.

BILL (*Glumly*): Neither did I.

MARY: Let's put it in the car, then we'll come back. (BILL *picks up stand. They exit.*)

MRS. FLETCHER (*Pointing at table, right*): I wonder when Jane Griffin will get here with her display.

MRS. ADAMS: She's donating everything her Uncle Abner left in his house.

MRS. FLETCHER (*Musing*): Abner Underwood. What a strange man!

MRS. ADAMS: You know, he told Jane that after he died she'd never have to worry about money.

MRS. FLETCHER: Well, Abner's lawyer told me that all Abner left was that old house. It needs a complete renovation, and I'm sure Jane can't afford that. (JOE *and* ALICE LACEY *enter right, walk over to table.* ALICE *picks up coffee mill.*)

ALICE: Oh, Joe, we've wanted one of these coffee mills for years.

JOE: We have? Maybe *you* have. I'm a tea drinker! (ALICE *puts coffee mill down, picks up small vase.*)

ALICE: I love this vase. How much is it, Mrs. Fletcher?

MRS. FLETCHER: Five dollars.

JOE: That's exactly three dollars more than we got for it when we sold it at our own garage sale last month.

ALICE: I thought it looked familiar. (*Hands* MRS. FLETCHER *money*) This is for the vase and the coffee mill.

MRS. FLETCHER: Thanks, Alice.

JOE: They'll make ideal gifts for some unlucky member of the family. (JOE *and* ALICE *exit.*)

MRS. ADAMS: Let's see how things are selling at the other tables. (MRS. FLETCHER *picks up money box and follows* MRS. ADAMS *to other tables, where they talk in pantomime with* EXTRAS. TOM *and* SUE PARKER *enter right.*)

SUE: Oh, Tom, I have a feeling we'll be able to find a lot of good things here.

TOM (*Glancing around*): This stuff looks pretty weird to me. (*He picks up woman's hat, puts it on, poses affectedly.*) How did I ever live without this creation? (SUE *grabs hat, laughs, puts it back on table.*)

SUE: Please be serious. (TOM *picks up unstrung tennis racket, sticks his hand through center.*)

TOM: This will come in handy if I ever play tennis with the Invisible Man! (*He puts it back on table.* JANE GRIFFIN *enters right, carrying shopping bag and pushing large chest with the initials* A.U. *displayed prominently on front.* JANE *begins putting articles, including tea kettle and telescope, on table, right. The chest, facing audience, remains near table.* SUE *and* TOM *walk over to her.*)

SUE: Hello, Jane. Nice to see you.

JANE (*Smiling*): Hello, Sue—Tom.

TOM: I'm sorry about your uncle, Jane. I never met him, but I heard a lot about him.

JANE (*Tearfully*): All these things belong to Uncle Abner.

SUE (*Sympathetically*): We know how hard it must be for you to put everything up for sale.

JANE: I have to. I can't afford the house. My uncle often told me that I'd be comfortable after . . . (*Her voice trails off; she shrugs.*) but there's nothing left.

SUE: Did you search the house?

JANE: Every nook and cranny. I even went through all the equipment in his melting room.

TOM (*Surprised*): Your uncle had a melting room?

JANE: His hobby was metallurgy. (*Sadly*) All I found was an envelope addressed to me. The note inside made no sense whatsoever. (*She takes paper from pocket, hands it to* TOM.)

TOM (*Reading*): "Aurum . . ." (*Looks up*) What does that mean?

JANE: I don't know. I thought it might be someone's name. I looked through all the phone books for the area, but I can't find anyone by that name. (*Sadly*) I shouldn't burden you with my troubles. I must be off. (*She quickly exits.*)

SUE (*Pointing*): Maybe Abner Underwood hid something among these things.

TOM: I doubt it. (*He picks up tea kettle.*) This old kettle is worth five bucks, at the most.

SUE: Let me see it. (*She takes kettle.*) It looks really old.

TOM (*Nodding*): Old and useless. (SUE *turns kettle over, studies bottom.*)

SUE: There's something inscribed on the bottom. (*She scrapes kettle with fingernail, reads.*) Paul Revere!

Tom (*Excitedly*): Really? I can't believe it! (*He examines kettle.*) You're right! Paul Revere! And here's a date. Seventeen something-or-other. I can't make out the rest.

Sue: Do you think it's valuable?

Tom: Absolutely! Jane's uncle probably meant this kettle to be her inheritance. We'd better find an antique expert.

Sue (*Brightly*): That's easy—Professor Gribble!

Tom: Old man Gribble, our neighbor?

Sue (*Nodding*): He wrote a book on American antiques.

Tom: I know, but he's such a strange character.

Sue: He might be a bit forgetful and eccentric, but he's tops in his field. (*Suddenly*) Listen, Tom, don't let anyone buy a thing on this table until I come back with the professor. (*She exits right. Several* Extras *enter, walk past table.* Tom *grins foolishly, stands in front of table, shielding objects from their inspection.*)

Tom: Hi, there. Nice day, isn't it? (*Puzzled, they look at* Tom, *then proceed to other tables.* Bill *and* Mary *re-enter.*)

Mary: Now, let's see what other goodies we can find.

Bill (*Sarcastically*): Great! I've always wanted to furnish our house in "early garage sale." (Mary *points at tea kettle.*)

Mary: Oh, I like that tea kettle. (Tom *steps in front of kettle.*)

Tom (*Shaking head*): You wouldn't want that old thing. (*He picks up kettle, hides it behind his back.* Mary *stretches around him for a better view.*)

Mary: I want to see it.

Tom: No, no! It's dented! It leaks! It's absolutely useless.

Mary: That's O.K. I'd use it as an *objet d'art*. (*Insistently*) Please let me see it!

Tom (*Quickly*): I already bought it. I bought all the things on this table.

Bill (*Suspiciously*): I don't see a "Sold" sign anywhere.

Tom: I—bought all the "Sold" signs, too! (Mrs. Fletcher *joins them. She carries money box.* Tom *reaches into his pocket, holds out handful of bills.*) Mrs. Fletcher, I want to buy everything on this table.

Mrs. Fletcher: Oh, Jane will be delighted. (*She counts money.*)

Thirty dollars! Why, that's very generous for these things.

TOM (*Wearily*): Thirty bucks! (*He hammers on table.*) Sold! (*To* MARY) I'm sure there are items on other tables you'd like to buy. (*He rushes to center table, picks up metronome.*) How about a metronome? No music lover can afford to be without one! (MARY *takes metronome.*)

MARY: It's charming. I'll buy it.

MRS. FLETCHER: It's a bargain at fifteen dollars.

BILL (*To* MARY): You can't even read music!

MARY: I've been thinking about taking piano lessons. I'll start next week. (BILL *shakes head, hands money to* MRS. FLETCHER, *who walks around to other tables.* MARY *hands metronome to* BILL *who, in hypnotic fashion, moves his head in time. They exit right.* TOM *sinks against table.* SUE *and a bewildered* PROFESSOR GRIBBLE *enter right.*)

TOM: Well, Professor Gribble. How are you, sir?

GRIBBLE: I've been better. (*Gruffly*) What have you to show me?

TOM (*Pointing at items on table*): Everything on this table. (GRIBBLE *adjusts his glasses, examines articles.*)

GRIBBLE: Junk! I don't think the whole lot is worth five dollars.

TOM: But I paid thirty!

GRIBBLE: Then you're a fool. (SUE *hands kettle to* GRIBBLE)

SUE: Read the inscription on the bottom of this kettle, Professor. It says "Paul Revere." (GRIBBLE *scrapes kettle bottom. He looks up.*)

GRIBBLE: You're right, but there's another name after Paul Revere. (*Hands kettle to* SUE) Look at the spot I just scraped.

SUE (*Reading; bewildered*): "Paul Revere *Rumplemeier!*"

GRIBBLE: He's been making duplicates of original pieces for years.

TOM (*Gesturing*): But there's a date below the name. It begins with seventeen. (GRIBBLE *looks at kettle, shakes his head.*)

GRIBBLE: That's not a date. It's Rumplemeier's address. Seventeen deKalb Avenue, Yonkers, New York!

TOM: Oh, no!

GRIBBLE: If someone told you this thing was an authentic antique, you should have the culprit arrested.

TOM: I can't do that. I married her! (GRIBBLE *turns, sees chest.*)

GRIBBLE (*Reading*): AU. Now, that's interesting.

SUE: That chest belonged to Abner Underwood.

GRIBBLE (*Musing*): AU. That reminds me of something. (*Shakes head*) I can't think what, though. (*Testily*) All this commotion over nothing! I'm going home! (*Exits*)

SUE: I guess I goofed, but I only wanted to help Jane.

TOM (*Sighing*): We'll chalk it up to the garage sale experience. (*He picks up telescope, looks through it.*)

SUE: You look like Captain Ahab.

TOM: Wait a minute. (*He adjusts telescope.*) There's something scratched on the outer lens. Maybe it's just a smudge. (*Pause*) No, it's definitely a word. Let me see. (TOM *spells slowly.*) S-E-A-C-H-E-S-T.

SUE: Sea chest! Maybe Underwood hid something in the chest. (*Tries to open chest*)

TOM: Jane must have checked it before donating it.

SUE: But she might not have realized there was something valuable in it. (*Fiddles with lock*) Drat! It's locked! Tom, we have to buy this chest before anyone else does.

TOM (*Firmly*): I'm not buying any more junk. (MRS. FLETCHER *and* MRS. ADAMS *join them.*)

SUE: We'd like to buy this chest.

MRS. ADAMS: Why, Harriet and I were just discussing the chest.

MRS. FLETCHER: And we had the most wonderful idea, but you'll have to hold off for now, Sue. We'll make our announcement later. (MRS. FLETCHER *and* MRS. ADAMS *walk to other tables.*)

SUE: Tom, what should we do? (JANE *enters right.*) Oh, Jane, I'm so glad you decided to come back.

JANE: I wanted to see if Uncle's things were selling.

SUE (*Urgently*): I tried to open this chest, but it's locked. There might be something valuable inside.

JANE (*Distracted*): Oh, it's just some old clothes. And I left the key at home. There are two more chests in Uncle Abner's attic—monogrammed just like this one—but they're full of clothes, too. (JOE *and* ALICE LACEY *re-enter, join* EXTRAS *at other tables.*)

SUE: Oh, no, it's Joe and Alice Lacey. Alice will buy anything and everything. We can't let her get this chest.

TOM (*To* JANE): Jane, do you remember anything at all that was special about the attic or the sea chest? Try to remember.

JANE (*Touching telescope*): When I was a little girl, I'd stand at the attic window and look through the telescope, imagining Main Street was an ocean.

SUE: We think your uncle may have left a clue to your inheritance in the telescope lens.

JANE (*Puzzled*): I don't understand.

SUE (*Quickly*): Why don't you get the key to the chest, and then ask Professor Gribble to come back here with you. If the chest has anything valuable in it, he'll recognize it.

JANE: O.K. I'll be back as soon as I can. (JANE *exits.*)

MRS. FLETCHER (*Clapping hands*): Attention, everyone. Mrs. Adams and I have a big surprise for you lucky shoppers. (*Pointing*) We're going to auction off this lovely old sea chest and its mysterious contents to the highest bidder. Isn't that exciting?

EXTRAS (*Ad lib*): I wonder what's in it? Aw, it's just junk. I want that chest. (*Etc.*)

TOM (*Groaning*): We'll never get the chest now.

SUE: We will, if we're the highest bidders.

TOM: But, Sue, we're broke.

MRS. FLETCHER: I'm sure everyone is anxious to start. Who has an opening bid?

JOE: Ten dollars.

MRS. FLETCHER: Very nice, Mr. Lacey. May I hear another bid? (BILL *and* MARY DENNY *rush in right.*)

MARY: Did I hear someone mention "bid"? (*Gasps*) Bill, that chest will look divine in the guest room. (*Calls out*) Twenty dollars! (BILL *groans.*)

SUE: Tom, we have to make a bid.

TOM (*Loudly*): But, Sue, I already bought everything on the table for thirty!

MRS. FLETCHER: Did I hear thirty dollars, Tom? Thank you. Anyone else?

TOM: But I wasn't—

MARY: Thirty-five!

TOM (*Relieved*): Oh, good. She took me off the hook. Well, Sue, we'll have something exciting to tell our grandchildren when we're sixty.

MRS. FLETCHER: Sixty dollars! Such generosity, Tom! (*To others*) Are there any more bids?

TOM: But—

ALICE: Seventy-five dollars!

JOE (*Exploding*): Alice, have you lost your mind?

ALICE: If Tom made such a high bid, the chest must be valuable.

SUE (*Urgently*): Tom, we can't give up now.

TOM: I'll never bid again, even if I live to be a hundred!

MRS. ADAMS: One-hundred dollars! Tom Parker has bid one-hundred dollars for the chest. Any further bids? (TOM *sags against table.*) Sold to our lucky neighbors, Tom and Sue Parker. (MRS. FLETCHER, MRS. ADAMS, BILL, MARY, JOE *and* ALICE *walk to other tables, conduct business in pantomime.*)

SUE (*Pleased*): We saved the chest for Jane!

TOM (*Miserably*): Bankruptcy court, here I come! (JANE *and* GRIBBLE *rush in right.*)

GRIBBLE: This is highly irregular! All this rushing! You disturbed my body clock.

TOM: We'll buy you a new one, Professor—battery-operated!

SUE: Professor, we need your opinion of this chest and its contents. (GRIBBLE *adjusts his glasses, raps on chest.*)

GRIBBLE (*Wryly*): Well, at least it wasn't designed by Paul Revere Rumplemeier. (*He rubs his hand across initials.*) But those initials. AU. I wonder. (JANE *takes key from pocket and opens chest.* GRIBBLE *removes dark coat, Hawaiian shirt, bathrobe, pair of boots, and socks.*) I'd hardly call these things treasures.

TOM: And I paid a hundred bucks for it! (GRIBBLE *shakes shirt; string of beads falls out.*)

SUE (*Pointing*): Oh, look! A necklace!

JANE: It looks like gold. (GRIBBLE *picks up necklace, examines it closely.*)

GRIBBLE (*Shaking head*): No, it's just an inexpensive set of copper beads.

JANE (*Sadly*): Uncle Abner probably got them on one of his expeditions to the South Seas.

GRIBBLE (*Suddenly*): Gold! (*Triumphantly*) I *knew* something attracted my attention. (*He points to chest's initials.*) Those initials—AU. That's the chemical symbol for gold!

SUE: You're right! I remember that from chemistry class.

GRIBBLE: The Latin word for gold is *aurum,* and it's identified by the symbol AU. (TOM *picks up paper, waves it.*)

TOM: *Aurum!* That was the word in Abner's note.

JANE: But I'm sure it's just a coincidence that AU are my uncle's initials.

GRIBBLE: Oh, no, Miss Griffin. Your uncle was a very clever man! (*Points*) He melted down gold ingots and turned them into these initials. (*He looks into chest.*) The hinges, the reinforcements—all the hardware is made of pure gold.

JANE (*Stunned*): I can't believe it. I've seen this chest a thousand times, but I never dreamed the hardware was gold.

SUE: Jane, you said there are two more trunks in the attic, each with the initials AU?

JANE: Yes, that's right.

TOM: Great!

JANE: But Tom, you bought the trunk. Rightfully, it's yours.

TOM: I bought it for you, Jane. Besides, I would never have known the importance of those initials.

JANE (*Gratefully; to* TOM *and* SUE): How can I ever thank you? Now I can stay in my uncle's house—and even fix it up!

GRIBBLE: Miss Griffin, let's go to your house and examine those other chests. (GRIBBLE *and* JANE *exit right.*)

TOM: Well, Sue, that sign says it all. (*Points to sign*) This really has been a whale of a garage sale! (MARY *rushes on right, carrying two umbrella stands. After a moment* BILL *enters left.*)

MARY (*Crossing to* BILL): Bill, I found two more umbrella stands!

BILL (*Weakly*): Ah, yes. They're really stunning, Mary. (*They exit, carrying stands.*)

TOM (*Laughing*): There's nothing like an umbrella stand in every room.

SUE: And you'd better not laugh again when I want to go bargain hunting at garage sales.

TOM: Sue, when I married you, I got the best bargain in the whole world! (*He picks up unstrung tennis racket, kisses* SUE *through the opening. Quick curtain*)

THE END

Skits and Curtain Raisers

Meet Miss Stone-Age!

by Lewy Olfson

A prehistoric beauty pageant . . .

Characters

ROCKY GRAVEL, *M.C.*
GLENDA GRANITE, *last year's winner*
BARBIE BOULDER ⎫
MARCIA MARBLE ⎬ *finalists*
SYLVIA SLATE ⎭

BEFORE RISE: *Drum roll, as* ROCKY GRAVEL *enters in front of curtain and addresses audience. He is a typical beauty pageant M.C., all smiles and charm. He wears a caveman outfit of animal skins, black bow tie, and top hat.*

ROCKY: In just a minute, ladies and gentlemen, the judges will have finished tallying their slates, and we will be introducing the finalists in tonight's Miss Stone-Age Pageant. But first, I want to introduce the girl who won last year's pageant, the girl who, for the past year, has been traveling around as our ambassadress of beauty, intelligence and womanhood. (*Drum roll or musical flourish*) Welcome, please, Miss Stone-Age of 9847 B.C., Glenda Granite! (GLENDA *enters wearing fur cave-*

179

woman costume, sash reading MISS 9847, *dark glasses, and very high-heeled shoes. She carries a huge bouquet of roses.*) Look at her! Isn't she lovely, folks? (*To* GLENDA) Glenda, it certainly is a pleasure to have you here with us on this, the last night of your reign as Miss Stone-Age.

GLENDA (*Deadpan, reciting earnestly and with difficulty*): As I pass on my crown to you, my beautiful and worthy successor—

ROCKY (*Interrupting*): No, no, Glenda. I'm not the new winner. I'm the M.C. You give that speech later in the program.

GLENDA (*Blankly*): Oh. What do I do now?

ROCKY (*Quickly*): Tell us, Glenda, what were some of the special thrills of being Miss Stone-Age?

GLENDA (*Declaiming*): Some of the special thrills of being Miss Stone-Age were winning the money and the new wardrobe. Especially the money. (*Beaming*) I won lots of money and that was a special thrill.

ROCKY: You made some personal appearances, didn't you, Glenda?

GLENDA: Yes. I was present at the official ribbon-cutting ceremony marking the opening of Stonehenge.

ROCKY (*Surprised*): Stonehenge? I don't believe it. You mean they finally got that thing built?

GLENDA: Yup, they did it. Don't ask me how, but they did it.

ROCKY: Well, Glenda, they've just given me the signal that this year's finalists are lined up, waiting to be introduced, so why don't you say a few final words to the audience.

GLENDA (*Declaiming*): As I pass on my crown to you, my beautiful and worthy successor—

ROCKY (*Trying to move her off*): Later, Glenda, later! (*He pushes her off into wings.*) Wasn't she lovely, folks? (*Applauds enthusiastically*) And now, to meet the finalists in tonight's pageant. Will you open the curtains, please! (*Curtains open.*)

* * *

SETTING: *A traditional beauty pageant set, with ramp leading up to risers, chairs, etc.*

AT RISE: *Three finalists,* MARCIA MARBLE, SYLVIA SLATE, *and* BARBIE BOULDER *stand on risers. They wear ugly wigs, and shabby fur cave-woman costumes with sashes giving the names of their regions. They should look as unattractive as possible. Each one holds a papier-mâché club.*

ROCKY (*Enthusiastically*): Aren't they gorgeous, folks? Let me introduce them in alphabetical order, naturally. First, from Upper Siberia, the very lovely Miss Barbie Boulder. (BARBIE *walks down ramp, forward.*)

BARBIE: I just want to say, Rocky, that I am the happiest girl in the whole world, and I want to thank the judges for picking me as one of the finalists.

ROCKY: That's very sweet, Barbie. (*She returns to risers.*) Next, from Outer Mongolia, the beautiful Miss Marcia Marble.

MARCIA (*Coming forward, waving enthusiastically*): Hi, Mom! Hi, Dad! Hi, Teddy and Lois and Phyllis and Chuck and Larry and Amy. . .

ROCKY: Thank you, Marcia. That's fine.

MARCIA: Oh, Rocky, may I please just say hello to my date for next Saturday night?

ROCKY (*Smiling*): Well, of course.

MARCIA: Hi, Nick and Tom and Ed and Barry and Ralph and Eric and Mark and Allen and Don.

ROCKY (*Pushing her up ramp*): Fine, Marcia. Our third finalist, weighing in at 164 pounds is Sylvia Slate. (SYLVIA, *clasping her hands over her head in boxer fashion, makes a triumphant tour of stage.*)

SYLVIA: That's me, folks! (*She returns to risers.*)

ROCKY: Now, girls, as you know, there are just two parts left to the competition before the judges decide who will be crowned the next Miss Stone-Age—the talent exhibition and the intelligence test. Barbie, are you all set for the talent part of the competition?

BARBIE (*Coming forward*): Yes, I certainly am.

ROCKY: Tell us, what special talent do you have?

BARBIE: Cooking, so I have decided to recite an original recipe I created.

ROCKY: I think that's wonderful! (*Turns to audience and applauds madly*) You go ahead, Barbie.

BARBIE (*Reciting*): This is a recipe for Brontosaurus Stew. Take eight hundred pounds of freshly killed brontosaurus, and season it with half a dozen lumps of coal. Preheat your cave to four hundred and fifty degrees, and let the brontosaurus simmer for about three-and-a-half days. Meanwhile, separate sixty-four dinosaur eggs—I like Triceratops eggs best, myself, but you can use Tyrannosaurus eggs if that's what you happen to have. Slice fine a couple of two-year-old elm trees. . .

ROCKY (*Clutching his stomach*): Er—Barbie—I'm afraid our time is up. Why don't you just write the recipe down on a card, and we'll let the judges read it.

BARBIE (*Disappointed*): Oh—I suppose I could do that. (*Walks back up ramp*)

ROCKY: Now, Marcia, are you ready for your talent exhibition?

MARCIA: Yes, I certainly am, Rocky. (MARCIA *goes to wings, where she gets a huge stone wheel, and rolls it down center.*) I would like to present as my talent—this! (*She thrusts the wheel at him.*)

ROCKY (*Staggering under its weight*): What—what is it?

MARCIA (*As though it were obvious*): Why, it's a wheel, of course.

ROCKY: A wheel? What's a wheel?

MARCIA: It's a block of stone with edges sort of rounded off. I invented it myself.

ROCKY: It's—it's very nice, I'm sure, but what does it do? What's it good for?

MARCIA: A wheel isn't good for anything! It's just an artistic object. I'm a sculptor.

ROCKY (*Pretending to understand*): Oh. Oh, I see.

MARCIA: I invented another sculpture. It's sort of a pole that I put two wheels on. I call it the axle. It doesn't do anything, either. Would you like to see it?

ROCKY: No, no, I'm sure the judges have seen enough. But, oh, just out of curiosity, tell me. What on earth gave you the idea for naming this thing a "wheel"? That's such an odd name for a piece of stone.

MARCIA: Well, it looked like a wheel, and it felt like a wheel . . . so what else would I call it? A ball bearing?

ROCKY: Thank you, Marcia Marble. (*Pushes wheel to the side. MARCIA sits.*) And now, our last finalist in the talent competition, Sylvia Slate. (SYLVIA *trots center, waving clasped hands over head again.*) Sylvia, what is your talent?

SYLVIA: It's a song of my own composition. Also, I wrote it myself. (*She sings—off key—to the tune of "Three Blind Mice," simultaneously doing a very clumsy dance.*)

Three blind dinosaurs.

Three blind dinosaurs.

See how they walk.

See how they walk. (*She lumbers awkwardly across stage.*)

They all walked up to the Lady Fink.

She clubbed them to death, so now they're extinct.

No wonder we can't find the missing link.

Three blind dinosaurs. (*She bows.*)

ROCKY (*Dumbfounded*): That was terrible. (SYLVIA *picks up her club and waves it at him threateningly.*) Terribly well done! Wasn't it, folks? (*Applauds madly.* SYLVIA *plods back to seat.*) I can see the judges are going to have a tough time making up their minds. And now we come to the final stage of the competition—the intelligence test! (GLENDA *enters majestically from the wings, declaiming.*)

GLENDA: As I pass on my crown to you, my beautiful and worthy successor—

ROCKY (*Running to her and turning her back toward wings*): Later, Glenda, later!

GLENDA (*Mimicking him, disgustedly*): "Later, Glenda, later!" (*Exits*)

ROCKY: And now for the intelligence test. I will read just once the question the judges have selected. Then each of you will answer it in turn. (*Turns toward wings*) May I have the envelope, please? (*Hand reaches out from wings holding huge block of stone. Then another hand reaches out with a chisel.* ROCKY *takes items, borrows club from* SYLVIA, *and kneels on floor. He makes an elaborate show of chiseling open the stone "envelope," then stands, holding tiny slip of paper.*) The question you are to answer is, (*Reading*) "What is a woman's true role in today's society?" First, let's hear from Marcia.

MARCIA (*Coming forward, wringing her hands*): Oh, I'm so nervous.

ROCKY: Now, just relax, Marcia, and remember you only have
sixty seconds.

MARCIA (*Panicky*): The question has been asked, what is a
woman's true role in today's society? And I am glad that the
question has been asked, because there is probably no question more important than that question that—er—has been
asked. And I would like to answer that question. My answer is
(*To* ROCKY)—I'm sorry, could you repeat the question?

ROCKY: Oh, I'm sorry, Marcia, your time is up. But I know the
judges were impressed with your protestation.

MARCIA (*Preening*): Oh, I'm sure they were too, Rocky. 'Cause I'm
the prettiest. (*Sits*)

ROCKY: Now, Barbie, could we have your answer?

BARBIE: I think in today's society a woman's place is in the cave. I
think that she should devote herself to the cooking and cleaning and scrubbing and all the other backbreaking, boring,
time consuming chores that make being a full-time cave-wife
such a noble profession. I thank you.

ROCKY (*Applauding enthusiastically*): Wonderful! Wonderful!
That's what I call real intelligence!

SYLVIA (*Leaping up*): Really? That's what I call real stupidity.
And anyone that goes for that line is a male chauvinist Tyrannosaurus rex!

ROCKY (*Taken aback by her aggressiveness*): Well, er, Sylvia, it's
your turn. What do you think is a woman's role in today's
society?

SYLVIA (*Militantly*): I think all that cave-wife business went out
with the Ice Age. You show me a home where the dinosaurs
roam, and I'll show you a very messy house! I think cave
women today are the equals of cave men, and I think we
should stand up for our rights!

BARBIE (*Shocked*): Women equal to men?

MARCIA (*To* BARBIE): Don't listen to Sylvia, dear. Next thing you
know she'll probably want women to have the vote.

ROCKY (*Indignantly*): I must say I don't think the judges are
going to care for what you're saying, Sylvia.

SYLVIA: You know something, Rocky?

ROCKY: What?

SYLVIA: You're gorgeous! (*She conks him on the head with her club. He falls to the floor unconscious.*) This one's mine, girls, but there are lots of others out there. (*Points to audience*)

BARBIE (*Horrified*): But—we can't go around clubbing any man we happen to like! It's—unladylike!

SYLVIA: It may be unladylike, but it sure beats sitting around the cave night after night, waiting for the phone to ring.

MARCIA (*Thinking*): Barbie . . . maybe Sylvia has a point. Why should we let men do all the chasing? Why don't we do a little selective dating?

BARBIE: You mean—?

MARCIA: I think Sylvia's right. We've got clubs. Let's use 'em!

SYLVIA (*Egging them on enthusiastically*): Right on, sisters. Go get 'em! (BARBIE *and* MARCIA *shoulder their clubs and go running down steps into audience.*)

BARBIE: I want the one with the cute dimples!

MARCIA: He'll never know what hit him! (*They run up and down aisles, pretending to conk men on heads with their clubs.* SYLVIA *watches from stage and cheers them on.* GLENDA *enters.*)

GLENDA (*Declaiming*): As I pass on my crown to you, my beautiful and worthy successor. . . (*Quick curtain*)

THE END

A Perfect Match

by Ron Charles, Jr.

A romantic fantasy . . .

Characters

LIZ MASON, *26-year-old advertising designer*
ALICE, *her friend and colleague*
JOHN, *a figment of Liz's imagination*

TIME: *The present.*
SETTING: *An office. Desk and chair are center. Telephone and intercom are on desk, which is covered with papers. Two chairs are in front of desk.*
AT RISE: LIZ MASON *is seated behind desk, talking to* ALICE.
ALICE (*Looking at her watch*): I have only a few minutes before my lunch meeting, Liz, but I wish you'd tell me what's bothering you.
LIZ (*Sighing*): Robert just called to tell me he's lost his job again.
ALICE: Oh, no. He didn't!
LIZ: Yes, and I hung up on him.
ALICE: Oh, no. You didn't!
LIZ (*Shaking her head*): He's got to be the worst salesman in the world.

ALICE: Oh, no he isn't.

LIZ: He's a great person, and I love him very much, but everything he touches seems to go wrong.

ALICE: Oh, no, it doesn't.

LIZ: I just don't know if I could ever marry a person like that. Basically, he's the sweetest guy I've ever known, and he's always doing things to make me happy. But I'm beginning to think that I might need someone who has more in common with me. Do you know what I mean, Alice?

ALICE: Oh, no, I don't. I mean, yes, of course, I do.

LIZ: Maybe I should call Robert back and tell him I'm sorry. But I'm not. I meant what I said. And maybe it's time the two of us went our separate ways.

ALICE: Oh, no. It isn't!

LIZ: You don't think so?

ALICE: Oh, no, I don't. I don't think you should do anything until you've considered what I've told you.

LIZ (*Gratefully*): You've been such a help, Alice, I'd be lost if I couldn't talk things over with you.

ALICE: Oh, no, you wouldn't. Just relax and think this through again. (*Looks at watch*) I wish I could stay and talk, Liz, but I've got to go.

LIZ: You go ahead. I'll be all right. Thanks again.

ALICE: O.K. We'll talk more later. (*She exits.*)

LIZ (*To herself*): I just wish I knew what to do. Sometimes I think I'm in love with him, and then other times I can't imagine what I ever saw in him. (*Pause*) How can I not like someone who pasted hearts all over my front door on Valentine's Day? (*Smiles*) But I'm beginning to wonder how I could possibly spend the rest of my life with him. (*Sighs and shakes her head*) I wish I weren't so confused. . . . (LIZ *stares off into space, lost in thought.* JOHN, *carrying briefcase, enters right. He walks up to* LIZ's *desk and taps on corner.*)

JOHN: Hello.

LIZ (*Startled*): Oh! Where did you come from?

JOHN: Would you marry me?

LIZ (*Alarmed*): How did you get in here? (*Into intercom*) Leslie, why did you let this man in?

JOHN: Oh, please, don't bring her in here. It'll be more romantic with just the two of us. (*Leans over desk*)

LIZ: Listen, Mr. . .

JOHN: Oh, please, Liz, call me John.

LIZ: You'd better get . . . (*Suddenly*) How do you know my name?

JOHN: I waited until the planet Jupiter was lined up with Saturn in the constellation of Aquarius. Then I sat in the lotus position in front of the large oak in Central Park.

LIZ (*Sarcastically*): A tree told you my name?

JOHN (*Smiling*): No, I read the nameplate on your door.

LIZ (*Trying to coax him out*): John, it's very nice meeting you, but I've got lots of work to do, and I'm afraid I'm going to have to cut our little visit short.

JOHN: First, tell me "yes."

LIZ (*Confused*): Yes?

JOHN (*Thrilled*): You've made me the happiest man in the world! Thank you, thank you, thank you. (*He grabs her hand and puts a ring on her finger.*) The invitations are already in the mail.

LIZ (*Visibly upset*): Invitations? You've got things all wrong. You have to take this ring back and leave—for good.

JOHN (*Pretending to be hurt*): How could you change your mind so soon?

LIZ: What do you mean, change my mind?

JOHN (*Angrily*): There's someone else, isn't there? I knew it! Well, he's not going to get away with it. Nobody's taking you away from me.

LIZ (*Putting her hand to her forehead*): I don't know what's going on here.

JOHN: You tell me; you're the one who's been cheating.

LIZ (*In disbelief*): I've been cheating?

JOHN: Ah-hah! A confession!

LIZ (*Trying to be patient*): Listen, I am trying to be reasonable with you. Now, please tell me what you're doing here and why you're harassing me like this.

JOHN: *I'm* harassing *you*?

LIZ (*Mockingly*): Ah-hah! A confession!

JOHN: That's good.

LIZ (*Pleased*): Thanks. (*Infuriated*) Why am I thanking *you?* What do you want from me?

JOHN: Your hand.

LIZ: Is this a soap commercial?

JOHN: Your hand in marriage.

LIZ: You want to marry me?

JOHN: Now, why couldn't I put it that way?

LIZ: This is absurd! Listen, John . . . (*Trying to compose herself*) If someone put you up to this, I don't think it's the least bit funny. Now will you please go and leave me alone.

JOHN: I suppose this means the engagement is off.

LIZ (*Yelling*): *Get out!*

JOHN: Don't I even get the ring back?

LIZ (*Trying to get ring off*): How did you get this on my finger? I can't seem to get it off.

JOHN: It looks great on you.

LIZ: Would you mind? (*She extends her hand to him.*)

JOHN: A pleasure. (*He kisses her hand.*)

LIZ: The ring.

JOHN: Yes, it's beautiful, isn't it?

LIZ: I'm beginning to lose my patience. I've had about all of this game I can take!

JOHN (*Reciting, as if he doesn't hear her*): "Let me not to the marriage of true minds admit impediments."

LIZ: If you aren't out of here immediately . . .

JOHN (*Continuing*): "Love is not love which alters when it alteration finds."

LIZ: I'm going to call the police.

JOHN (*Continuing*): "Or bends with the remover to remove."

LIZ (*Amazed*): You know Shakespeare?

JOHN: Not personally.

LIZ: That's a beautiful poem.

JOHN: Next to you it's plain.

LIZ (*Flattered*): That's very kind. Thank you.

JOHN: Look, Liz, I can tell you're under a lot of pressure.

LIZ: Yes, I am.

JOHN: You still haven't finished that advertising campaign, have you?

LIZ: No, and it's due at three o'clock, and . . . How did you know that?

JOHN: Well, I was in the middle of a large field, when suddenly this huge cucumber-shaped object shot over the horizon and hovered over me.

LIZ (*Sarcastically*): An outer-space pickle told you I was behind in my work?

JOHN (*Sheepishly*): No. Actually, your secretary told me.

LIZ: What about this thing from the cosmic delicatessen?

JOHN: How can you think about all that when you have a big project due in three hours?

LIZ: I don't understand any of this.

JOHN: Let's see what you've got so far. (*He starts looking through papers on her desk.*) Ah, good. Very good. (*Looks up*) You'll never finish in time.

LIZ: I won't if you keep bothering me.

JOHN: All right, all right. (*He picks up briefcase and pulls out several pages.*) Here.

LIZ: Here what?

JOHN: Your advertising campaign. It's finished.

LIZ: What?

JOHN (*Loudly*): Your advertising campaign is finished!

LIZ: I heard you. I can't—I just don't believe it. (*She flips through pages.*) How did you know I was working on this account?

JOHN: I was swimming down the Amazon River, when suddenly . . .

LIZ: Skip it.

JOHN: Your secretary told me.

LIZ: Why would my secretary tell you all these things?

JOHN: You know how friends are. Everybody wants to help out people in love.

LIZ: We are not in love. I have never seen you before.

JOHN: We're perfect for each other.

LIZ: We're strangers.

JOHN: Ah, something in common already!

LIZ: I don't know anything about you.

JOHN: Of course you do. I'm everything you've always wanted.

LIZ: I have never, even momentarily, wanted some kook to come running into my office and make me lose my job.

JOHN: Our favorite food is Chinese food.

LIZ: There are a billion people on this planet who eat Chinese food at every meal. Go bother one of them.

JOHN: Your favorite color is light blue.

LIZ: I'm beginning to see red.

JOHN: You love to ski.

LIZ: I'll have lots of opportunities to ski once I lose my job.

JOHN: Your favorite author is F. Scott Fitzgerald, and you love poetry, especially Shakespeare. They're my favorites, too.

LIZ: So we both have good taste in books. So what?

JOHN: Our favorite fruit is watermelon.

LIZ (*Sarcastically*): A match made in heaven.

JOHN: I thought so.

LIZ: I think this is crazy, your waltzing in here professing your love for me.

JOHN: We both hate lima beans.

LIZ (*Ignoring him*): I've tried to be polite. . . .

JOHN: We want a small family.

LIZ (*Holding up hands*): Please stop. Right now.

JOHN: We'd rather live in the country than in the city.

LIZ: Stop! Stop! Stop! (*Pause*) Now, listen to me. You must leave. I must finish this account. Do you hear me? These two events must take place in that order, beginning immediately.

JOHN: But I've already finished your campaign for you.

LIZ: I can't use that.

JOHN: Why not? I just handed you a finished copy, photos and all. Isn't it good enough?

LIZ: Well . . . that's not it. It's just that I need to do my own work. (*Looks at papers*) Actually . . .

JOHN: What?

LIZ (*Amazed*): This is exactly what I'd planned on doing myself, if I'd only had the time.

JOHN: Well, I had the time.

LIZ: No one knew what I had in mind . . . How could you. . . ?

JOHN: We're perfect for each other, Liz. Forget this salesman Robert and come with me.

LIZ: Robert?

JOHN: You remember Robert. He's shorter, brown hair, unemployed.

LIZ: This can't be happening. Things like this just don't happen!

JOHN: People don't fall in love?

LIZ: I'm not in . . .

JOHN: We're perfect for each other. I knew it the moment I met you.

LIZ: When did you meet me?

JOHN: Don't you remember? It was just a few minutes ago. It's love, don't you see? We're a cliché come true. Just be glad we found each other.

LIZ (*Bewildered*): Somehow . . . I *am* glad. But it doesn't make any sense.

JOHN: It doesn't have to make sense. We're talking about love, not a math problem.

LIZ: But how can I possibly love you?

JOHN: How can you help it? Your life's been a mess. You've been spending so much time running interference for Robert that you've been missing your deadlines month after month. Let's face it, that salesman-boyfriend of yours couldn't sell a banana to a monkey.

LIZ (*Defensively*): Wait a minute! You don't have to be so nasty! Robert and I have had some good times together—and he'll be a good salesman someday. He just needs time.

JOHN: Maybe someday his mother will need a car, and Robert will manage to sell her one.

LIZ: He needs me, you know. And he really cares about me.

JOHN: Liz, ten minutes ago you told Alice you weren't sure you could marry someone like Robert.

LIZ: He loves me very much.

JOHN: But you and I have everything in common.

LIZ (*Slowly*): When you first came in, somewhere in the back of my mind, even though I thought you were crazy, I knew there was something about you . . . (*Pause*) I can't quite put my finger on it.

JOHN: We're a perfect match.

LIZ: Is that it?

JOHN: You believe me, don't you?

LIZ: I believe that with you I would have absolutely everything I ever wanted.

JOHN: That's what everybody's after: happiness, satisfaction.

LIZ: And would you have everything you ever wanted?

JOHN: Everything.

LIZ: It sounds marvelous, doesn't it? Two people absolutely, instantly happy. Never a disagreement, never a difference to cause any problems.

JOHN: No aggravating little habits, no conflicting interests.

LIZ: Nothing to have to work out between us. Nothing to give up.

JOHN: That's right. (*Telephone rings.* LIZ *answers it.*)

LIZ: Hello, Liz Mason. . . . Yes, hello, Robert.

JOHN: Tell him now, Liz. Tell him now.

LIZ (*Pleased*): You got your job back? Oh, that's fantastic, Robert. I'm so glad. (*Pause*) I know you'll do better this time. I believe in you. (*Pause*) Robert? I'm sorry I hung up on you before. I was aggravated about something here at work. It's just that for a minute I didn't think that . . . Well, I just didn't think, that's all, and I'm sorry.

JOHN: Liz, tell him.

LIZ: Oh, that's just a client here in the office. No, it's all right. I'm glad you called. I was worried about you. . . . Dinner tonight? Well. . . . O.K. Bye, Robert. (*She hangs up.*)

JOHN: How could you do that?

LIZ: Do what?

JOHN: Lead him on like that.

LIZ: I wasn't leading him on.

JOHN: What about us?

LIZ: That man is my best friend. I can't leave him.

JOHN: That doesn't make any sense.

LIZ: Remember, this is love, not a math problem. (*Pause*) On my last birthday, Robert spent the entire night before filling my office with red balloons.

JOHN: But your favorite color is blue.

LIZ: During the subway strike, he came down here every afternoon, spending hours in traffic, just so he could drive me home.

JOHN: So what?

LIZ: I suppose it isn't much.

JOHN: No, it isn't.

LIZ: But there are other things. Years of things—sacrifices, and gifts, and silly inside jokes—things we've done because we cared about each other regardless of the little arguments and differences that come up now and then.

JOHN: But you don't have anything in common with him.

LIZ: I love him, and he loves me. That's a lot to have in common.

JOHN: I'm perfect for you.

LIZ: I'm perfect for someone who needs me. You don't. (*Pause*) Please go . . . and don't come back. (*Takes ring off finger, hands it to* JOHN)

JOHN (*Relieved*): Good. (*He puts his papers back into his briefcase.*)

LIZ (*Puzzled*): What?

JOHN: I'm through here.

LIZ (*Puzzled*): I don't get it. What really made you come through my door in the first place?

JOHN (*Smiling*): I thought I heard someone in trouble.

LIZ: You did all this for me?

JOHN: He was wrong, you know.

LIZ: Who?

JOHN: Parting isn't such *sweet* sorrow.

LIZ (*Smiling*): You knew all along it would end like this, didn't you?

JOHN: I hoped it would. (LIZ *looks away for a moment as* JOHN *exits.*)

LIZ (*To herself*): I've got to call Robert back and tell him all about this. He'll never believe that a total stranger helped me realize how much I love him. (*She turns to speak to* JOHN *who has already left.*) Maybe you could . . . Thank you, Whoever-You-Were. (*She laughs quietly as she picks up phone. Curtain*)

THE END

A Fish Story

by *Alida E. Young*

A comic monologue. . . .

FISHERMAN'S WIFE *enters and addresses audience. Stool is placed downstage.*

FISHERMAN'S WIFE: I'm tired of fishwife jokes. Nobody realizes how hard it is to be married to a fisherman. For one thing, everyone always asks me for my favorite fish recipes—and I don't cook! Listen, do you have some time to listen to my side of the story? I just have to tell this to someone. (*Sits on stool*)

It all started when my husband Herman was out fishing on the Santa Monica pier in California. He came home and, as always, I asked him (*Sweetly*), "How were they biting today, dear?"

Herman usually grumbles about the surfers and the tourists who scare the fish away, but this time (*Chuckling*) he said, "Today a flounder spoke to me." Well (*Shrugs*), when you live near Hollywood, you get used to some pretty weird characters, but . . . (*Rolls her eyes upward*) a talking flounder? Not a mermaid or a dolphin . . . (*Shakes her head*)

I thought poor Herman had been out in the sun too long

because he claimed the flounder said, "Fisherman, let me go! Put me back into the sea!"

Herman said he was so surprised by hearing a fish talk (*Sarcastically*)—one would certainly hope so—that he threw the fish back. Then—you won't believe this—Herman said the flounder claimed to be an enchanted prince! (*Roars with laughter*)

When I could stop laughing, I said, "Herman, you've been had. Somebody's a ventriloquist."

"No," he said. "I was the only person on the pier—just the enchanted flounder and me."

Now, you know how it always works in the fairy tales. You find a fish or a frog who's enchanted and you get a wish. But I was only kidding when I asked him, "What did you wish for? A condominium?" (*Matter of factly*) You see, we live in a trailer so small, we have to sleep on the table. (*Pause*) Herman took me very seriously and said, "Why should I wish for anything?"

Still managing to keep my face straight, I said, "Because I hate this tiny trailer. There's not even room for my surfboard. You go right back and tell that flounder I want a nice little condominium." The next morning Herman actually went back. I followed him and hid. He went to the end of the pier and started yelling (*Holds hand to mouth to yell*), "Oh, enchanted flounder or prince, come out of the sea!" Using this wild kind of talk he went on to say that his wife wanted a house. Well, I didn't stay around to listen to any more. I figured he knew I was listening and was putting me on.

I decided to go shopping and was gone for a long time. When I got back to our trailer lot, I thought I was lost. Our trailer was gone, and standing there instead was a lovely mobile home. It even had a picket fence around it! Herman tried to pass it off as if the enchanted fish had done it. Of course, I didn't believe him.

It was fine at first, but it took me only a few weeks to realize what a lemon that house was. (*Indignantly*) Talk about poorly built! Nothing worked right. The faucets dripped, the doors stuck. (*Outraged*) Why, it didn't have a dishwasher or a microwave oven. Can you imagine? Not even a garbage disposal. The last straw was the day I found termites. (*Disgustedly*) When I fell through the floor, I yelled at Herman, "I hate this place! Why don't you ask your stupid flounder for a stone castle? At least it wouldn't have termites."

That night I got a call from my sister in Walla Walla, asking me to visit her for a week or so. (*Leans forward and speaks confidentially*) I *know* you won't believe me, but, when I got home a stone house was sitting in place of the mobile home. (*Shakes head, amazed*) Not exactly a castle, but it did have a tower.

I looked around and only half jokingly said to Herman, "With a mansion like this you ought to run for mayor." Herman has about as much ambition as a gnat, and he said, "I don't know anything about politics."

And I said, "When did *that* ever stop anyone from running for office?" Then it occurred to me that *I* could run for office. So I said to Herman. "You just go out to the pier and talk to your magic fish. Tell him your wife wants to be mayor. And while you're asking, tell him a queen might be fun, too."

That day Herman went fishing, and when he came home, I caught him staring at me in an odd way. Trying to get him to smile, I said, "Well, what did your enchanted flounder say?"

I'm telling you, he gave me a real chill when he said, in a very serious, quiet way (*Pauses and lowers voice*), "It will come to pass."

(*Stands and puts hands on hips*) This wasn't funny anymore. Herman went up to his tower and stayed there for a week. He didn't even come down for meals. Now I was really getting worried. Maybe he believed his fish story, and if he did, he had problems.

I decided to go to the new supermarket in the mall, to get away from it all. At first, I didn't notice all the cameras and people standing around and staring at me, until somebody shouted, "You have chosen the secret grocery item—pickled artichoke hearts. You're the supermarket queen for a day!"

I nearly fell over my cart. The coincidence was spooky. A

supermarket queen for a day is hardly the same as a real queen, but then, I hadn't been specific, had I?

I hurried home and told Herman I was going to be on the evening news, but he wouldn't speak to me, even when I told him I was fixing pickled artichoke hearts, his favorite food.

That night I couldn't sleep so I decided to take a walk. I went to the pier. There was a full moon and the sea was silvery. (*Looks all around*) I made sure I was alone, and then I whispered, "Flounder—can you hear me?"

The waves lapped gently against the wooden pilings and I swear it sounded like a voice saying (*Whispers*), *I hear you. . . . I hear you. . . .* I felt stupid talking to a fish, but I had no choice. "Flounder, I don't believe in you, but somehow my wishes have come true. So, *please,* whoever or whatever you are, I don't want a stone house. I just want my husband back the way he was before he met you."

Suddenly the pier began to shake. Earthquake! I started to run. I had to get to Herman. If the stone house collapsed, and Herman was in it, I'd never forgive myself. (*Breathless*) I raced faster. My heart was pounding.

In the moonlight I could see the huge pile of stones that used to be a house. "Herman!" I screamed. Frantically I pawed through the rubble. I couldn't find him. Suddenly I saw our old trailer, the only thing now standing. If only I'd been content to live in it! Suddenly the door opened and a sleepy-eyed Herman peered out. Relieved beyond belief to see him, I cried, "Are you all right?"

He seemed a bit dazed as he said, "I have a little headache."

Laughing and crying with relief, I hugged him. Then Herman said abruptly, "Let's go to an all-night seafood restaurant. I'm starved." But when we got there and he looked at the menu, he said, "You know, for some reason, I don't feel like eating fish."

I could hardly blame him. As for me, I ordered a vegetable plate. No way was I going to eat fish.

Back in our old trailer, I found I couldn't sleep. I slipped out and headed for the pier. I was wondering why Herman didn't remember anything that had happened since he caught the flounder. (*Looks all around*) "Flounder? Are you still out there?"

The waves lapped against the pilings. "If you can hear me, Flounder (*Whispers*), thanks. As long as I live I'll never, never wish for another thing." (*Exits; curtain*)

THE END

Harvey the Hypochondriac

by Juliet Garver

Abby gives her boyfriend a dose of his own medicine and cures their ailing romance. . . .

Characters

HARVEY WALKER
ABBY TYLER
MR. GEORGE TYLER ⎫
MRS. JOAN TYLER ⎭ *her parents*
DR. JASON PALMER, *neighbor*

SCENE 1

TIME: *The present.*

SETTING: *Living/dining room of the Tyler family. Dining table and chairs are left; couch and coffee table are right. Exit left leads to kitchen; exit right, to front door.*

AT RISE: ABBY TYLER *and* MRS. TYLER *are setting table for dinner.* MR. TYLER *is on couch, reading newspaper.*

MRS. TYLER: I can't start broiling the salmon until Harvey gets

200

file on, wearing caps and gowns. NEDRA *carries trophy.*) And
this year's valedictorian is . . . Nedra! (NEDRA *holds trophy
high as* PORCINE *and* SIZZLEAN *cheer and clap.*)

SIZZLEAN (*To* PORCINE): Just think, Porcine, Nedra was named
the smartest pig in the whole school!

NEDRA (*To pigs*): Oh, you're too kind! (*Pigs shed caps and gowns
and drop them off stage. They wear high school jerseys, pink
jogging pants, and sneakers. They line up in cheerleader for-
mation.*)

PORCINE: Gimme a P!

SIZZLEAN: Gimme an I!

NEDRA: Gimme a G!

PORCINE: What does it spell?

ALL: Pig! Swine! Hogs! Pork-Pigs-Yeah!

PORCINE: Well, now that we've graduated, it's time to move to the
Big Apple!

NEDRA (*Dreamily*): New York!

SIZZLEAN (*Excitedly*): The city that never sleeps! (*In lofty tone*)
There I can fulfill my lifelong dream and break into show
business!

PORCINE: I can get rich!

NEDRA: And I can go to college!

PORCINE and SIZZLEAN (*Ad lib*): Come on. Let's go! (*Etc.* PORCINE
and SIZZLEAN *grab suitcases, start off.*)

NEDRA: Wait a minute, you two. I want to remind you of the
warning our dear mother gave us.

PORCINE: Oh, you mean about that silly Strump the Wolf?

NEDRA: He's not silly, he's the most evil wolf in all of New York
City.

SIZZLEAN: Oh, Nedra, that's hogwash! That gnarly wolf Strump
must be a hundred years old by now!

PORCINE: Yeah, who cares about him?

NEDRA: You will, if you don't watch out, and he comes breathing
down your neck! Don't say I didn't warn you. Now, come on.
Let's go!

ALL: New York, here we come! (*They exit left.*)

* * *

SETTING: *New York City. Backdrop optional; see Production Notes.*

AT RISE: *Pigs enter, carrying suitcases, gawking and pointing.*

SIZZLEAN: Here we are!

NEDRA: New York!

PORCINE: I'm in hog heaven.

NEDRA: Well, girls, what do you want to do first?

SIZZLEAN and NEDRA (*Talking at once*): I want to go to Macy's, Windows on the World, Trump Tower, Radio City Music Hall. (*Etc.*)

NEDRA: Whoa! Hold on, you knuckleheads! I think you're forgetting one important thing. We don't have anywhere to live.

PORCINE: Oh, yeah. You're right.

SIZZLEAN: Good point there, Nedra.

PORCINE: Well . . . since you're so smart, what are we gonna do about that? (PORCINE *and* SIZZLEAN *look at* NEDRA *expectantly.*)

NEDRA: We could all move into the Times Sqaure Motor Hotel and Pigsty.

SIZZLEAN: Oh, no. I've heard that place is very low class.

NEDRA: It was just an idea. Or, we could all get a place together—

PORCINE (*Protesting*): In a pig's eye!

SIZZLEAN: No, I have to, like, have my own space, you know, to explore my own creativity. I am, after all, a performing *artiste*.

PORCINE (*In sardonic tone*): Actually, you're a pig with three years of ballet, tap, and jazz. But I agree with you. I think it's time we all had our own places.

NEDRA: O.K., but remember what I told you about the Big Bad Wolf! Be on the lookout, or you'll make a nice meal for him.

SIZZLEAN and PORCINE (*Together, sweetly*): Yes, Nedra dearest.

NEDRA: Good luck, and be careful. I'm off to build a house! (*They ad lib goodbyes.* NEDRA *exits. Once she is off,* PORCINE *and* SIZZLEAN *dissolve into laughter.*)

PORCINE: Goodbye and good ridance!

SIZZLEAN (*In affected tone*): So sorry you couldn't stay! (*Exasperated*) Oh, she drives me crazy!

PORCINE: She thinks she's so clever. Can you imagine what she'll do without us around to hassle?

SIZZLEAN (*Musing*): She may have a point about the wolf, though.

PORCINE: How could you fall for that? She's just trying to scare us. *I'm* not scared of any old wolf, big, bad, or otherwise.

SIZZLEAN (*Shaking her head*): Neither am I! But I think I'd better be off to build my house. Catch you later. (*Exits*)

PORCINE: I guess it's time for me to build my house, too. (*Muses*) What should I make it out of? (*Pauses; suddenly*) I know—straw! Straw is nice and *cheap*. If I'm going to get rich, I can't waste all my money on expensive building materials! (*Brief blackout; "house" is rolled onstage—see Production Notes. When lights come back up,* PORCINE *is sitting in house, telephone and books next to her.*) Here I am in my very own home! I'd better make a few calls to get my finances in order. (*Dials phone*) Hello, Chase Manhattan Bank? This is Porcine the Pig. Can you tell me the minimum balance for a checking account? . . Hm-m . . . What are your rates for long-term CDs? . . . That's good . . . Yes, please. It's Porcine the Pig, 549 W. 85 St. Thank you very much. (*Hangs up*) With that taken care of, I'll sit down and read! (*She picks up book,* Get Rich, You Pig. STRUMP THE WOLF *enters right.*)

STRUMP: I could have sworn I smelled a nice, fresh, young pig around here. I'm so hungry. (*He creeps around stage in front of house, sniffing the air.*) Aha! Just what I thought! There's a pig in there for sure. (*Rubs stomach*) Pork chops tonight! Look at that flimsy house! It'll be fun to knock over. (*He knocks.*) Knock, knock!

PORCINE (*Putting book down*): Who's there?

STRUMP: Candygram.

PORCINE: C'mon, you've got to do better than *that*. No one sends candygrams anymore.

STRUMP: Telegram.

PORCINE: Can't be. I moved in only an hour ago.

STRUMP: Avon calling.

PORCINE: I don't use Avon. I use Clinique.

STRUMP: All right, let's cut the cute stuff. My name is Strump the Wolf, and I want in!

PORCINE (*Terrified*): Strump?! Oh, no!

STRUMP: Little pig, little pig, let me in!

PORCINE: Not by the . . . um, not by the . . . I always forget this part. (*She picks up book,* The Three Little Pigs, *and flips through pages. She reads.*) "Not by the hair of my chinny, chin, chin"? That's the silliest thing I've ever heard.

STRUMP: Little pig, little pig, let me in!

PORCINE (*Calling to* STRUMP): Not by the hair of my chinny, chin, chin! (*Rubs her chin, frowning*)

STRUMP (*To audience*): I love this part. (*Faces house*) Then I'll huff, and I'll puff, and I'll blow your house in! (*He huffs, puffs, and "blows" house over. Note: Stagehand offstage pulls string attached to house, or* STRUMP *pushes house over.* STRUMP *lunges at* PORCINE *and misses. They creep around fallen house from opposite directions and back into each other.* STRUMP *bellows,* PORCINE *squeals. He chases her right.* PORCINE *stops him by holding up her hand and pointing off.*)

PORCINE: Wait! Look! It's Miss Piggy!

STRUMP (*Stopping*): Where?

PORCINE: There! (*When he cranes his neck to look off, she stomps on his foot. As he yells in pain and hops,* PORCINE *runs out right.* STRUMP *follows her off. As he is running off,* SIZZLEAN's *house is set stage left.* SIZZLEAN *is doing exercises.* PORCINE *runs on right.*)

PORCINE (*Shrieking*): Help! Oh, help! Sizzlean, let me in!

SIZZLEAN (*Letting her in*): What in the world is the matter, Porcine?

PORCINE: It's Strump, the Big Bad Wolf! He's after me!

SIZZLEAN: *What?*

PORCINE: He wanted to eat me for dinner! When I wouldn't let him in, he huffed, and he puffed, and he blew my house in!

SIZZLEAN: Blew your house in? What was your house made of?

PORCINE: Well, uh—straw.

SIZZLEAN: Oh, you're so gauche. I knew your penny-pinching would get you into trouble someday!

PORCINE: Well, Miss Perfect, what did you make your house out of?

SIZZLEAN: Sticks, of course. Lots of Broadway stars have stick houses. It's very chic.

PORCINE: Well, I hope your sticks are stronger than my straw was.

SIZZLEAN (*Horrified*): You think the wolf is coming here?

PORCINE: I don't know. I think I lost him.

STRUMP (*Running on*): Think again, Bacon Bits! (SIZZLEAN *and* PORCINE *scream.*) I'm hungry enough now to eat *two* pigs! Little pigs, little pigs, let me in!

SIZZLEAN: What should we do? (PORCINE *whispers into* SIZZLEAN's *ear.*) Are you sure?

PORCINE (*Shrugging*): I looked it up!

SIZZLEAN (*Sighing affectedly*): Only a pig with star quality could pull off a line like that.

STRUMP: Little pigs, little pigs, let me in!

SIZZLEAN *and* PORCINE (*Together*): Not by the hair of my chinny, chin, chin!

STRUMP: Then I'll huff, and I'll puff, and I'll blow your house in! (*He does so. When house is down,* STRUMP *lunges at pigs and misses.*)

PIGS (*Running around stage; ad lib*): Hey! Over here! Behind you! (*Etc.* PORCINE *picks up large box labeled* ACME TACKS, *and pretends to pour tacks out onto stage.*)

SIZZLEAN: Oh, wolfie!

PORCINE: Mr. Strump! (STRUMP *turns around and charges toward pigs. He yells with pain as he runs over "tacks." Pigs cheer in triumph and race off right. After a brief pause,* STRUMP *follows them off. Meanwhile* NEDRA's *house is set up on stage.* NEDRA *enters.*)

NEDRA: Well, now that my house is finished, it's time to read this book by my favorite author, Carl Sagan! (*She pulls out* Cosmos *and begins reading.* SIZZLEAN *and* PORCINE *enter left, screaming, then run into* NEDRA's *house.*) What's all this commotion? (SIZZLEAN *and* PORCINE *babble at once, unintelligibly.*) Wait, wait, slow down! You're both hyperventilating. Now, Porcine, exactly what happened?

PORCINE (*Breathlessly*): Strump the Wolf blew our houses down.

NEDRA: You're both too cheap and lazy for your own good. I told you to be on the lookout for the Big Bad Wolf, didn't I? Now, why in the world would you build houses of straw and sticks when you know there's a wolf around, just waiting to eat silly, little pigs like you?

PORCINE: Well, Miss Bigbrain, what did you build your house out of?

NEDRA: Bricks, of course!

PORCINE: Bricks are so expensive.

SIZZLEAN: And it takes so much work to build a house with them.

NEDRA: Well, you see how your laziness and cheapness almost cost you your lives. You have to use your brains. I know you each have one—somewhere.

PORCINE: Well, what do we do now? What if he comes here?

NEDRA: Oh, don't you worry your little snout about that. Even a wolf as big and bad as Strump can't blow down a house made of bricks. I think we should have a party to celebrate!

PORCINE *and* SIZZLEAN: Good idea!

NEDRA: How about some popcorn? (*She produces a bowl of popcorn, which* SIZZLEAN *and* PORCINE *grab for it.*) Wait a minute. Where are your manners? (*She calms them down and holds bowl between them.*) O.K. Go ahead. (SIZZLEAN *and* PORCINE *again lunge for popcorn, ravaging it quickly. There is popcorn everywhere.*) All right. Now I think it's time we played our favorite game, Pig Trivia! (*She pulls out deck of cards and reads.*) The first question is for you, Porcine. What Shakespearean play concerns a young pig seeking revenge?

PORCINE: Hamlet?

NEDRA: Correct! Now you, Sizzlean. What year were Bacos invented? (STRUMP *enters disguised as Little Bo Peep. He knocks.*)

STRUMP (*In high voice*): Knock, knock!

NEDRA: Who's there?

STRUMP: I'm Little Bo Peep, and I've no place to sleep. (SIZZLEAN *and* PORCINE *head for the door, but* NEDRA *blocks them.*)

NEDRA: Wait a minute! (*Calls*) How do we know you're Little Bo Peep?

STRUMP (*In own voice*): Because I said—(*Catches himself; in high voice*) Because I said so!

PORCINE *and* SIZZLEAN (*Ad lib*): I've always wanted to meet her! I've read all about her! (*Etc. They head for door.*)

PORCINE: It *is* Bo Peep. Let her in.

NEDRA: You two are so gullible! How can we be sure it's really Little Bo Peep? I know! I'll quiz her.

SIZZLEAN: Great idea!

NEDRA (*To door*): Oh, Miss Peep. If you're really who you claim to be, *what did lose?*

STRUMP (*In own voice, aside*): Curses! I can't remember all the silly details of that story! (*Back to door, in high voice*) I'm little Bo Peep and I've lost my—tuna casserole.

NEDRA: Wrong.

STRUMP: I'm Little Bo Peep, and I've lost my frisbee!

NEDRA: Wrong again.

STRUMP (*In own voice*): My name is Strump the Wolf, and I've lost my pigs! (*Pigs scream.*) Little pigs, little pigs, let me in!

PIGS: Not by the hair of my chinny, chin, chin!

STRUMP: Then I'll huff, and I'll puff, and I'll blow your house in!

PIGS: Go for it! (STRUMP *huffs and puffs repeatedly, but can't blow house down. He collapses.*)

NEDRA: You see? He can't blow down a brick house! (*Pigs cheer.*)

STRUMP: Humph. Think you're pretty smart, eh? Well, there's more than one way to peel a pork rind. I'll be back! (*Exits*)

PORCINE: What'll we do now?

NEDRA: Huddle! (*Pigs get into football huddle, mumbling loudly.*) PIGS (*Together*): Swine, hogs, pork, pigs, yeah! (NEDRA *produces rope, three tin pie plates, three spray cans of whipped cream. Pigs ceremoniously make three pies. STRUMP appears above back of house.*)

STRUMP: Since I can't *blow* this house down, I'll slide down the chimney, just like Santa Claus! (*He disappears and crawls into house. As soon as he stands up, pigs throw pies in his face, then produce three feathers and begin tickling him.*)

SIZZLEAN: What's the matter, Wolfie?

PORCINE: Ticklish? (*They tickle him until he is on the ground, helpless. Then they pull him upright and wind rope around him, toss him onto rug, and roll him up in it. They begin to drag him off.*)

SIZZLEAN: I think we'll go visit the Brooklyn Bridge! (*They exit, then reenter a moment later, cheering and laughing.*)

PORCINE: We showed him!

SIZZLEAN: I guess ol' Strump learned his lesson, huh?

NEDRA: Wait a minute. He's not the only one who needed to learn a lesson. (SIZZLEAN *and* PORCINE *exchange glances.*) So, what did you learn?

PORCINE: Well . . . I learned to take warnings seriously.

SIZZLEAN: And not to be cheap or lazy where safety is at stake.

NEDRA: Very good. I guess we learned a lesson after all. Now, why don't the two of you move in here with me until you get new, *safer* places to live?

PORCINE: Great!

SIZZLEAN: Thanks, Nedra.

PORCINE: Now I can get back to figuring out how to get rich.

SIZZLEAN: And I can get on with becoming a major Broadway star.

NEDRA: And I can go register at Columbia University. And remember, safety first! (*Quick curtain*)

THE END

Great Caesar's Ghost!

by Lewy Olfson

Crystal ball gives mixed messages in this spoof of history. . . .

Characters

JULIUS CAESAR
LUCIUS, *his secretary*
SOOTHSAYER
MARC ANTONY

SETTING: *Julius Caesar's office. Chair and desk with telephone on it stand center. There is chair beside desk, and several other chairs around room. Working door is right.*

AT RISE: JULIUS CAESAR *stands near desk.* LUCIUS *sits beside desk, holding pad and pencil.*

CAESAR: Lucius, take a letter. (*Dictating*) To Augustus Claudius, President and Publisher, Papyrus Press, Main Street, Rome. Dear Augie: Thank you for your scroll dated the seventh of March. I am delighted to learn that my book, *The Gallic Wars,* has hit the best-seller list. I look forward to receiving my royalty check soon, as I am short of ready cash. Do you have any idea when you will be rendering unto Caesar? Paragraph.

As for your suggestion that I consider writing a new book, I cannot make up my mind. Do you really think anyone is interested in my memoirs of Cleopatra? Personally, I regard that as ancient history. However, if you think there might be a movie sale, I'd be willing to think it over. Sincerely yours, Julius Caesar, Imperial Ruler of the Roman World, General Triumphant, Best-selling Author, etc. etc. Got that?

LUCIUS: Yes, Caesar. You're a great dictator.

CAESAR: Thank you, Lucius. Now, then, what's next on the agenda?

LUCIUS: Your soothsayer is here to see you.

CAESAR: By Jupiter! Is it the fifteenth of the month already?

LUCIUS: Yes, it's March 15, 44 B.C.

CAESAR: How time flies! Very well, show the Soothsayer in. (LUCIUS *rises, goes to door, opens it.*)

LUCIUS (*Calling out*): You can come in, Soothsayer. The great Caesar will see you now. (SOOTHSAYER *enters, carrying crystal ball.*)

SOOTHSAYER (*Approaching* CAESAR *and saluting*): Hail, Caesar!

CAESAR (*With casual salute*): Welcome, Soothsayer. Sorry I kept you waiting, but I had some urgent correspondence to take care of.

SOOTHSAYER: Don't apologize, Caesar. I know what life is like for you dictators—busy, busy, busy!

CAESAR (*Sighing*): Yes, it's a regular Roman circus around here. Maybe from now on you could schedule your appointments for the weekend, when I have more time. You could come out to the villa some Saturday.

SOOTHSAYER (*Indignantly*): Please—Irving the Soothsayer does not make house calls.

CAESAR: You don't have to get so huffy. It was just a suggestion. Now, what does your crystal ball have to say to me this month?

SOOTHSAYER (*Striking dramatic pose*): Silence! I am about to say the sooth! (*Looks into crystal ball*) Hm-m. Very interesting! Caesar, would you like to become rich? The crystal ball shows how you can make a fortune.

CAESAR (*Eagerly*): How? How?

SOOTHSAYER: They're holding races at the Colosseum. Go and bet on Ben Hur in the fifth. He's a sure thing.

CAESAR (*Disappointed*): Oh, I can't. My wife and I have to go to a wedding tonight.

SOOTHSAYER (*Horrified*): A wedding? (*Melodramatically*) No! No! That must not be, great Caesar!

CAESAR: Why not?

SOOTHSAYER (*Intoning*): The crystal ball says, "Caesar, beware! Beware the brides of March!"

CAESAR: But that's silly! What possible harm could befall me at a wedding?

SOOTHSAYER (*Shrugging*): Maybe you'll get hit on the head with the bride's bouquet. (*Ominously*) The crystal ball is seldom wrong.

CAESAR: That's true. Your crystal ball called the last election right, and everyone else got it wrong—even the Gallic Poll. (*Pauses*) O.K. I won't go to the wedding. Lucius, get my wife on the phone, would you?

LUCIUS: Yes, Caesar. (*Goes to phone and dials*)

CAESAR (*Musing*): Maybe I'll go swimming instead. There's nothing like a dip in the Tiber.

SOOTHSAYER: Swimming? Bad idea, Caesar. The crystal ball says, "Caesar, beware! Beware the tides of March!"

CAESAR (*Sourly*): Soothsayer, that crystal ball of yours is just full of warnings today!

LUCIUS (*Into phone*): Hello, Mrs. Caesar? Just a minute, please. Mr. Caesar wants a word with you.

CAESAR (*Taking phone from* LUCIUS): Hello, dear, how are you? (*Pause*) Listen, I'm afraid I won't be able to go to that wedding tonight. I've got to work late. (*Pause*) Yes, I know you bought a new toga. (*Pause*) Yes, dear, I know you've been cooped up in the atrium all day and were looking forward to going out, but I just can't make it, and that's that. (*Pause*) Oh, one other thing. I'd like to invite Cassius over for dinner soon. Nothing fancy— just a Caesar salad. I bumped into him today, and he had a lean and hungry look. (*Pause*) O.K., dear, I'll see you later. 'Bye. (*Hangs up*)

SOOTHSAYER (*Admiringly*): Caesar, you certainly got out of that neatly.

LUCIUS: That's Caesar for you. He called, he convinced, he conquered.

CAESAR (*Pleased*): Say, that's catchy, Lucius! Maybe I'll use it in my next book. Well, Irving? What else does your crystal ball have to tell me?

SOOTHSAYER (*Peering intently into crystal*): Hm-m. There's *something* there, but I can't quite make it out. It looks like, "Beware the guides of March." Were you planning a trip?

CAESAR: Well, I was thinking of taking the family on a chariot ride. I can't believe the crystal ball would worry about *that*.

SOOTHSAYER (*Looking closely into ball*): Maybe that's it . . . "Beware the *rides* of March."

CAESAR (*Angrily*): Come on, Irving, for what I pay you, I expect you to come up with something better than this nonsense.

SOOTHSAYER: You have to be patient, Caesar. Rome wasn't built in a day, you know.

CAESAR: That's because I wasn't the construction engineer on the job! (*Knock at door*) See who that is, Lucius. (LUCIUS *walks to door.*) And as for you, Irving, I want you to come up with a message that makes some sense. (SOOTHSAYER *shakes crystal ball, looks puzzled.* LUCIUS *opens door to admit* MARC ANTONY, *who strides in.*)

ANTONY (*Saluting and declaiming*): Hail, Caesar! Friends, Romans, countrymen, lend me your ears. . . .

CAESAR (*Irritated*): Marc Antony, can't you ever just walk into a room and say hello in plain, ordinary Latin?

ANTONY (*Shrugging*): I only wanted to make a good impression.

CAESAR: Asking people to lend you their ears does *not* make a good impression. It sounds unhygienic.

ANTONY (*Sulking*): You just don't like it when anyone besides you gets some attention.

CAESAR (*Angrily*): Are you suggesting that I'm not telling you the truth?

ANTONY (*Placatingly*): No, no. Everyone knows that Caesar is an honorable man. But I didn't come here to praise Caesar.

SOOTHSAYER (*Blurting out*): You came to bury him.

CAESAR, ANTONY, *and* LUCIUS (*Outraged*): *What?*

SOOTHSAYER (*Confused*): Did I say something wrong? (*Defen-*

sively) I am a soothsayer. I'm not responsible for the sooth I say.

CAESAR: But you *are* responsible for what's in that crystal ball of yours. Have you figured out yet what it's trying to tell you?

SOOTHSAYER (*Staring into crystal ball, then exclaiming happily*): I have it! I have it!

CAESAR: Well?

SOOTHSAYER: It says, "Caesar, beware! Beware the *prides* of March!"

CAESAR (*Happily*): Now, *that's* a message that makes sense!

LUCIUS (*Blankly*): It does?

CAESAR: Of course. It's telling me that just because I'm the Emperor, the greatest man in all of ancient Rome, I shouldn't be filled with pride and hold myself aloof. I should join my fellowmen in a show of good nature and humility.

LUCIUS (*To* SOOTHSAYER): Is *that* what the message means?

SOOTHSAYER (*Shrugging*): How do I know? I just tell you what the crystal ball says. If you want interpretation, write to Dear Abby.

CAESAR (*Thoughtfully*): "Beware the prides of March." You know, Marc Antony, I *have* been a little stand-offish with the other guys lately.

ANTONY: As a matter of fact, Caesar, Brutus was complaining of that the other day. He and some of the other fellows are getting together tonight, but they decided not to invite you.

CAESAR (*Upset*): Why not?

ANTONY: They felt you were too high and mighty to join them.

CAESAR (*Strutting about*): Well, I'll show them whether I'm high and mighty or not. Where are they meeting?

ANTONY: On the steps of the Senate. They'll probably go out for pizza later.

CAESAR: Since my evening is free, I say let's join them! (*Chuckling*) "Beware the prides of March!" Good advice, Irving! I don't know what I'd do without you. Coming, Marc Antony? (CAESAR *exits.*)

ANTONY (*At door, looking out*): Say! There go some of the fellows now! (*Calls out dramatically*) Friends, Romans, countrymen, lend me your ears! (*He exits.*)

LUCIUS: Whew! *That* was a narrow escape!

SOOTHSAYER: You can say that again! For a minute there, I thought Caesar was really going to let me have it for not coming up with a message he could understand.

LUCIUS: Yeah, it's a good thing you finally got it right. Caesar puts a lot of stock in that soothsaying stuff, you know. Why, if you hadn't given him the right message today, I think it would have killed him! (*Quick curtain*)

THE END

The Midnight Ride of . . . Who?

by Bill Majeski

What *really* happened "On the eighteenth of April, in Seventy-five. . . ."

Characters

HENRY WADSWORTH LONGFELLOW, *a poet*
JONATHAN DANDRILL, *a Revolutionary War veteran and friend of Paul Revere*
PAUL REVERE, *patriot, silversmith, and sometime jockey*
ABIGAIL REVERE, *Paul's wife*
PAUL REVERE, JR., *Paul's teenage son*
MRS. DANDRILL, *Jonathan Dandrill's forceful wife*

TIME: *After the Revolutionary War.*
SETTING: *Area down right is lighted and contains small writing desk and two chairs. At center is the Revere house, furnished simply with tables, chairs, etc. There is a window against backdrop.*
AT RISE: *Spotlight is on area down right.* HENRY WADSWORTH

225

LONGFELLOW *sits at desk, writing, pausing, then writing. He smiles in satisfaction, then stands and reads his composition.*

LONGFELLOW:
Listen my children, and you shall hear
Of the midnight ride of Paul Revere.
On the eighteenth of April, in Seventy-five;
(*Unseen by* LONGFELLOW, JONATHAN DANDRILL, *an elderly gentleman, enters and listens intently.*)
Hardly a man is now alive
Who remembers that famous day and year.

DANDRILL (*To audience*): I remember it. I was there.

LONGFELLOW (*Reading*):
He said to his friend,
(DANDRILL *points to himself.*)
If the British march
By land or sea from the town tonight,
Hang a lantern aloft in the belfry arch
Of the North Church tower as a signal light—
One, if by land, or two, if by sea;
And I on the opposite shore will be,
Ready to ride and spread the alarm
Through every Middlesex village and farm,
For the country folk to be up and to arm.
Then he said "Good night," and with muffled oar
silently rowed to the Charlestown shore,
Just as the moon rose over the bay,
Where swinging wide at her moorings lay
The *Somerset,* British man-of-war;
A phantom. . . .
(LONGFELLOW *stops as he notices* DANDRILL, *who crosses to desk area and sits.*)

DANDRILL (*Smiling at* LONGFELLOW): It's very good so far. Nice imagery. And it scans.

LONGFELLOW: Who are you?

DANDRILL (*Surprised*): Who am I? You write about me in your poem, and you don't recognize me?

LONGFELLOW: I'm writing about Paul Revere.

DANDRILL: And his friend?

LONGFELLOW: That's right.

DANDRILL: I'm the friend. Jonathan Dandrill of the Quincy Dandrills. Patriot and town barber. (*He rises, steps forward and shakes hands with* LONGFELLOW.)

LONGFELLOW: I'm Henry Wadsworth Longfellow. Poet.

DANDRILL: I've read about you. You wrote the poem about the Indian . . . what's the name?

LONGFELLOW: You mean Hiawatha.

DANDRILL: That's it . . . . On the shores of Hootchie-Kootchie . . .

LONGFELLOW: That's Gitchee Gumee . . .

DANDRILL: Whatever . . . but go ahead with this one. What else have you written about me?

LONGFELLOW (*Scanning his manuscript*): I have you wandering through alley and street . . . then you hear the muster of men at the barracks door, and you hear—quote—measured tread of the grenadiers—unquote.

DANDRILL: Hey, that's good. And it's true, too.

LONGFELLOW (*Continuing*): They march down to their boats on the shore.

DANDRILL: Nice scene. But what about me? Where am I?

LONGFELLOW: You're next. I have you climbing to the tower of the church . . .

DANDRILL: That was a killer. Me with my rheumatism and fear of heights! I had to pay for my own lantern, too. Seventy-five shillings. Plus tax. I said it then and I meant it—that King has got to go.

LONGFELLOW (*Reading*):
By the wooden stairs, with stealthy tread,
To the belfry-chamber overhead,
And startled the pigeons from their perch.

DANDRILL (*Shaking his head*): I never did like pigeons. They scared the life out of me that night. I almost fell off the ladder. (DANDRILL *takes paper from* LONGFELLOW *and reads to himself.*) Not bad. But you couldn't get my name in it—Jonathan Dandrill—could you?

LONGFELLOW: Hm-m-m . . . Hard to find a rhyme for Dandrill.

DANDRILL: I guess so. Anyway . . . (*He continues reading and mutters aloud a few key phrases.*) ". . . sentinel's tread . . . like a bridge of boats . . . impatient to mount and ride . . . opposite shore walked Paul Revere . . ." (DANDRILL *shakes his head and frowns.*) You go off here, I'm afraid.

LONGFELLOW (*Upset*): What do you mean?

DANDRILL: Don't get me wrong. I like the poem. It'll thrill people for a long time to come. But you have to get the facts straight. It didn't happen like this.

LONGFELLOW: It didn't?

DANDRILL: No. Paul Revere didn't stand on the shore patting his horse's side. He wasn't here.

LONGFELLOW (*Confused*): Where was he?

DANDRILL: He was home with his wife and children.

LONGFELLOW: Are you sure?

DANDRILL: Listen, I was his closest friend. He told me the whole story later. The way it *really* happened.

LONGFELLOW: Suppose you tell me. I don't want to distort history. I want to write the true story.

DANDRILL: Good! Sit down and I'll tell you all about it. (*Area down right darkens.* LONGFELLOW *and* DANDRILL *sit and watch.* PAUL *and* ABIGAIL REVERE *enter, and as spotlight comes up on center stage,* PAUL *is pacing floor nervously, stopping every so often to gaze out the window apprehensively.* ABIGAIL *sits at table cleaning silverware.*)

PAUL (*Muttering*): One if by land, two if by sea. . . . One if by land, two if by sea. . . .

ABIGAIL (*Stopping her cleaning*): What's the problem, Paul? Why are you looking out that window? All you can see from it is the Old North Church.

PAUL (*Hesitating*): Well . . . it's pretty at night. (ABIGAIL *shrugs and sets out silverware in place setting.*)

ABIGAIL: Paul, something's wrong with you. I can always tell.

PAUL (*Reluctantly*): Well . . . the British might be coming tonight.

ABIGAIL: The British! Why didn't you tell me? (*Patting her hair*) My hair's a mess.

PAUL: Aren't you frightened? There might be trouble. Fighting. Shooting, and all that.

ABIGAIL (*Casually*): Oh, you mean the British *Army*. Too bad. (PAUL JUNIOR *enters, wearing tricorn hat, which he takes off and tosses toward chair. He sprawls into another chair.*)

JUNIOR: Hi, gang. What's up?

PAUL: Nothing yet, son.

JUNIOR: How about doing a favor for a nice lad?

PAUL: Anybody I know?

JUNIOR (*Smiling*): Me.

PAUL (*Sighing*): What is it this time?

JUNIOR: I'd like to borrow the horse tonight, Dad.

PAUL (*Firmly*): Not tonight.

JUNIOR: Aw, Dad. Why not?

ABIGAIL: Why not take the mule instead?

JUNIOR: You don't take a girl like Priscilla Bradford anywhere on a mule. All the other guys will have powerful stallions, and you want me and Priscilla Bradford to go on a mule?

PAUL (*Sharply*): Priscilla deserves a mule. At least a kick from one. And so does her father. He's a Tory, one of the King's men.

JUNIOR (*Sighing*): Yes, but Priscilla has a way about her that just doesn't go with a mule. Please, Dad?

PAUL: No. You *can't* borrow the horse. And for that matter, I'm not so sure I want you going out at all tonight.

JUNIOR (*Taken aback*): Whoa! Nothing can keep me from Priscilla Bradford, Dad. And the horse would make it so much better. I promise I won't ride over twenty miles an hour and I'll pay for his oats and. . . .

PAUL: No horse, and that's final.

JUNIOR (*Grumbling*): No wonder I never get any good dates. Here I have a chance with Priscilla Bradford and I'm supposed to go calling on a mule!

ABIGAIL: Maybe next time you can have the horse, son.

JUNIOR: I don't think there'll be a next time when Priscilla sees the mule. Why can't we have *two* horses, like the Adamses?

PAUL: It's too showy, and besides, we can't afford it. This is a one-horse family, and it will *stay* a one-horse family! The trouble today is too many people are trying to keep up with the Adamses.

JUNIOR: I never have any fun. (*He takes his hat.*) O.K., I'll saddle up Jenny. (*Exits*)

ABIGAIL (*Going to exit and calling off*): Don't forget to hang onto her ears when you turn a corner. (*Pauses*) I mean *Jenny's* ears, not Priscilla's! (ABIGAIL *comes back to center stage.*)

PAUL: One if by land, two if by sea.

ABIGAIL: You could have let him borrow the horse this one time.

PAUL (*Firmly*): No, I could not. *I'm* using the horse tonight.

ABIGAIL (*Surprised*): Whatever for?

PAUL: I told you, the British are coming. It's up to me to warn the countryside.

ABIGAIL: Why do you always get stuck with the dirty work? (*Shaking her head*) Honestly. . . .

PAUL (*Stopping, suddenly*): Sh-h-h! There it is! (PAUL *and* ABIGAIL *freeze, and spotlight comes up on stage right;* LONG-FELLOW *is reading aloud to* DANDRILL.)

LONGFELLOW (*Reading*):
And lo! as he looks, on the belfry's height
A glimmer, and then a gleam of light!
He springs to the saddle, the bridle he turns,
But lingers and gazes, till full on his sight
A second lamp in the belfry burns.
(*Spotlight dims on area down right.* PAUL *and* ABIGAIL *resume action on center stage.* PAUL *takes one last look out of window, picks up hat and whip.*)

PAUL: Two! They're coming by sea!

ABIGAIL: I hope they get their boots wet!

PAUL: 'Bye, Abby. Don't wait up for me! (PAUL *exits.* ABIGAIL *looks out after him, and freezes as light dims center and comes up on* LONGFELLOW *and* DANDRILL.)

LONGFELLOW (*Reading:*)
It was twelve by the village clock
When he crossed the bridge into Medford town.
He heard the crowing of the cock,
And the barking of the farmer's dog,
And felt the damp of the river fog,
That rises after the sun goes down.

It was one by the village clock,
When he galloped into Lexington.
He saw . . .

DANDRILL (*Stepping forward*): You're making this thing up out of whole cloth!

LONGFELLOW: I have it on good authority it happened just this way.

DANDRILL: Well, now you have it on *better* authority it didn't. Watch and listen. . . . (LONGFELLOW *and* DANDRILL *look center stage, as spotlight dims down right and comes up center.* ABIGAIL *goes to window and looks out.*)

ABIGAIL: I don't see any lantern. (*Resignedly*) The things men say just to get out of the house. (*Sound of galloping hooves is heard, as if slowing and coming to a stop, then horse's whinny is heard from offstage.* PAUL *comes in slowly, weakly, clutching his stomach.*) Paul! What's wrong?

PAUL (*Slumping into a chair*): My stomach again. You know what always happens when I gallop—I get horse-sick.

ABIGAIL: Honestly, you're like a child—always in such a rush when you're out for a good time.

PAUL (*Annoyed*): Good time? Good time? I'm about to ride like a madman through the villages and farms of Medford, Lexington, and Concord to warn everybody that the British are coming. You call that a good time?

ABIGAIL: Then it's true? You really were going to wake the countryside and warn the citizens?

PAUL: Would I lie to you? Of course, it's true. I was the man to do it. And now . . . oh, what's going to happen to us? We're doomed! (ABIGAIL *goes to* PAUL *and takes off his hat. She pulls the whip from his hand.*)

ABIGAIL: Don't worry about a thing. You finish the silver, and I'll finish your route.

PAUL (*Astonished*): You?

ABIGAIL: Just straighten me out on one thing. What do I tell the Colonials? How do I give the warning?

PAUL (*Upset*): No, no, that's out! No woman can do my job. This is serious business. This calls for a man!

ABIGAIL: A man who is horse-sick?

PAUL: It doesn't matter. You're not going. (*Clutches stomach*)

ABIGAIL: What's more important, your pride or the future of our country? (PAUL *paces floor, then sighs.*)

PAUL: All right. You go. But be careful.

ABIGAIL: O.K., what do I say? How do I warn them?

PAUL: Just say—to arms! To arms! The British are coming by sea!

ABIGAIL: To arms! To arms! The British are coming by sea! (*She exits quickly.* PAUL *slumps into chair. Sound of galloping hooves is heard followed by sound of* ABIGAIL *shouting offstage.*) To arms! To arms! The British are coming by sea! Hey, wake up, you bunch of lazy, no-good loafers. Those bad guys with the red coats are coming and you'll die in bed unless you shape up right now! Come on! Move it, move it, move it! (*Center stage darkens. Lights come up down right on* LONGFELLOW *and* DANDRILL, *seated.*)

LONGFELLOW: So that's the story!

DANDRILL: Right. Abby Revere was the one.

LONGFELLOW: Hm-m-m. Even if that is the truth, I'm not sure anyone will believe it. (*Shrugs*) Meanwhile, back to the Village Blacksmith. . . . (*Poem in hand,* LONGFELLOW *retires to his desk. He begins to write.* MRS. DANDRILL, *a sturdy, determined woman, comes onstage and goes to* DANDRILL.)

DANDRILL (*Anxiously*): Did I do all right, lambie pie?

MRS. DANDRILL: Not bad, Jonathan, not bad at all.

DANDRILL: Now can I go down to the club and play cards with the fellows?

MRS. DANDRILL: Yes, I guess so. Just don't get caught. You know the Blue Laws. Humph! Let men run things, and there's nothing but trouble.

DANDRILL (*Meekly*): Right, dear. Thanks, honey. I'll be careful, sugar. Don't worry, loveykins. (*He exits quickly.*)

MRS. DANDRILL (*Shaking her head, watching him go*): He's a little strange, but he's all I have. (*To audience*) Longfellow never rewrote his poem to give credit to Paul's wife. But I just wanted to set the record straight for you. Now if you'll excuse me, I have a meeting with another Revolutionary War historian. I have to straighten him out on the crossing of the Delaware River. It wasn't George Washington at all, you know . . . (*Conspiratorially*) It was someone *else* in his family. (*Walks off quickly as curtain falls*)

THE END

Adaptations

The Importance of Being Earnest

by *Oscar Wilde*
Adapted by *Lewy Olfson*

Mistaken identity almost upsets romance, in this turn-of-the century comedy. . . .

Characters

ALGERNON MONCRIEFF
LANE, *a butler*
JACK WORTHING, *alias Ernest*
LADY BRACKNELL
GWENDOLEN FAIRFAX
CECILY CARDEW
MISS PRISM
DOCTOR CHASUBLE
MERRIMAN, *a butler*

SCENE 1

TIME: *Late nineteenth century. A spring afternoon.*

SETTING: *The drawing room of Algernon's apartment, London, furnished with sofa, tea table, chairs, desk, etc. Tea set, cups and saucers, small bell, and two platters of tea sandwiches are on table. Door at right leads outside; door at left, to music room.*

AT RISE: ALGERNON, *in his mid-twenties, is stretched out on sofa, eating a sandwich.* LANE, *the butler, is just going to door, right, to open it.*

LANE (*After opening door, turning and announcing*): Mr. Worthing. (*As Lane exits,* JACK WORTHINGTON, *also known as Ernest, enters. He is a few years older than* ALGERNON.)

JACK (*Walking over to* ALGERNON): Algy, my good fellow, how nice to see you. (*They shake hands.*)

ALGERNON: How are you, my dear Ernest? What brings you to town?

JACK: Pleasure, of course. What else should bring one anywhere?

ALGERNON: Where have you been since last Thursday?

JACK: In the country.

ALGERNON: What on earth do you do there?

JACK: When one is in town, one amuses oneself. When one is in the country, one amuses other people. It is excessively boring. (*Gestures*) But why all these cups, Algy? Are you expecting people to tea?

ALGERNON: Merely Aunt Augusta and Gwendolen.

JACK (*Pleased*): How perfectly delightful!

ALGERNON: Yes, that is all very well. But I am afraid Aunt Augusta won't quite approve of your being here.

JACK (*Amused*): May I ask why not?

ALGERNON: My dear fellow, the way you flirt with Gwendolen is perfectly disgraceful. It is almost as bad as the way Gwendolen flirts with you.

JACK: But I am in love with Gwendolen. I have come up to town expressly to propose to her.

ALGERNON (*Wryly*): I thought you had come up for pleasure. I call that business.

JACK: How utterly unromantic you are!

ALGERNON: Oh, it's very romantic to be in love. But there's nothing romantic in a definite proposal. (JACK *reaches out to take a sandwich.* ALGERNON *stops him.*) Please don't touch the cucumber sandwiches. They are specially for Aunt Augusta. (ALGERNON *takes one and eats it.*)

JACK (*Annoyed*): I see it's all right for you to eat them, however.

ALGERNON: This is quite a different matter. She is my aunt. (*He passes a different plate to* JACK.) Have some bread and butter. Gwendolen adores bread and butter. (JACK *takes sandwich.*)

JACK (*Munching*): Very good bread and butter it is, too.

ALGERNON: You behave as if you were married to her already. I don't think you ever will be. I don't give my consent.

JACK: *Your* consent!

ALGERNON: My dear fellow, Gwendolen is my first cousin, and before I allow you to marry her, you will have to clear up the whole question of Cecily. (*He rings small bell on tea table.*)

JACK: Cecily? What do you mean, Algy? I don't know anyone by the name of Cecily. (LANE *appears in doorway.*)

LANE: You rang, sir?

ALGERNON: Yes, Lane. Bring me the cigarette case Mr. Worthing left in the smoking room the last time he dined here.

LANE: Yes, sir. (*He exits.*)

JACK: Do you mean to say you have had my cigarette case all the time? I was very nearly offering a reward for its return.

ALGERNON: I wish you *would* offer one. I happen to need cash.

JACK: There is no good offering a reward now that it has been found. (LANE *enters, carrying cigarette case, which he hands to* ALGERNON.)

LANE: The cigarette case, sir. (*He exits.*)

ALGERNON (*Looking at it*): No need for you to offer a reward, Ernest, for I see, now that I look at the inscription, that the case isn't yours at all.

JACK: Of course it's mine.

ALGERNON: But this is a present from someone named Cecily, and you said that you didn't know anyone by that name.

JACK (*Impatiently*): If you must know, Cecily happens to be my aunt.

ALGERNON: Then why does she call you her uncle? The inscription reads, "From little Cecily, with her fondest love to her dear Uncle Jack." Besides, your name isn't Jack. It's Ernest.

JACK: My name, dear Algy, is really Jack.

ALGERNON: How can it be? You've always told me your name is Ernest. I've introduced you to everyone as Ernest. You answer to the name of Ernest. You are the most earnest-looking person I ever saw in my life. It's perfectly absurd your saying that your name isn't Ernest. It's on your card. Here is one of them. (*Taking card from case*) Mr. Ernest Worthing, B.4, The Albany. I'll keep this as proof that your name is Ernest if ever you attempt to deny it to me or to Gwendolen or anyone else.

JACK: That's my town card. At The Albany, here in town, I'm Ernest. But in the country I'm always Jack. And the cigarette case was given to me in the country.

ALGERNON (*Exasperated*): Will you kindly explain yourself?

JACK: Give my cigarette case to me first. (ALGERNON *hands case to* JACK.) Thank you. Now, listen closely to what I am about to say. In his will, old Mr. Cardew, who adopted me when I was a little boy, made me guardian to his granddaughter, Miss Cecily Cardew. Cecily, who addresses me as her uncle, lives at my place in the country under the charge of her admirable governess, Miss Prism.

ALGERNON: Where is this place in the country?

JACK: That is nothing to you. You are not going to be invited.

ALGERNON: Even so, how does that explain why you are Ernest in town and Jack in the country?

JACK: In order to be a good guardian to Cecily, I must adopt a high moral tone regarding everything while I am in the country. This becomes rather boring at times, so I have always pretended to have a younger brother by the name of Ernest, living in The Albany. He gets into the most dreadful scrapes. But the fact of the matter is, I think I shall soon have to kill off Ernest altogether.

ALGERNON: But why, my dear fellow? He seems a most useful sort.

JACK: I suspect my ward, Cecily, is becoming rather too interested in Ernest. So I shall just get rid of him and be Jack in the country and Jack in the city. It's rather a bore, but that's the whole truth, pure and simple.

ALGERNON: The truth is rarely pure, and never simple. (LANE *enters, followed by* LADY BRACKNELL *and* GWENDOLEN FAIRFAX. LADY BRACKNELL *is an overbearing dowager;* GWENDOLEN *is a lovely girl of twenty.*)

LANE: Lady Bracknell and Miss Fairfax. (*He exits.*)

LADY BRACKNELL: Good afternoon, dear Algernon. I hope you are behaving very well.

ALGERNON: I'm feeling very well, Aunt Augusta.

LADY BRACKNELL: That's not quite the same thing. Ah, Mr. Worthing, good afternoon.

JACK: Good afternoon, Lady Bracknell.

ALGERNON: How are you today, Gwendolen?

GWENDOLEN (*Coyly*): How do I look?

JACK (*Beaming*): You're quite perfect, Miss Fairfax.

ALGERNON: Will you have tea, Aunt Augusta?

LADY BRACKNELL: First things first, Algernon. I asked you to prepare the program for my musicale this evening.

ALGERNON: I have laid the music out on the piano. You can select whatever you prefer. Please come to the music room.

LADY BRACKNELL: Will you excuse us, Mr. Worthing? Gwendolen, while I am gone I expect you to think constructive thoughts.

GWENDOLEN (*Meekly*): Yes, Mama.

ALGERNON: This way, Aunt Augusta. (ALGERNON *ushers* LADY BRACKNELL *out.* GWENDOLEN *sits with poise, and stares sweetly ahead.* JACK *is obviously at a loss as to what to say.*)

JACK (*Falteringly, after a pause*): Charming day, Miss Fairfax.

GWENDOLEN: Pray don't talk to me about the weather, Mr. Worthing. When people talk to me about the weather, I always feel quite certain they mean something else.

JACK: I do mean something else. I would like to take advantage of Lady Bracknell's absence—

GWENDOLEN: I would advise you to do so. Mama has a way of coming back into a room so suddenly.

JACK (*Nervously*): Miss Fairfax, ever since I met you I have admired you more than any other young woman . . . I have ever met since . . . I met . . . you.

GWENDOLEN: Yes, I am quite aware of that fact. And even before I met you, I must confess, I was far from indifferent to you. We live, as you know, in an age of ideals. My ideal has always been to love someone by the name of Ernest. There is something in that name that inspires confidence. The moment Algernon mentioned to me that he had a friend named Ernest, I knew that I was destined to love you.

JACK (*Taken aback*): You don't really mean, do you, that you couldn't love me if my name weren't Ernest? Personally, darling, to speak quite candidly, I don't care much about the name Ernest. In fact, I don't think it suits me at all.

GWENDOLEN: It suits you perfectly. It is a divine name. It has a music of its own. It produces vibrations.

JACK: I think there are lots of other much nicer names. Jack, for instance, is a charming name.

GWENDOLEN (*Considering*): Jack? No, there is very little music in the name Jack. It does not thrill. It produces absolutely no vibrations. No, darling, I truly feel I must marry someone by the name of Ernest. It is the *only* really safe name.

JACK (*Going down on his knees before her, impetuously*): Gwendolen, I must get christened at once . . . I mean, we must get married at once.

GWENDOLEN (*Coyly*): But you haven't proposed to me yet.

JACK: Well, then, may I propose to you now?

GWENDOLEN: I think it would be an admirable opportunity. And to spare you any possible disappointment, Mr. Worthing, I think it only fair to tell you that I am fully determined to accept you.

JACK (*Rapturously*): Gwendolen!

GWENDOLEN: Yes, Mr. Worthing? What have you to say to me?

JACK: Gwendolen, will you marry me?

GWENDOLEN: Of course I will, darling. Really, how long you took! (LADY BRACKNELL *enters. She takes in the situation at once and explodes.*)

LADY BRACKNELL: Mr. Worthing! Rise, sir, from your knees. Such a position is most indecorous.

GWENDOLEN (*Happily*): Mama, I am engaged to Mr. Worthing.

LADY BRACKNELL: When you become engaged, Gwendolen, your

father and I will inform you of the fact. Now, I have a few questions to put to Mr. Worthing. While I am making these inquiries, you, Gwendolen, will wait for me in the carriage.

GWENDOLEN (*Protesting*): But, Mama!

LADY BRACKNELL (*Imperiously*): To the carriage, Gwendolen.

GWENDOLEN (*Smiling at* JACK *as she moves to door*): Yes, Mama. (GWENDOLEN *exits.* LADY BRACKNELL *sits majestically.* JACK *squirms.*)

LADY BRACKNELL: Now, then, Mr. Worthing, how old are you?

JACK: Twenty-nine.

LADY BRACKNELL (*Approvingly*): A very good age to be married. Now, about your parents . . . ?

JACK: I have lost both my parents.

LADY BRACKNELL: Both? That seems like carelessness. Who was your father?

JACK (*Embarrassed*): I'm afraid I really don't know. The fact is, Lady Bracknell, I was . . . well, found in the cloakroom of a station on the Brighton Line, by a gentleman named Mr. Thomas Cardew. He gave me the name of Worthing because he happened to have a first-class ticket to Worthing in his pocket. Yes, I was found, Lady Bracknell, in a large black handbag.

LADY BRACKNELL (*Indignantly*): I'm sure that you can hardly consider that an assured basis for recognition in good society.

JACK: May I ask, then, what you would advise me to do?

LADY BRACKNELL (*Rising imperiously*): I would strongly urge you, sir, to try to acquire some relations as soon as possible. You can hardly imagine that I would allow my only daughter to marry into a cloakroom, and form an alliance with a parcel! Good afternoon, Mr. Worthing. (LADY BRACKNELL *sweeps out the door.*)

JACK (*Calling out, miserably*): It's all right, Algy. You can come in now.

ALGERNON (*Entering from left*): What's the matter? Didn't it go off all right? Gwendolen didn't refuse you, did she?

JACK: Oh, Gwendolen is perfect. But her mother is unbearable.

ALGERNON: Did you tell Gwendolen the truth about your being Ernest in town and Jack in the country?

JACK: My dear fellow, the truth isn't the sort of thing one tells a nice young lady like Gwendolen. And besides, as I say, I plan to rid myself of the name Ernest by the end of the week. He shall die of a chill in Paris.

ALGERNON: Won't your poor little ward, Miss Cecily, feel his loss a good deal?

JACK: I doubt it. Cecily is not a silly romantic girl, I'm glad to say. She has a capital appetite, goes on long walks, and pays no attention at all to her lessons.

ALGERNON: I would rather like to see Cecily.

JACK: I will take very good care you never do. She is excessively pretty, and she is just eighteen. (LANE enters.)

LANE: Miss Fairfax. (He exits as GWENDOLEN re-enters.)

GWENDOLEN (Rushing to JACK): Ernest, Mama has just told me all, and from the expression on her face I fear we never shall be married. But although she may prevent us from becoming man and wife, nothing she can possibly do will ever alter my eternal devotion to you.

JACK: My darling!

GWENDOLEN: The story of your romantic origin has naturally stirred the deeper fibres of my nature. The simplicity of your character makes you exquisitely incomprehensible to me, and your name has an irresistible fascination for me.

JACK: Dear Gwendolen!

GWENDOLEN: It may be necessary to do something desperate. I shall write you daily. If you will just give me your country address . . .

JACK (In a loud stage whisper): I don't want Algy to know, but it's the Manor House, Woolton, Hertfordshire. (ALGERNON overhears and writes address on his cuff.)

GWENDOLEN: What is it, again? I can't hear.

ALGERNON (Blandly): He said he didn't want me to hear, but it's the Manor House, Woolton, Hertfordshire.

JACK (Outraged): Oh bother, Algy! Come along, Gwendolen, I'll escort you to the door.

ALGERNON (Pleasantly): Goodbye, Cousin Gwendolen. Goodbye, Ernest. (JACK and GWENDOLEN exit. Pause, then ALGERNON calls off) Oh, Lane.

LANE (Entering): Yes, sir.

ALGERNON: I'm going visiting tomorrow—to Mr. Worthing's country home.

LANE: Yes, sir.

ALGERNON: I shall probably not be back till Monday. Pack my dress clothes and my summer suits. I do hope tomorrow will be a fine day.

LANE: It never is, sir. It never is. (ALGERNON *pops a tea sandwich into his mouth, curtain falls*)

* * * * *

SCENE 2

TIME: *Afternoon, the next day.*

SETTING: *Garden of the Manor House, Woolton, Hertfordshire.*

AT RISE: CECILY CARDEW *is writing in her diary. After a pause,* MISS PRISM's *voice is heard.*

MISS PRISM (*Offstage*): Cecily! Cecily! Where are you? (CECILY *continues writing, unperturbed.* MISS PRISM, *a prim, elderly maiden lady, dressed plainly, enters.*) Ah, here you are. Put away that diary and come in for your German lesson. You know your Uncle Jack put particular stress on your German lesson before he left for town yesterday. I really don't see why you waste time on your diary.

CECILY: I keep a diary, Miss Prism, to enter the wonderful secrets of my life.

MISS PRISM: Memory is the diary we all carry about with us.

CECILY: I believe it is memory that is responsible for those horrible three-volume novels everyone reads nowadays.

MISS PRISM (*Loftily*): Please do not speak slightingly of the three-volume novel. I wrote one myself in earlier days. Alas, I lost the manuscript and so I was never able to finish it. (DR. CHASUBLE, *the portly, elderly rector, enters at rear of garden.*)

CECILY: That is a shame, Miss Prism. But look, here is dear Dr. Chasuble.

MISS PRISM (*As he approaches*): Ah, Dr. Chasuble. This is indeed a pleasure.

CHASUBLE: Has Mr. Worthing returned from town yet, Miss Prism?

MISS PRISM: No, we don't expect him until Monday.

CHASUBLE: I'll be on my way, then. Would you care to walk a way with me, Miss Prism?

MISS PRISM (*Simpering*): Gladly. Now, study your German, Cecily. (*With a beatific smile, she takes* DR. CHASUBLE's *arm, and they stroll out.*)

CECILY (*Pushing book off the table*): Oh, horrid, horrid German! (MERRIMAN, *the butler, enters, followed immediately by a jovial* ALGERNON. MERRIMAN *stands stiffly.*)

MERRIMAN: Excuse me, Miss Cardew. A Mr. Ernest Worthing is calling. (ALGERNON *advances, his hand outstretched, as* MERRIMAN *exits.*)

ALGERNON: You must be my little cousin Cecily, I'm sure.

CECILY (*Shaking his hand*): And you are Uncle Jack's brother, my cousin Ernest—(*Coyly*) my wicked cousin Ernest. I don't understand how you happen to be here. Uncle Jack won't be back until Monday afternoon.

ALGERNON: What a shame, then, that I must leave on Monday morning.

CECILY: Can't you wait for him? He is eager to talk to you about emigrating. He said he's sending you to Australia—you do look awfully pale.

ALGERNON: I expect it's because I'm so awfully hungry.

CECILY: How thoughtless of me. Won't you come in for tea? (*She rises and moves toward house.*)

ALGERNON: Thank you. You know, cousin Cecily, you're the prettiest girl I ever saw.

CECILY: Miss Prism says that all good looks are a snare.

ALGERNON: They *are* a snare—one every sensible man wants to be caught in.

CECILY: I don't think I would care to catch a sensible man. I shouldn't know what to talk to him about. (*She leads* ALGERNON *off left. Immediately,* JACK *enters from right, followed by* MISS PRISM *and* DR. CHASUBLE. JACK *is in full mourning, and his manner is almost sepulchral.*)

MISS PRISM: We didn't expect you back until Monday, Mr. Worthing. . . . (*Looks closely at* JACK) But—but what is this? You are in mourning?

JACK (*Sighing heavily*): My poor brother Ernest.

CHASUBLE: Still leading his shameful, wicked life, is he?

JACK (*Mournfully*): Alas, he is leading no life at all. He's dead—of a chill, in Paris.

MISS PRISM: How sad! My deep sympathies, Mr. Worthing.

CHASUBLE: My sympathies, sir. I shall mention this in Sunday's service.

JACK: Ah, that reminds me. I should like to be christened, Dr. Chasuble. This afternoon, if convenient.

CHASUBLE: Have you never been christened before?

JACK: I don't know. At any rate, I should like to be christened this afternoon. Will half-past five do? (CECILY *enters in the highest spirits.*)

CECILY (*Excitedly*): Uncle Jack! How nice to see you back! Who do you think is in the dining room? Your brother Ernest. He arrived just a few minutes ago, and he has already proposed marriage to me! Of course I have accepted him. And he's promised to be wicked no more.

MISS PRISM (*In horror*): But Mr. Worthing's brother Ernest is dead, Cecily. (ALGERNON *enters, eating a sandwich.*)

ALGERNON: I am no such thing, madam. (*Extending his hand cordially to* JACK) Dear brother Jack!

JACK (*Astonished*): Algernon! (*Catching himself*) I mean Ernest!

CHASUBLE: I think it is so touching to see this family reunion. Come, Cecily, Miss Prism—we shall leave them alone.

CECILY (*Going to* JACK): You *will* forgive cousin Ernest, won't you, Uncle Jack? You must, for my sake. I must confess, ever since I heard you had a brother named Ernest I was determined to love him. There is something in the name Ernest that inspires a woman so.

ALGERNON (*Sputtering*): Do you—do you mean, Cecily, that you couldn't love me if my name were not Ernest?

CECILY (*Sweetly*): But your name is Ernest. So what is the matter?

CHASUBLE: Come along, Cecily. We must leave these brothers to their joyous reunion. (CECILY, *smiling sweetly over her shoul-*

der at ALGERNON, *follows* DR. CHASUBLE *and* MISS PRISM *out.*)

JACK (*Exploding as soon as they are out of sight*): Algy, you scoundrel. You must leave at once.

ALGERNON: Don't be silly, Jack. I'm engaged to Cecily and I'm staying.

JACK (*Calling off*): Merriman! (JACK *glowers at* ALGERNON. MERRIMAN *enters.*)

MERRIMAN: Yes, sir?

JACK: Merriman, send for the dogcart. Mr. Worthing is leaving.

ALGERNON (*Airly*): Never mind, Merriman. He's decided to stay after all.

JACK: Oh, no, he hasn't!

ALGERNON: Oh, yes, he has!

JACK (*After a moment, with disgust*): Oh, what's the use? (JACK *throws himself into chair, disgruntled.* ALGERNON *smiles triumphantly.* MERRIMAN *looks from one to the other in amazement, as curtain falls.*)

* * * * *

SCENE 3

TIME: *Later, the same day.*

SETTING: *The garden.*

AT RISE: CECILY *is writing feverishly in her diary. After a moment,* MERRIMAN *enters, followed by* GWENDOLEN.

MERRIMAN: Miss Gwendolen Fairfax. (*He exits.*)

CECILY (*Rising*): Pray let me introduce myself. I am Cecily Cardew.

GWENDOLEN: How do you do, Miss Cardew? I am Gwendolen Fairfax.

CECILY: How do you do?

GWENDOLEN: Are you on a visit here at Mr. Worthing's country home?

CECILY: Why, no. I am Mr. Worthing's ward.

GWENDOLEN (*Taken aback*): His ward! He never told me that he had a ward. Though I must say, I'm not jealous. Ernest is so dependable.

CECILY: Oh, it is not Mr. Ernest Worthing who is my guardian. It is his elder brother, Jack. You see, Mr. Ernest and I are engaged.

GWENDOLEN (*Icily*): My darling Cecily, I think there must be some error. Mr. Ernest Worthing is engaged to me.

CECILY (*Icily*): My dearest Gwendolen, it is you who are mistaken. Ernest proposed to me just an hour ago.

GWENDOLEN: It is certainly quite curious; he asked me to be his wife yesterday afternoon at 5:30. Therefore, I have the prior claim.

CECILY: I should say it was quite clear that he has since changed his mind.

GWENDOLEN: Here he comes now. I'll ask him myself. (JACK *enters.*) Ernest, dear.

JACK (*Delighted to see* GWENDOLEN): Gwendolen, darling, this is a surprise. (*They embrace.*)

CECILY: I knew there must be some mistake, Miss Fairfax. The gentleman whom you are now embracing is my dear guardian, Uncle Jack.

GWENDOLEN (*Drawing back in horror*): Jack!

CECILY: Here comes *Ernest* now. (ALGERNON *enters, munching a sandwich.*)

ALGERNON: You know, Cecily, I have never eaten such delicious cucumber sandwiches.

CECILY (*Putting her arm around his waist*): May I ask, Ernest, if you are engaged to this young lady?

ALGERNON: To what young lady? (*Seeing her for the first time*) Good heavens, Gwendolen!

CECILY (*Dryly*): Yes, to good heavens, Gwendolen. I mean, to Gwendolen.

GWENDOLEN: I knew there was an error, Miss Cardew. The gentleman about whose waist you now have your arm is my cousin, Mr. Algernon Moncrieff.

CECILY (*Horrified; stepping back*): Algernon!

GWENDOLEN (*Pointing to* JACK *and* ALGERNON *in turn*): Well, then if *you* are not Ernest, and if *you* are not Ernest, who on earth *is* Ernest?

JACK (*Slowly, hesitatingly*): Gwendolen—Cecily—it is very painful for me to say this, but I'm afraid the truth is—there is no Ernest. (Gwendolen *and* CECILY, *both crushed, rush into each other's arms.*)

GWENDOLEN: Poor Cecily!

CECILY: Poor Gwendolen! (MERRIMAN *enters, followed by* LADY BRACKNELL.)

MERRIMAN: Lady Bracknell. (*He exits.*)

ALGERNON: Good lord, it's Aunt Augusta.

GWENDOLEN: Heavens, it's Mama!

LADY BRACKNELL (*Glancing at others; imperiously*): Mr. Worthing! Why have you spirited off my daughter?

GWENDOLEN: He didn't spirit me off, Mama. I came of my own free will. Mr. Worthing and I are engaged.

LADY BRACKNELL: You are no such thing. (*Turning to* ALGERNON) Algernon, who is the young woman around whose waist your left arm is twined?

JACK: Allow me to present my ward. Lady Bracknell, Miss Cecily Cardew. (CECILY *curtsies.* LADY BRACKNELL *is unmoved.*)

ALGERNON: Cecily and I are engaged.

LADY BRACKNELL: You are no such thing. There must be something invigorating in the air, hereabouts. There seems to be a peculiar number of engagements. (DR. CHASUBLE *enters, followed by* MISS PRISM, *who timidly hides behind him.*)

CHASUBLE: Gentlemen, about the christenings . . .

GWENDOLEN, CECILY *and* LADY BRACKNELL (*In unison*): Christenings?

CHASUBLE: Yes. Mr. Jack Worthing is to be christened Ernest at 5:30. Mr. Ernest Worthing is to be christened—er, I don't know what—at 6:00.

GWENDOLEN (*Radiantly*): Do you mean you were prepared to make this sacrifice for us?

CECILY (*Delighted*): Darlings!

CHASUBLE: Ahem . . . about the christenings. Might they be postponed?

JACK: Whatever for?

CHASUBLE: Well, sir, the fact is—(*Looks fondly at* MISS PRISM) Miss Prism and I have just become engaged.

LADY BRACKNELL (*Hopelessly confused*): May I have the honor of knowing what is going on here? (*Suddenly sees* MISS PRISM *and explodes*) Miss Prism!

MISS PRISM (*Horrified*): Lady Bracknell!

LADY BRACKNELL (*Slowly, emphatically and menancingly*): Miss Prism, where is that baby? (*The others gasp in amazement.*) Twenty-eight years ago, Miss Prism, you left Lord Bracknell's house in charge of a perambulator containing a baby of the male sex. You never returned. A few weeks later, the police discovered the perambulator standing by itself in a remote corner of Bayswater. It was empty, except for the unfinished manuscript of a dreadful three-volume novel. Miss Prism! Where is that baby?

MISS PRISM (*Humiliated*): I don't know, I admit it. I only wish I did. The plain facts are these. By mistake, I put the manuscript for a book I was writing into the perambulator, and I put the baby into a large, black handbag that I had intended for the manuscript.

JACK (*Urgently*): Where did you deposit the handbag?

MISS PRISM: I left it in the cloakroom of one of the larger railway stations in London.

JACK (*Eagerly*): What railway station?

MISS PRISM (*Crushed*): Victoria. The Brighton Line.

JACK (*Excitedly*): Excuse me for one moment. (*He dashes wildly off.*)

LADY BRACKNELL (*Sternly*): I need not tell you, Miss Prism, of the weeks—nay, years—of anguish your error has caused.

MISS PRISM (*Looking down; abjectly*): I can imagine!

LADY BRACKNELL: Can you, indeed! (JACK *enters, carrying large handbag.*)

JACK: Miss Prism, is this the handbag? Examine it carefully before you speak. Is this the handbag?

MISS PRISM (*Looking it over carefully*): It seems to be mine. Yes, here are my initials on the clasp. Thank you so much for restoring it to me.

JACK: Miss Prism, more has been restored to you than that handbag. I am the baby you placed in it.

LADY BRACKNELL (*Shocked*): Mr. Worthing! Then you are the son of my dear dead sister, and therefore Algernon's elder brother.

JACK (*Amazed*): Algy's elder brother! Then I have a brother after all. I always said I had a brother. Miss Prism, Dr. Chasuble, meet my unfortunate younger brother.

GWENDOLEN (*Throwing her arms about* JACK): My own! (*Puzzled*) But what own are you? What *is* your name, now that you have become someone else?

JACK: Good heavens, I almost forgot. Can you not love me but under that one name?

GWENDOLEN: Alas, no. Cecily and I have both resolved to marry men by the name of Ernest.

LADY BRACKNELL: That's it! You were named after your father, Mr. Worthing. His name was General Ernest John Moncrieff.

JACK (*Calmly*): I always told you my name was Ernest, didn't I, Gwendolen?

GWENDOLEN: Ernest, my own! I felt from the first you could have no other name. I forgive you now for all that has gone before.

ALGERNON: Cecily, do you forgive me?

CECILY: Yes, Algernon, I do—if you promise to be rechristened.

ALGERNON: I do, my love, I do. And now—may I kiss you?

CECILY: But of course! (*She stretches out her hand. He bows low and kisses it.*)

LADY BRACKNELL (*Overcome*): My dear nephew, you seem to be displaying a dreadful amount of triviality.

ALGERNON: On the contrary, Aunt Augusta, I've only just realized for the first time in my life, the vital importance of being earnest! (*He kisses* CECILY's *hand.* DR. CHASUBLE *kisses* MISS PRISM's *hand.* LADY BRACKNELL *looks on with dismay as curtain falls.*)

THE END

She Stoops to Conquer

by Oliver Goldsmith
Adapted by *Paul T. Nolan*

Nothing is what it seems to be in this lively version of a famous 18th-century play. . . .

Characters

HARDCASTLE, *a country gentleman*
MRS. DOROTHY HARDCASTLE, *his wife, and Miss Neville's aunt*
KATE, *his daughter*
CHARLES MARLOW, *a young man*
GEORGE HASTINGS, *his friend*
MISS CONSTANCE NEVILLE, *Kate's friend*
MAID
SIR CHARLES, *Marlow's father*

SCENE 1

SETTING: *An old-fashioned eighteenth-century English parlor. The setting should be representational, with painted backdrops and a few elegant pieces of furniture. A screen stands upstage.*

251

AT RISE: HARDCASTLE *and* MRS. HARDCASTLE *sit center.*

MRS. HARDCASTLE: I swear, Mr. Hardcastle, you're a very peculiar man. Everybody in the whole country but ourselves makes a trip to London now and then.

HARDCASTLE: Yes, and they bring back enough vanity to last the whole year. Wasn't so bad when men walked, but now with the rapid stage coaches, they fly around like birds.

MRS. HARDCASTLE: Oh, your olden times were fine indeed. You tell us about them often enough. Here we live in a rambling old mansion, that looks for all the world like an old inn. I hate old things.

HARDCASTLE: I love everything that's old: old friends, old times, old manners, old books; and, Dorothy (*Taking her hand*), I have been pretty fond of my old wife.

MRS. HARDCASTLE (*Pleased but embarrassed*): Oh, fie, Mr. Hardcastle. I'm not as old as you make me. You just think I'm older because Kate has now become a young lady. But I must remind you that Kate is the daughter of your first wife. Why, I was scarcely a babe myself when your Kate was born. (KATE, *fashionably dressed, enters at rear.*)

HARDCASTLE (*To* KATE): Here she is now. Kate, you look dressed for a ball.

KATE: You know our agreement, Father. I dress to please myself during the day, and then in the evening, to please you, I put on old-fashioned country clothes.

MRS. HARDCASTLE: Remind him, Kate, about his old-fashioned ways. He needs the advice of young women like us. (*Rises and exits*)

HARDCASTLE: I must admit I do like the old ways best.

KATE: Don't worry, Father. This evening, I shall be dressed as simply as a serving girl in a village inn.

HARDCASTLE: I'm pleased to hear that, Kate, for tonight I expect a visitor—a young gentleman I hope will be your husband.

KATE (*Upset*): What am I supposed to do? I know I won't like him, anyway. Our meeting will be so formal that I shall never be able to fall in love.

HARDCASTLE: I won't make you marry anyone against your will. But this young man, Mr. Marlow, is the son of my old friend,

Sir Charles, and he is said to be a serious fellow.

KATE (*Sighing*): Oh, dear, I was afraid of that.

HARDCASTLE: He is young and brave.

KATE: I may like him.

HARDCASTLE: And very handsome.

KATE: I'm sure I shall like him.

HARDCASTLE: And. . . .

KATE: My dear Papa, say no more. (*Kisses* HARDCASTLE *on forehead*) He's mine. I'll marry him.

HARDCASTLE: And—as I was about to say—he's one of the most bashful and reserved fellows in all the world.

KATE (*Dismayed*): Oh! You have frightened me to death again. That word *reserved* has undone all the rest of his accomplishments. A reserved man makes a grumpy husband.

HARDCASTLE: I don't think so. In fact, nothing that I know about him pleases me more. I like shyness in a man.

KATE: Well . . . if he's young and very, *very* handsome, I believe he'll still do. I might still accept him.

HARDCASTLE (*Teasing*): Of course, Kate, he may not want you.

KATE: My dear papa, you are a tease. But if he refuses me, it won't break my heart. I'll just set my cap for another.

HARDCASTLE: That's my sensible Kate. I'll warn the servants. We have so little company they won't know how to treat a guest. (*Exits*)

KATE (*Pacing*): This news of Papa's puts me all in a flutter. Young and handsome, but sensible and bashful. Perhaps I can cure him of his shyness. But maybe I can't. (MISS NEVILLE *enters.*)

MISS NEVILLE: My dear Kate, I've been looking for you.

KATE: Constance, guess what? Papa is bringing a man here tonight to meet me.

MISS NEVILLE: Charles Marlow?

KATE: How did you know?

MISS NEVILLE: He's the best friend of my friend, Mr. George Hastings. They are coming together.

KATE: What's he like, Mr. Marlow?

MISS NEVILLE (*With some hesitation*): He's rather unusual. Among women of society, he's modest and bashful. But I have been told that with servants and country girls, he's witty and clever—almost a man-about-town, if you understand me.

KATE: That is unusual. I'll never be able to handle a man like that. But I might try, if you will help.

MISS NEVILLE: You must help me, too. I've decided that if I can get Aunt Dorothy's permission—for she is against us—I shall marry Mr. Hastings.

KATE: Then let us go and prepare for the gentlemen! (*They exit. Lights dim and rise to denote the passage of time.* MARLOW *and* HASTINGS, *two handsome young men, enter, carrying traveling bags.*)

MARLOW: This doesn't look as bad as I feared.

HASTINGS: After what we've been through trying to find the Hardcastle home, this old inn looks good enough. True, it's a little antique, but not bad for a country inn.

MARLOW: If we can get a decent night's lodging here, tomorrow we can start looking for the Hardcastle home.

HASTINGS: We'll probably be cheated. These country innkeepers always take advantage of strangers.

MARLOW: One is cheated in all inns. In good inns, you pay dearly for comforts. In bad inns, you're both fleeced and starved.

HASTINGS: For a man who has spent most of his life in school, Marlow, you sound like a world traveler.

MARLOW (*Smiling*): I read a great deal.

HASTINGS: It is not only books that have educated you. You certainly sounded like a man of the world when you were joking with the serving girl in that inn last night.

MARLOW: But I freeze every time I'm around a fine lady. They utterly petrify me.

HASTINGS (*Laughing*): If you feel that way, how do you ever expect to marry?

MARLOW (*Shrugging*): I guess I never will. I would like to be married, but I can't go through the terrors of formal courtship. Such an ordeal would utterly destroy me.

HASTINGS: Then how do you intend to behave toward this Miss Hardcastle?

MARLOW: I'll bow a great deal, answer yes or no to all her demands, and escape as quickly as possible. I agreed to meet Miss Hardcastle only so that you could see Miss Neville again.

HASTINGS (*Patting him on the shoulder*): You're a good friend, Marlow. If I make a favorable impression on Miss Neville's aunt—Miss Hardcastle's stepmother—she may agree to the match. I think Miss Neville will accept me.

MARLOW: You have talent and art to capture any woman, while I can only stammer and turn red. (MR. HARDCASTLE *enters*.) Ah, here is the innkeeper, from the looks of him.

HASTINGS: Watch him, Marlow. He looks shifty.

HARDCASTLE (*Hurrying toward them*): Gentlemen, you are welcome. Which one is Mr. Marlow? I have been looking forward to meeting you.

MARLOW (*Aside, to* HASTINGS): He's crafty. He never heard of me until a minute ago, when he heard you call me by name, and already he acts as if we are old friends. (*To* HARDCASTLE) Your abode's a little run down, isn't it old fellow?

HARDCASTLE (*To* MARLOW): Surely, you are not Mr. Marlow?

MARLOW: Surely, I am. Would you fetch me a glass of punch?

HARDCASTLE (*Aside, to audience*): Is this the shy Mr. Marlow? He insults my home, calls me "old fellow," and orders a glass of punch as if he were a traveler visiting a run-down inn. (*To* MARLOW) I have prepared some hot chocolate. (*Exits*)

MARLOW: What a strange fellow, Hastings. I suppose this inn doesn't have many guests.

HASTINGS: And I can understand why.

HARDCASTLE (*Returning with three cups of chocolate on a tray*): Sirs, will you join me in a cup of chocolate?

MARLOW: Why not? (*All three men take cups.*)

HARDCASTLE (*Proposing a toast*): To your good health, gentlemen.

MARLOW: I hope so. (*Drinks; pleasantly surprised*) Why, my fat friend, this is excellent.

HARDCASTLE (*Almost choking with rage*): Fat friend! (*Aside*) If this is modesty, I would hate to meet an impudent fellow these days. I wonder if my friend, Sir Charles, has lost his mind, or if he simply does not know his son. (*To* MARLOW *and* HASTINGS) There is nothing like a cup taken together to help friends discover a common philosophy.

HASTINGS: Philosophy! (*Aside to* MARLOW) Philosophy in a country innkeeper! What has happened to England?

MARLOW (*Aside, to* HASTINGS): Not so loud. He amuses me. (*To* HARDCASTLE) To your health, old philosopher. (*Drinks*) What's for supper?

HARDCASTLE: Supper!

MARLOW: Yes, sir, supper. I'm hungry.

HARDCASTLE (*Aside*): I never heard of such impudence in my life. (*To* MARLOW) Well, sir, I don't know what's for supper. My Dorothy and the maid take care of such matters.

MARLOW: Well, when I travel, I order my own meals. No offense, I hope, sir.

HARDCASTLE: Oh, no, none at all. But I don't know how the cook will take it.

MARLOW: I'd like to see the menu.

HARDCASTLE (*Aside*): I'd like to see some manners, but I'll try to be a good host, even with these guests. (*To* MARLOW) Mr. Marlow, you remind me of my uncle, Colonel Wallop. He said no man was sure of his supper until he had eaten it.

HASTINGS (*Aside, to* MARLOW): Now he has a colonel for an uncle. Are you still going to humor him?

MARLOW (*Aside, to* HASTINGS): I'll try again. (*To* HARDCASTLE) Sir, I think I'll talk to the cook now. (*Starts off*)

HARDCASTLE: Egad, Mr. Marlow, you can't do that! (*Runs after* MARLOW) Wait a minute, I'll go with you. (MARLOW *exits, and* HARDCASTLE *follows him off.*)

HASTINGS: This is a strange inn. (*Looks offstage*) But what's this? Miss Neville! (MISS NEVILLE *enters and sees him.*)

MISS NEVILLE: My dear Mr. Hastings, it's so good to see you.

HASTINGS: What are you doing in this inn, my dear Constance?

MISS NEVILLE: Inn? You've made a mistake. My guardian, Aunt Dorothy, lives here. What made you think it was an inn? This is the Hardcastle home.

HASTINGS: The Hardcastle home? When we saw this place, we assumed it was an inn. Good heavens, Marlow will be mortified when he finds out our mistake.

MISS NEVILLE: I'm so pleased we are to be together, anyway.

HASTINGS: I'm afraid it won't be for long. When Charles discovers his mistake, he won't be able to face his host. (*Pauses*)

But why should we tell him? It will do him no good and us harm.

MISS NEVILLE: But he'll know where he is soon enough. Miss Hardcastle is here, too. (MARLOW *enters.*)

MARLOW: Hastings, this is a madhouse. Our host won't leave me alone, and he insists that I meet his wife, Dorothy. He talks about joining us at supper.

MISS NEVILLE (*Aside to* HASTINGS): He means my Aunt Dorothy.

HASTINGS: My dear Charles, we're in good luck. Who do you think is staying here at the inn? The ladies we seek most in the world—your Miss Hardcastle and my Miss Neville. Allow me to introduce Miss Constance Neville.

MARLOW (*Embarrassed, bowing stiffly*): My pleasure, Madam. (*Aside to audience*) It's no pleasure for me at all. And if I feel like such a fool with Niss Neville, what will I feel when I meet Miss Hardcastle?

HASTINGS: Isn't this indeed a fortunate meeting?

MARLOW (*Uncomfortably*): Indeed. But George, we look terrible—dusty from the road, clothes wrinkled. Would it not be much more proper if we waited until tomorrow to pay our respects?

MISS NEVILLE: No, indeed, sir. Miss Hardcastle is not a formal lady. Besides, she knows you are here, and she will join us shortly.

MARLOW: Here? (*Aside*) What am I going to say? (*To* HASTINGS) Hastings, stay here. I just know I'll make a fool of myself.

HASTINGS (*Aside*): Don't worry, Marlow. She's only a woman.

MARLOW: And of all women, the one I dread the most to meet. (KATE *enters, carrying her bonnet.*)

HASTINGS (*Going to her*): Miss Hardcastle, this is indeed a pleasure. (*Leads her toward* MARLOW) You have no idea, Miss Hardcastle, how pleased I am to bring together two persons of such merit—you and my friend, Charles Marlow. (MARLOW *looks up at ceiling, down at floor, then out at audience.*)

MARLOW (*Aside*): I wish I were dead.

KATE (*Aside*): He's either modest or numb. (*To* MARLOW) I'm glad of your safe arrival, Mr. Marlow. Did you have a pleasant journey?

MARLOW (*Looking everywhere but at* KATE): Fairly unpleasant. I mean, unfairly pleasant. I mean, I thank you, Madam, for your . . . your. . . .

HASTINGS (*Stage whispers to* MARLOW): You're doing fine, Charles. You never spoke better in your whole life.

MARLOW (*Gathering courage*): I have traveled quite a bit, Madam. I have done little, but I have seen much.

MISS NEVILLE: I have been told that's the best way to travel.

HASTINGS (*Stage whisper to* MARLOW): Keep going, Charles.

MARLOW (*Stage whisper to* HASTINGS): Don't leave me, George. If I start to flounder, throw me a word.

KATE: An observer like you, Mr. Marlow, must lead a pleasant life.

MARLOW: Most things are pleasant enough, if one learns to be amused by one's traveling companions.

HASTINGS (*Stage whisper to* MARLOW): Good, good, Charles. Just keep it up. (*To* KATE) I know that you and Mr. Marlow are going to be excellent company. I believe our being here will simply slow down your getting acquainted.

MARLOW (*Frightened*): Not at all, not at all, George. We don't know what we would do without you.

HASTINGS: Miss Neville and I will take a short walk about the garden. We shall see you presently. (*To* MARLOW) Don't worry, Charles. (*To* MISS NEVILLE) Shall we, Miss Neville? (*Offering his arm*)

MISS NEVILLE (*Taking his arm*): By all means, Mr. Hastings. (MISS NEVILLE *and* HASTINGS *exit.* KATE *looks at* MARLOW, *who first starts to follow* HASTINGS, *then returns to stand near* KATE. *He doesn't look at her.*)

KATE: You were saying, Mr. Marlow, that your traveling companions keep you amused. Did your observations include the ladies?

MARLOW: I . . . I . . . Pardon me, Madam, I . . . as yet have studied . . . only—how to please them.

KATE: Some people say that is the very worst way.

MARLOW: I talk only to sensible, grave ladies. (*Pauses*) I'm afraid that I'm boring you.

KATE: Not at all, sir. I like a sensible, grave conversation. I could listen to it forever. Indeed, I am shocked when men speak foolishness to ladies—of dances and concerts, London gossip, and . . . (*Pauses and looks at him closely*) Do you know what I mean, Mr. Marlow?

MARLOW: Indeed, yes, Madam. Just what I meant to say.

KATE (*Aside, to audience*): Is this a man of the world? (*To MARLOW*) You were saying?

MARLOW: I was saying . . . (*Aside*) What the devil was I saying? (*To her*) I was saying, Madam. . . . Small talk comes from a lack of courage, and . . . er . . .

KATE: I agree entirely—a lack of courage. Please go on.

MARLOW: Well, er, I would like to, but I'm sure I heard Miss Neville calling us.

KATE: Then, you must join them! I'll follow in a moment.

MARLOW (*Bowing*): Your servant, Madam. (*Rushes off*)

KATE (*Laughing*): Ha! ha! ha! Was there ever such a sober meeting of lovers? He did not look at my face once. But—except for his unaccountable bashfulness—Mr. Marlow is a charming, handsome man. If I could teach him some confidence, I might make him a perfect husband for some lovely girl. (*Pauses*) And who would that lovely girl be? (*Thinks*) Maybe me. But it is time for me to change my costume. Papa wants me to look like a country maid in the evening. (*Exits as curtain falls*)

* * * * *

SCENE 2

TIME: *Several hours later.*

SETTING: *The Hardcastle parlor, the same as Scene 1.*

AT RISE: HARDCASTLE *and* MRS. HARDCASTLE *are at center, talking.*

HARDCASTLE: How could Sir Charles describe his son as a modest man? I find him to be the most impudent piece of brass that ever spoke with a tongue. Why, he just took off his boots, dropped them in the hall, and told me to have them back in a half-hour, shined. I'm sure Kate has found him to be impudent, too.

MRS. HARDCASTLE (*Laughing*): Oh, Mr. Hardcastle. You're entirely too hard on *us* young people. Both young men are utterly charming. I must go and speak to Mr. Hastings now.

HARDCASTLE: Be careful, wife, or he'll have you washing his shirts. (*She exits.* KATE *enters, in a servant's dress.*) Ah, Kate, I see you're dressed in country style.

KATE: I try to please you, Father, even when I do not share your taste.

HARDCASTLE: Do you mean the dress or young Mr. Marlow?

KATE: Both, but you warned me he was extraordinary.

HARDCASTLE: He is, indeed. I was never so surprised in all my life.

KATE: I would think that with all the traveling he has done. . . .

HARDCASTLE: Travel has never taught a young man modesty.

KATE: Oh, it's natural with him—that bashful manner.

HARDCASTLE: Whose bashful manner?

KATE: Why, Mr. Marlow's. He's so modest, it's painful.

HARDCASTLE: You can't be serious. He's the most impudent puppy that ever barked in another man's house.

KATE: What! He treated me with shyness and respect.

HARDCASTLE: He treated me like a handyman in my own house.

KATE: One of us must surely be mistaken.

HARDCASTLE: But we're agreed—he's rejected as your suitor.

KATE: Yes, but with one condition. If you should find him less impudent—and I find him more presuming—if you find him more respectful—

HARDCASTLE: All right, if we should both find him improved. . . . But that's impossible. I know men.

KATE: One of us is wrong. Let's investigate further.

HARDCASTLE: I agree, but you'll see that I'm right. Now I must to get his boots back to him. (*Exits.* KATE's MAID *enters.*)

MAID: Really, Miss Hardcastle, that Mr. Marlow's the most impertinent thing!

KATE: He is?

MAID: And what is more, Madam, he saw you dressed in your present costume, and he mistook you for the maid.

KATE: Did he? (*Pauses*) I hope you didn't tell him differently. Do you think I could fool Mr. Marlow into thinking I'm the maid here?

MAID: I think so, Madam, for you have a kind of spirit that one doesn't often find in women of quality. (MARLOW *enters*.)

MARLOW (*In confident manner*): Ah, here are a couple of lovelies.

MAID: Oh, it's that Mr. Marlow.

KATE (*Aside to* MAID): Leave us. (MAID *exits*. *To* MARLOW) You must be Mr. Marlow, sir. Miss Hardcastle told me you were in the house.

MARLOW (*Going to* KATE): That must have been a serious conversation. Your Miss Hardcastle is a serious woman.

KATE: Oh, that she is, sir.

MARLOW: Too serious for me. Besides, from the glimpse I had of her, I think she squints.

KATE (*Starting off*): I thought I heard someone call me.

MARLOW: You heard only the murmuring of my heart, sweet girl. No one called. (*Looking at her*) You're a pretty one.

KATE: Oh, sir, you embarrass me.

MARLOW: What's your name?

KATE: My name, sir?

MARLOW: Yes, yes, what do people call you?

KATE: Oh, that depends upon the people and what I've done. In the eighteen years I've spent in this house, I've been called many things.

MARLOW: Eighteen years? Were you a maid the day you were born?

KATE: Oh, sir, I must never tell you my age. They say women and music should never be dated.

MARLOW: It's difficult to judge either from too great a distance. (*Tries to catch her and kiss her*)

KATE (*Ducking to avoid him*): Pray, sir, keep your distance. One would think you wanted to know my age as they do with horses, by their teeth.

MARLOW: If you keep so far from me, we shall never get acquainted.

KATE: Who wants to be acquainted with you? I want no acquaintance with any man who treats women the way you treated

Miss Hardcastle. You didn't try to kiss her, but kept bowing and hedging like a criminal before a judge.

MARLOW (*Aside*): Egad, she got me that time. (*To* KATE) Oh, that was all a game. Miss Hardcastle and I laughed and joked a bit, but she is too serious. I like lively women like you. (*Grabs her and tries to kiss her*)

KATE: Sir! Sir! What are you trying to do? (HARDCASTLE *enters and stands, surprised.* MARLOW *turns and sees him, and* KATE *escapes from him.*)

MARLOW: What a house for a man who likes privacy. (*Exits*)

HARDCASTLE (*Going to* KATE): This is your modest lover? Kate, aren't you ashamed to deceive your father so?

KATE: Do not believe your eyes, Papa. He really is modest. Give me an hour to prove it, and even you'll agree.

HARDCASTLE: You've never deceived me before; so you'll have your hour. But don't trifle with me, child.

KATE: Not with *you,* Papa. Not with you. (*She takes his arm, and they exit.* HASTINGS *and* MISS NEVILLE *enter.*)

HASTINGS: I hate deceiving Charles. But if your aunt gives us permission to marry, even Charles may agree it's worth it.

MISS NEVILLE: We have but an hour to win her over. Charles' father will be here tonight.

HASTINGS: Egad! As soon as young Marlow meets his father, he'll learn this is no inn, and all will be exposed.

MISS NEVILLE: Then I'll talk to my aunt now. She's a flighty woman, but she wants me to be happy. And she likes you.

HASTINGS: Charm her as you do me.

MISS NEVILLE: I'll try. (*She exits.* MARLOW *enters.*)

MARLOW: Is the old innkeeper about?

HASTINGS: I don't think so.

MARLOW: He's been spying on me. I met a pretty little maid, and I was just about to steal a kiss, when he interrupted us.

HASTINGS: Heavens, Charles, are you trifling with the maids again?

MARLOW: Don't be a snob, George. She's pretty, and I like her.

HASTINGS: I wasn't thinking about you. It's fine for a gentleman to trifle with a maid. But what of her?

MARLOW: I hadn't thought of that.

HASTINGS: The girl has feelings, you know. Besides, what would Miss Hardcastle think?

MARLOW: I couldn't care less. (*Muses*) But you're right, George. The girl does have feelings. George, do you think I've offended the poor child?

HASTINGS: I wouldn't go that far, Charles.

MARLOW: It's low to use people for one's own advantage.

HASTINGS (*Aside*): What will Charles say when he learns I've used him? (*To* CHARLES) Now, it's not as bad as that. Excuse me, Charles. I must go. (*Exits*)

MARLOW: What's wrong? Could I have offended George by my behavior with the maid? Am I a brute, who—too timid to speak to women of my own class—plays the man of the world at the expense of some poor working girl? I'm going to leave this inn. I have made a fool of myself again. (MR. HARDCASTLE *enters.*)

HARDCASTLE: Mr. Marlow, a word with you.

MARLOW (*Sternly*): And I would have a word with you. I want my bill.

HARDCASTLE: Your what, sir?

MARLOW: My bill. And don't cheat me.

HARDCASTLE: This is too much, sir. For a man to enter my house and call for whatever he wants, to order me and my wife about, to try to kiss. . . . Well, sir, you go too far.

MARLOW: I can't go far enough. Bring me my bill.

HARDCASTLE: Young man, from your father's letter to me, I expected a well-bred, modest man as a visitor here, but you are rude, boorish, and a bully. Your father will be here presently and shall hear about this. (*Exits*)

MARLOW: Wait! My father? What's this? Certainly there is some mistake. He speaks as if. . . . Good heavens, is it possible that this is *not* an inn? It looks like an inn. (KATE *enters.*) Just a minute, miss. I want to ask you something.

KATE: Well, be quick about it. I'm in a hurry.

MARLOW: It seems . . . it would appear. . . .

KATE (*Aside*): Has he begun to discover his mistake?

MARLOW: What is your position in this house?

KATE: A poor relation of the family, sir.

MARLOW: And you serve as a maid for this inn?

KATE: An inn, sir? This is Mr. Hardcastle's house.

MARLOW: What! The Hardcastle home? Good heavens, what have I done? To mistake this house for an inn, and my father's old friend for an innkeeper! What an insolent puppy Mr. Hardcastle must think me. And you, my dear, what you must think of me! I've got to leave here. Now.

KATE: I would be sorry, sir, if anything I've said is forcing you to leave good Mr. Hardcastle's home. (*Pretends to cry*)

MARLOW: Don't weep. You are the only one I mind leaving. If it were not for the difference in our birth, fortune, and education—all of which would make marriage between us impossible—I would stay and seek your hand.

KATE (*Aside*): He proves to be a decent man. (*To* MARLOW) I'm sure my family is as good as Miss Hardcastle's, and although I'm poor, I'm respectable. If I had money, I'd give it to you.

MARLOW (*Aside*): Oh, she is just the woman I want, but the son of Sir Charles Marlow cannot marry a maid. (*To* KATE) If I had my choice, you would be my wife. But I owe too much to my father to marry against his wishes. I wish I could say more. But I can't. (*Exits*)

KATE (*Aside to audience*): He *will* say more! I'll see to that. I must find Father. (*Exits.* HARDCASTLE *and* HASTINGS *enter.*)

HASTINGS: It's really all my fault, sir. I should have told Charles as soon as I discovered our error.

HARDCASTLE (*Laughing*): He took my home for an inn, did he, and me for an innkeeper? That, indeed, is quite amusing!

HASTINGS: I am afraid, sir, that I used him to further my own romance.

HARDCASTLE: All may come out well yet.

HASTINGS: Your wife has given Miss Neville permission for our marriage. So it has gone well for me, but I won't be happy until Charles forgives me. Will you excuse me, Mr. Hardcastle?

HARDCASTLE: Certainly, my boy. Certainly. (HASTINGS *exits.*) Took me for an innkeeper, imagine that. And my Dorothy for the innkeeper's wife (*Laughs.* MARLOW *enters, sees* HARDCASTLE *and starts to leave.*)

HARDCASTLE: Mr. Marlow, just one moment, please.

MARLOW (*Seeking an exit*): Mr. Hardcastle, I want to apologize—to explain, but I don't know how.

HARDCASTLE: It's all right. Hastings has explained everything.

MARLOW: Everything?

HARDCASTLE (*Laughing*): Yes, everything. You are taking a very humorous mistake too seriously. See my daughter and spend an hour or two laughing. She'll enjoy the joke.

MARLOW (*Unaware that* KATE *and the "Maid" are the same*): Thank you, sir. Miss Hardcastle is so serious that I think she will be displeased by my behavior.

HARDCASTLE: Kate? I don't think so. She likes you.

MARLOW: Sir, I shall be always proud of her approbation. Thank heavens, I was always a gentleman in her presence.

HARDCASTLE: Approbation? That's a cold word, Mr. Marlow. If I'm not mistaken, I thought you showed her more than approbation when I saw the two of you together.

MARLOW: Really, sir, you are mistaken. I have seen your daughter but once, and then under the most formal conditions.

HARDCASTLE: Now, young man, I'm an old fellow and all that. But I know what I saw. Don't worry. You have my approval.

MARLOW: Really, sir, I assure you—no matter how impudent I have been to you, your daughter received from me nothing but the most proper—and serious—and. . . .

HARDCASTLE: Good heavens, man, stop explaining. You have my approval, and I'm sure you shall have hers for the asking.

MARLOW: Really, sir, I never even held her hand.

HARDCASTLE: What are you saying? I saw with my own eyes. . . .

MARLOW: Sir, I speak the truth. I saw the lady once without emotion, and parted without reluctance. Now, sir, I think I should leave your home, where I have behaved so outrageously. Good day, sir. (*Exits*)

HARDCASTLE (*Aside, to audience*): Now, what am I to make of that? He tells me that there's nothing between my Kate and him. And I saw him with my own naked eyes trying to steal a kiss. (KATE *and* SIR CHARLES *enter.*)

SIR CHARLES: Am I still welcome in your home, old friend?

HARDCASTLE (*Going to him and shaking his hand*): Sir Charles, it's good to see you. I see Kate has told you.

SIR CHARLES: She has told me all.

HARDCASTLE: Then maybe she will be so good as to do the same for me. Your son, sir, informs me that he has seen my Kate but once and that upon the most formal terms. Yet I, myself, saw him trying to kiss her.

SIR CHARLES (*Surprised*): My son, Charles, tried to kiss Kate? Well, that surprises me and pleases me.

HARDCASTLE: But he denies it. (*To* KATE) Kate, has Mr. Marlow made any professions of love to you?

KATE: Yes, I think he has.

HARDCASTLE (*To* SIR CHARLES): You see, Sir Charles.

SIR CHARLES: Did he indicate marriage?

KATE: He said, as I remember, that he would seek my hand.

SIR CHARLES: That's blunt enough. But it doesn't sound like my son. Kate, I'm afraid you are mistaken.

KATE: If you and Papa will hide yourselves there (*Points to screen*) until he returns, I'll show you how he behaves with me.

SIR CHARLES: All right. Come, sir, let us hide. (HARDCASTLE *and* SIR CHARLES *go behind screen.* MARLOW *enters.*)

MARLOW: I'm ready to leave now, but I couldn't go until I told you how sorry I am that we are parting.

KATE: You aren't sorry—or you wouldn't be leaving.

MARLOW: I can't stay. I have made a fool of myself, and it also seems that I am being compromised with a most unpromising young lady.

KATE: The one that squints?

MARLOW (*Taking her hand*): If only you were she.

KATE: I can squint, too, if necessary.

MARLOW: By heavens, this has gone too far for me to retreat. I love you. I'll stay and face my father. When he sees you, he'll know why of all women, you must be the one to be my wife. (HARDCASTLE *and* SIR CHARLES *comes from behind screen.*)

HARDCASTLE (*Roaring*): Tell me, young man, tell me again that you never spoke of marriage to my daughter.

MARLOW: Good heavens! Mr. Hardcastle and my father. Well, so be it. Mr. Hardcastle, I am sorry that you should learn of this matter in this way. But I do not love your daughter, and I never spoke to her of marriage.

HARDCASTLE (*To* SIR CHARLES): You heard him! You saw him!

SIR CHARLES: This is the most brazen behavior I've ever seen. Charles, Mr. Hardcastle and I heard you just now.

MARLOW: It's just as well, Father.

HARDCASTLE: Just as well? Just as well that you talk of love to my daughter in private and deny it in public!

MARLOW: Daughter! This lady couldn't be your daughter!

HARDCASTLE: My only daughter, Kate. Who else would she be?

KATE: Yes, sir, I am the squinting lady.

MARLOW: I have made a fool of myself one time too often. I can say nothing but farewell. (*Starts to leave*)

HARDCASTLE (*Catching his arm*): Wait a minute. I see it all now—it was another mistake. I am glad of it, and I know Kate is, too.

MARLOW: How can she ever forgive me? I'm such a fool.

KATE (*Taking his arm*): Well, having stooped to conquer with success, and gaining a husband without aid of dress, I'd be a fool to let you go until the parson makes us one. Now, you may kiss me, Charles. (*Holds out hand, which he kisses.*)

SIR CHARLES: Well, I'm grateful I have only one son.

HARDCASTLE: And I one daughter, if all marriages are arranged this way. Modern courtships are too much for me! (*Curtain*)

THE END

The Wizard of Oz

by L. Frank Baum
Adapted by Lynne Sharon Schwartz

The adventures of Dorothy and friends on their trip down the Yellow Brick Road. . . .

Characters

NARRATOR
DOROTHY
WITCH OF THE NORTH
THREE MUNCHKINS
SCARECROW
TIN WOODMAN
COWARDLY LION
SOLDIER
WIZARD OF OZ
LOVELY LADY
WICKED WITCH OF THE WEST
KING OF THE WINGED MONKEYS
WINGED MONKEYS
GLINDA, *the Good Witch of the South*
AUNT EM

Scene 1

Before Rise: Narrator *enters and goes to a lectern at one side in front of curtain.*

Narrator: Once upon a time there was a little girl named Dorothy, who lived in the great Kansas prairie with her Uncle Henry, who was a farmer, and her Aunt Em, and her dog, Toto.

One day, they heard a whistling sound in the air, and they knew that a great storm, a cyclone, was coming. (*Howling sound of wind is heard from offstage*) Uncle Henry ran out to take care of the cattle, and Aunt Em ran to a trapdoor in the floor, calling to Dorothy to follow her. But at that moment, Toto jumped out of Dorothy's arms and hid under the bed. As Dorothy reached to get him, the house shook so hard that she lost her footing and fell down on the floor. Then the house whirled around and rose slowly through the air. The house was in the exact center of the cyclone, and it was carried miles and miles up into the air. The wind was shrieking loudly, but soon the house felt very calm, and Dorothy crawled into her bed and fell asleep. When she awoke, she found herself in a strange place. (Narrator *exits as curtain rises.*)

Setting: *A field. A backdrop portrays the front of a cottage. Two silver shoes can be seen sticking out from under the house.*

At Rise: Dorothy *is standing near the doorway holding her dog, Toto.*

Dorothy: I wonder where I am? All I can remember is whirling around and around. (*Looks around.* Witch of the North *and* Three Munchkins *enter.*)

Witch of the North (*Going to* Dorothy *and bowing*): You are welcome, most noble Sorceress, to the land of the Munchkins. We are so grateful to you for having killed the Wicked Witch of the East, and for setting our people free.

Dorothy: You are very kind, but there must be some mistake. I have not killed anyone.

Witch of the North (*Laughing*): Your house did, anyway, and that is the same thing. See? (*She points to corner of house.*)

There are her two feet, sticking out from under the house.

DOROTHY (*Dismayed*): Oh, dear. The house must have fallen on her. Whatever shall we do?

WITCH OF THE NORTH: There is nothing to be done. She was the Wicked Witch of the East, and she made the Munchkins her slaves. Now they are set free, and are grateful to you.

DOROTHY: Who are the Munchkins?

WITCH OF THE NORTH: They are the people who live in this land of the East. These are three of my Munchkin friends. (THREE MUNCHKINS *bow to* DOROTHY.) I am the Witch of the North.

DOROTHY: Oh, gracious! Are you a real witch?

WITCH OF THE NORTH: Yes, indeed. But I am a good witch.

DOROTHY: I thought all witches were wicked.

WITCH OF THE NORTH: Oh, no, that is a great mistake. There were four witches in all the Land of Oz, and two of them, those who live in the North and the South, are good witches. Those who lived in the East and the West were wicked witches, but now there is only one wicked Wicked Witch left—the Wicked Witch of the West.

1ST MUNCHKIN (*Who has been peering at the feet of the Wicked Witch*): Look! Look! Her feet have disappeared. (*All run to look.*)

WITCH OF THE NORTH: She was so old that she dried up quickly in the sun. That is the end of her. (*To* DOROTHY) But the silver shoes are yours, and you shall have them to wear. (*Gives shoes to* DOROTHY)

2ND MUNCHKIN: There is some charm connected with these silver shoes, but what it is, we never knew.

DOROTHY: Thank you. (*Puts shoes on*) Now, can you help me find my way back to my aunt and uncle?

3RD MUNCHKIN: There is a great desert all around this land, and no one who tries to cross it can live.

WITCH OF THE NORTH: I am afraid, my dear, that you will have to live with us.

DOROTHY (*Starting to cry*): But I want to go back to Kansas.

WITCH OF THE NORTH (*Taking off her cap and looking inside*): Perhaps we will get a magic message from the cap to help us.

(*Reading*) It says, "Let Dorothy go to the City of Emeralds." Is your name Dorothy, my dear?

DOROTHY: Yes. Where is the City of Emeralds?

WITCH OF THE NORTH: It is in the center of the country, and is ruled by Oz, the Great Wizard.

DOROTHY: Is he a good man?

WITCH OF THE NORTH: He is a good Wizard. Whether he is a man or not I cannot tell, for I have never seen him.

DOROTHY: How can I get there?

WITCH OF THE NORTH: You must walk. It is a long journey, through a country that is sometimes pleasant and sometimes dark and terrible. However, I will use all the magic arts I know of to keep you from harm, and I will give you my kiss. No one will dare injure a person who has been kissed by the Witch of the North. (*Kisses* DOROTHY *on the forehead*) The road to the City of Emeralds is paved with yellow brick, so you cannot miss it. When you get to Oz, do not be afraid of the Wizard. Just tell him your story and ask him to help you. Goodbye, my dear.

MUNCHKINS (*Bowing*): Goodbye, Dorothy.

DOROTHY: Goodbye, and thank you. I will start on my journey right away. (WITCH *and* MUNCHKINS *exit. Lights dim to indicate the passage of time. While the stage is dark, the* SCARECROW *enters and stands on a high stool at one side. There is a pole in back of stool which he pretends to be attached to. When lights come up,* DOROTHY *is crossing stage, holding Toto. Suddenly she notices the* SCARECROW.) I'm sure I saw the Scarecrow wink at me, but it couldn't be. He's just made of straw.

SCARECROW: Good day.

DOROTHY (*Surprised*): Did you speak?

SCARECROW: Certainly. How do you do?

DOROTHY: I'm pretty well, thank you. How do you do?

SCARECROW: I'm not feeling well. It's very tedious being perched up here night and day to scare away crows.

DOROTHY: Can't you get down?

SCARECROW: No, because this pole is stuck up by back. If you will please take away the pole, I shall be greatly obliged to you.

(DOROTHY *goes to* SCARECROW *and pretends to lift him off pole. He steps down and lowers his arms.*) Thank you very much. I feel like a new man. (*Stretches and yawns*) Who are you, and where are you going?

DOROTHY: My name is Dorothy, and I am going to the Emerald City to ask the great Wizard of Oz to send me back to Kansas.

SCARECROW: Where is the Emerald City? And who is Oz?

DOROTHY: Don't you know?

SCARECROW (*Sadly*): No, indeed; I don't know anything. You see, I am stuffed, so I have no brains at all.

DOROTHY: Oh, I'm awfully sorry.

SCARECROW: Do you think if I go to the Emerald City with you, Oz would give me some brains?

DOROTHY: I cannot tell, but you may come with me if you like.

SCARECROW: I think I shall. You see, I don't mind my legs and arms and body being stuffed, because I cannot get hurt. But I don't like to be thought a fool. (*As they talk,* TIN WOODMAN *enters, unseen by others. He stands at one side of the stage with his ax raised. He groans, first softly, then louder.*)

DOROTHY (*Looking around*): I'm sure I heard someone groan. (*Sees* TIN WOODMAN *and goes to him*) Did you groan?

TIN WOODMAN: Yes, I did. I've been groaning for more than a year.

DOROTHY (*Sympathetically*): What can I do for you?

TIN WOODMAN: Get an oilcan and oil my joints. They are rusted so badly that I cannot move them at all. You will find an oilcan right in front of my cottage a few steps further in the woods.

DOROTHY: Very well. You wait here. (*She runs off-stage and returns immediately carrying oilcan.*) Where are your joints?

TIN WOODMAN: Oil my neck, first (DOROTHY *does so.* SCARECROW *helps by moving* TIN WOODMAN'S *head from side to side gently.*) Now oil the joints in my arms. (DOROTHY *does so.* SCARECROW *bends* TIN WOODMAN'S *arms.* TIN WOODMAN *sighs and lowers his ax.*) This is a great comfort. I have been holding that ax in the air ever since I rusted in a rainstorm. Now, if you will oil the joints of my legs, I shall be all right once more. (*They oil his legs.*) Thank you so much, I might have stood there forever if you had not come along, so you have certainly saved my life. How did you happen to be here?

DOROTHY: We are on our way to the Emerald City to see the great Oz. I want him to send me back to Kansas, and the Scarecrow wants him to put a few brains into his head.

TIN WOODMAN (*After thinking for a moment*): Do you suppose Oz could give me a heart?

DOROTHY: Why, I guess so. It would be as easy as giving the Scarecrow brains.

TIN WOODMAN: True. If you will allow me to join your party, I will also go to the Emerald City and ask Oz to help me.

SCARECROW: We'd be pleased to have you. But if I were you, I should ask for brains instead of a heart, for a fool with no brains would not know what to do with a heart if he had one.

TIN WOODMAN: I shall take the heart, for brains alone do not make one happy. (*A great roar is heard, and the* COWARDLY LION *rushes in. He knocks* SCARECROW *over and strikes* TIN WOODMAN, *who falls to ground.* DOROTHY *drops Toto, in her surprise, and* LION *rushes toward him.* DOROTHY *snatches him up, and then slaps the* LION *on the nose.*)

DOROTHY: Don't you dare to bite Toto! You ought to be ashamed of yourself, a big beast like you, biting a poor little dog!

LION (*Rubbing his nose*): I didn't bite him.

DOROTHY: No, but you tried to. You are nothing but a big coward.

LION (*Hanging his head in shame*): I know it, but how can I help it?

DOROTHY: I'm sure I don't know. To think of your striking a stuffed man like the poor Scarecrow!

LION: Is he really stuffed?

DOROTHY (*Helping* SCARECROW *up*): Of course he's stuffed.

LION: That's why he went over so easily. Is the other one stuffed also?

DOROTHY (*Helping* TIN WOODMAN *up*): No, he's made of tin.

LION: Then that's why he nearly blunted my claws.

SCARECROW: What makes you a coward?

LION: It's a mystery. I suppose I was born that way. All the other animals in the forest naturally expect me to be brave, for the

Lion is the King of Beasts. I learned that if I roared very loudly every living thing was frightened. If the elephants and the tigers and the bears had ever tried to fight me, I should have run myself—I'm such a coward. But when they hear me roar, they all run away, and of course I let them go.

SCARECROW: But that isn't right. The King of Beasts *shouldn't* be a coward.

LION: I know it. (*He wipes a tear from his eye with the tip of his tail.*) It makes my life very unhappy. But whenever there is danger, my heart begins to beat fast.

TIN WOODMAN: You ought to be glad of that, for it proves you have a heart. I have no heart at all, so it cannot beat fast. But I am going to the great Oz to ask him for one.

SCARECROW: And I am going to ask him to give me brains, for my head is stuffed with straw.

DOROTHY: And I am going to ask him to send Toto and me back to Kansas.

LION: Do you think Oz could give me courage?

SCARECROW: Just as easily as he could give me brains.

TIN WOODMAN: Or give me a heart.

DOROTHY: Or send me back to Kansas.

LION: Then, if you don't mind, I'll go with you, for my life is simply unbearable without a bit of courage.

DOROTHY: You will be very welcome, for you will help to keep away the other wild beasts. (*They start to exit, as curtain falls.*)

* * * * *

SCENE 2

TIME: *A few days later.*

SETTING: *Outside* WIZARD'S *throne room.*

BEFORE RISE: DOROTHY, SCARECROW, TIN WOODMAN, *and* LION *enter, all wearing green spectacles.*

DOROTHY: I am so tired. I thought we would never arrive.

TIN WOODMAN: I hope the great Oz will see us. The soldier said no one had asked to see Oz in many years. (SOLDIER *enters.*)

DOROTHY (*To* SOLDIER): Have you seen Oz and asked him about us?

SOLDIER: Oh, no, I have never seen him, but I gave him your message. When I mentioned your silver shoes he was very much interested. He said he would grant you an audience, but if you come on an idle or foolish errand he may be angry and destroy you all in an instant.

SCARECROW: But it is not a foolish errand, nor an idle one.

SOLDIER: Very well, then. But each of you must enter his presence alone. And you must not remove the green spectacles.

DOROTHY: Why?

SOLDIER: Because that is the rule. Otherwise the brightness and glory of the Emerald City would blind you.

DOROTHY: Thank you. (*Bell rings.*)

SOLDIER: That is the signal. You must go into the throne room by yourself. (SOLDIER *exits with* SCARECROW, TIN WOODMAN *and* LION, *as curtain rises to reveal the throne room. All the furnishings are green. Suspended over the throne at center is a tremendous papier mache head, with a mouth that moves. Screen stands at one side.* DOROTHY *walks hesitantly into room.*)

OZ (*Speaking from behind screen*): I am Oz, the great and terrible. Who are you, and why do you seek me?

DOROTHY (*Speaking to the head*): I am Dorothy, the small and meek. I have come to you for help.

OZ: Where did you get the silver shoes?

DOROTHY: I got them from the Wicked Witch of the East, when my house fell on her and killed her.

OZ: What do you wish me to do?

DOROTHY: Send me back to Kansas, where my Aunt Em and Uncle Henry are. I am sure Aunt Em will be dreadfully worried over my being away so long.

OZ: Why should I do this for you?

DOROTHY: Because you are strong, and I am weak; because you are a great Wizard and I am only a helpless little girl.

OZ: But you were strong enough to kill the Wicked Witch of the East.

DOROTHY: That just happened. I could not help it.

OZ: Well, you have no right to expect me to send you back to Kansas unless you do something for me in return.

DOROTHY (*Fearfully*): What must I do?

Oz: You wear the silver shoes which have a powerful charm. There is now only one Wicked Witch left in all this land, and only when you can tell me that she is dead will I send you back to Kansas.

DOROTHY (*Beginning to weep*): I never killed anything, willingly, and even if I wanted to, how could I kill the Wicked Witch of the West? If you are great and terrible, can't you kill her yourself?

Oz: Silence! Until the Wicked Witch of the West dies, you will not see your aunt and uncle again. Now go, and do not ask to see me again until you have done your task. (*Blackout, during which* DOROTHY *exits; head is removed, and* LOVELY LADY *enters and sits on throne. Lights come up.* SCARECROW *enters and bows.*)

LADY: I am Oz, the great and terrible. Who are you, and why do you seek me?

SCARECROW: I am only a Scarecrow, stuffed with straw, and I have no brains. I come to you praying that you will put brains in my head so I may become as much a man as any other.

LADY: Why should I do this for you?

SCARECROW: Because you are wise and powerful, and no one else can help me.

LADY: I never grant favors without some return, but this much I will promise. If you will kill the Wicked Witch of the West for me, I will bestow upon you so many brains that you will be the wisest man in all the Land of Oz.

SCARECROW (*Surprised*): I thought you asked Dorothy to kill the Witch.

LADY: So I did. I don't care who kills her. Until she is dead I will not grant your wish. Now go, and do not seek me again until you have earned the brains you so greatly desire. (*Blackout during which* SCARECROW *and* LADY *exit;* Oz *appears as a horrible beast and sits on throne. Lights come up.* TIN WOODMAN *enters.* Oz *roars.*)

Oz: I am Oz, the great and terrible. Who are you, and why do you seek me?

TIN WOODMAN: I am a Woodman, and made of tin. Therefore I

have no heart and cannot love. I pray you to give me a heart
that I may be as other men are.

Oz: Why should I do this?

TIN WOODMAN: Because you alone can grant my request.

Oz: If you indeed desire a heart, you must earn it.

TIN WOODMAN: How?

Oz: Help Dorothy kill the Wicked Witch of the West. When the
Witch is dead, I will give you the biggest and kindest and most
loving heart in all the Land of Oz. (*He roars again, as lights
black out, and he goes behind screen.* TIN WOODMAN *exits.
When lights go on again, there is a great "Ball of Fire" hanging
over the throne.* COWARDLY LION *enters, frightened.*)

Oz (*Behind screen*): I am Oz, the great and terrible. Who are you,
and why do you seek me?

LION: I am a Cowardly Lion. Though I am supposed to be King of
the Beasts, I am frightened of everything I see. I have come to
ask you to give me courage.

Oz: Why should I do this for you?

LION: Because you are great and powerful, and you alone can
help me.

Oz: I will grant you courage only if you help Dorothy kill the
Wicked Witch of the West.

LION: But how can I do that if I am a coward?

Oz: I do not know, but after the Witch is dead, you may come
back to me, and I will make you the most courageous beast in
all the forest. (*Ball of Fire shakes, and* LION *cringes, as curtain
falls.*)

* * * * *

SCENE 3

BEFORE RISE: NARRATOR *enters.*

NARRATOR: The next morning the four friends met and marveled
at the many forms the Great Wizard could take. Then they
started for the castle of the Wicked Witch of the West. At
night, Dorothy and Toto and the Lion lay down to sleep, while
the Scarecrow and the Tin Woodman kept watch.

Now the Wicked Witch of the West had an eye so powerful, she could see everywhere. As she stood in front of her castle and looked out, she saw Dorothy asleep with her friends all around her. She was furious to find them in her country and tried in many ways to capture them, but was unsuccessful. Finally, she thought of one last idea. (*Curtain opens slowly.*)

SETTING: *Before castle of the Wicked Witch of the West. A backdrop shows front of castle.*

AT RISE: WICKED WITCH *enters with broom and a bucket of water. She wears a gold cap.*

WICKED WITCH: The only way left to destroy these strangers is with my Golden Cap. I have only one command left to the Winged Monkeys. (*Sets down pail and broom, puts one hand on cap and recites, standing on left foot*) Ep—pe, pep—pe, kak—ke! (*Stands on right foot*) Hil—lo, hol—lo, hel—lo! (*With both feet on ground, shouts loudly*) Ziz—zy, zuz—zy, zik! (*A low rumbling sound is heard, and* WINGED MONKEYS *enter.*)

KING OF MONKEYS: You have called us for the third and last time. What is your command?

WICKED WITCH: Destroy the strangers within my land, all except the Lion. Bring that beast to me, for I shall harness him like a horse and make him work.

KING OF MONKEYS: Your commands shall be obeyed. (MONKEYS *run out.*)

NARRATOR: The Monkeys flew to Dorothy and her friends. First they seized the Tin Woodman and dropped him in a valley covered with sharp rocks, where he lay battered and dented. Then they caught the Scarecrow and pulled the straw out of his clothes. They made a small bundle of his hat and clothes and threw it into the branches of a tall tree. (NARRATOR *exits as* WINGED MONKEYS *enter with* DOROTHY, *who holds Toto.*)

KING OF MONKEYS (*To* WICKED WITCH): We have obeyed you as far as we are able. The Tin Woodman and the Scarecrow are destroyed, and the Lion is tied up in your courtyard. We dare not harm the little girl or her dog, for the Witch of the North has kissed her forehead. Your power over our band is now ended. (MONKEYS *exit.*)

WICKED WITCH (*To* DOROTHY): Aha! I have tried many ways to capture you, and at last I have you for my slave. If you don't obey me in everything, I will make an end of you. You will clean the pots and kettles and sweep the floor and tend the fire.

DOROTHY: You are a very wicked witch for destroying my friends and tying up the Lion, but your power cannot last long. I have a special charm in my silver shoes that I got from the Wicked Witch of the East, and it will help me destroy you.

WICKED WITCH (*Staring at shoes*): The silver shoes! Give them to me!

DOROTHY: No!

WICKED WITCH (*Pushing* DOROTHY *down and grabbing one shoe*): There, you silly, little girl. You cannot struggle against my power. Now that I have your shoe, your charm will be useless.

DOROTHY: You are wicked! You have no right to take my shoe from me.

WICKED WITCH: I shall keep it, just the same and someday I shall get the other one from you, too. (DOROTHY *seizes bucket of water and dashes it over* WICKED WITCH *who begins to "shrink."* NOTE: *She does this by curling up slowly under her wide cloak and sinking to floor, so that soon she is completely hidden under the cloak.*)

DOROTHY: There, you mean, cruel creature!

WICKED WITCH: See what you have done? In a minute I shall melt away.

DOROTHY (*Frightened and astonished*): I'm very sorry!

WICKED WITCH: Didn't you know water would be the end of me?

DOROTHY (*Upset*): Of course not. How could I?

WICKED WITCH: In a minute, I shall be all melted, and you will have the castle to yourself. I have been wicked in my day, but I never thought a little girl like you would be able to put an end to my wicked deeds . . . (*Her voice trails off, and she shrinks, completely hidden under her cloak.*)

DOROTHY (*Taking broom*): I may as well get her out of here. And take my shoe, too. (*Puts shoe back on*) Perhaps I shall take her Golden Cap also. (*Puts cap on*) It fits perfectly! (*She "sweeps" the* WICKED WITCH *offstage.*) Now I must go back to the Emerald City for my reward. But how can I save the Scarecrow and the Tin Woodman and the Lion? (*She looks away.*) And I am afraid I am hopelessly lost. What can I do? (*She sits down wearily, takes off cap, and idly looks inside it.*) Oh, look! There's a charm in the cap! It's a magic rhyme. Maybe it will help me. (*Puts cap on and recites, standing on left foot*) Ep—pe, pep—pe, kak—ke! (*Stands on right foot*) Hil—lo, hol—lo, hel—lo! (*Louder, standing on both feet*) Ziz—zy, zuz—zy, zik! (*A low rumbling sound is heard, and* WINGED MONKEYS *enter.*)

KING OF MONKEYS: What is your command? We can take you anywhere within the Land of Oz in a moment's time.

DOROTHY: I wish to go to the Emerald City, but I must rescue my friends and take them with me.

KING OF MONKEYS: We will carry you there, and we will find your friends and take them with us, have no fear. (MONKEYS *lead* DOROTHY *offstage, as curtain falls.*)

* * * * *

SCENE 4

SETTING: *Oz's throne room.*

AT RISE: Oz *is hidden behind screen.* DOROTHY, SCARECROW, TIN WOODMAN, *and* LION *are onstage.*

LION: How lucky it was, Dorothy, that you took that magic cap!

DOROTHY: I wonder where Oz is.

OZ (*From behind screen*): I, the great and terrible Oz am here. Why do you seek me?

DOROTHY: We have come to claim our rewards, great Oz.

OZ: What rewards?

DOROTHY: You promised to grant us all our wishes when the Wicked Witch was destroyed.

OZ: Is she really destroyed?

DOROTHY: Yes, I melted her with a bucket of water.

OZ: Dear me! This is all very sudden! Come to see me tomorrow, for I must have time to think everything over.

DOROTHY: You must keep your promise to us. (LION *lets out a great roar;* DOROTHY *jumps, drops* TOTO *and tips over screen*

*with a crash, revealing a little old man with a bald head who
sits on a stool.*)

TIN WOODMAN (*Raising his ax and rushing toward* Oz): Who are
you?

Oz: I am Oz, the great and terrible (*Trembles*), but don't strike
me—please don't—and I'll do anything you want me to.

DOROTHY (*Dismayed*): I thought Oz was a great head.

SCARECROW: And I thought Oz was a lovely lady.

TIN WOODMAN: And I thought Oz was a terrible beast.

LION: And I thought he was a ball of fire.

Oz (*Timidly*): No, you are all wrong. I have been making believe.
I'm supposed to be a great wizard, but I'm really just an
ordinary man.

SCARECROW: You're a humbug, a fake!

Oz: Please don't speak so loudly or you will be overheard, and I
shall be ruined.

TIN WOODMAN: But this is terrible. How shall I ever get my
heart?

LION: Or I my courage?

SCARECROW: Or I my brains?

Oz: I pray you not to mention these little things. Think of the
terrible trouble now that you've found me out.

DOROTHY: Doesn't anyone else know you're a humbug?

Oz: No one but the four of you.

DOROTHY (*Bewildered*): But I don't understand. How was it that
you appeared to me as a great head?

Oz: That was one of my tricks. Everything has been a trick.

SCARECROW: You ought to be ashamed of yourself.

Oz: I am—I certainly am—but it was the only thing I could do.
You see, I was born in Omaha—

DOROTHY: Why, that isn't very far from Kansas!

Oz: No, but it's farther from here. (*Shakes his head sadly*) I
worked in a circus as a balloonist to draw a crowd. One day the
ropes of my balloon got twisted, and I couldn't come down
again. I floated for miles through the air until I landed in this
strange country. The people who saw me come down from the
clouds thought I was a great wizard. They were afraid of me
and promised to do anything I wished, so to amuse myself and

to keep the good people busy I ordered them to build this city and my palace. Because the country was so green and beautiful, I called it the Emerald City. I have been good to the people, and they like me. But one of my greatest fears was the witches, who had magical powers, while I had none at all. That is why I was so pleased to hear that your house had fallen on the Wicked Witch of the East, and why I was so willing to promise anything if you would do away with the other witch. But I am ashamed to say now that I cannot keep my promises to you.

DOROTHY: I think you are a very bad man.

OZ: Oh, no, my dear. I'm really a very good man, but I'm a very bad wizard, I must admit.

SCARECROW: Can't you give me brains?

OZ: You don't need them. You are learning something every day. A baby has brains, but it doesn't know much. Experience is the only thing that brings knowledge, and the longer you are on earth the more experience you are sure to get.

SCARECROW: That may all be true, but I shall be very unhappy unless you give me brains.

OZ: Then I will try to give you brains. I cannot tell you how to use them, however; you must find that out for yourself. (Oz goes to cabinet and fills a cup with powder, then goes to SCARECROW and pretends to pour the powder into his head.) Hereafter you will be a great man. Now you have a great many brains.

SCARECROW: Oh, thank you, thank you. And I'll find a way to use them well.

LION: Now, how about my courage?

OZ: You have plenty of courage, I am sure. All you need is confidence in yourself. True courage is facing danger when you are afraid, and you have plenty of true courage.

LION: Perhaps I have, but I'm scared just the same. I shall really be very unhappy unless you give me the sort of courage that makes me forget I am afraid.

OZ: Very well, I will get some for you. (Goes to cupboard, takes down green bottle, and pours contents into a green dish. He offers it to the LION, who sniffs at it disdainfully.) Drink.

LION: What is it?

Oz: Well, if it were inside of you, it would be courage. Courage is always inside a person. Therefore, I advise you to drink it as soon as possible. (LION *drinks*) How do you feel now?

LION (*Happily*): Full of courage!

TIN WOODMAN: How about my heart?

Oz: I think you are wrong to want a heart. It makes most people unhappy. You are lucky not to have a heart.

TIN WOODMAN: That must be a matter of opinion. I will bear all the unhappiness without a murmur, if you will give me a heart.

Oz: Very well. (*Goes to cabinet, takes out paper heart and pins it carefully on* TIN WOODMAN's *chest*) Isn't it a beauty?

TIN WOODMAN (*Looking down at it*): It is, indeed. But is it a kind heart?

Oz: Oh, very kind. It is a heart that any man might be proud of.

TIN WOODMAN: I am very grateful to you, and shall never forget your kindness.

DOROTHY: And now, how am I to get back to Kansas?

Oz (*Sighing*): We shall have to think about that for a while. (*Curtain*)

* * * * *

SCENE 5

BEFORE RISE: NARRATOR *enters and goes to lectern.*

NARRATOR: Oz thought for several days, and finally decided that he and Dorothy should leave in a balloon, and it was soon ready, but at the moment they were to take off, she realized that she had lost Toto. By the time she found him, the balloon was already sailing overhead, and she was very sad. She cried because she thought she would never get back to Kansas. Finally, a soldier who felt sorry for Dorothy came and told her that Glinda, the good Witch of the South, might help her. Glinda was the most powerful of all the Witches, and ruled over the Quadlings. The road to her castle was full of dangers to travelers, but Dorothy decided to go nevertheless, because it was her last hope, and her faithful friends went along to protect her. (NARRATOR *exits as curtain rises.*)

TIME: *A few days later.*
SETTING: *Glinda's castle.*
AT RISE: DOROTHY, SCARECROW, TIN WOODMAN, *and* LION *enter.*

DOROTHY: This must be Gilda's castle. Isn't it beautiful?

TIN WOODMAN: She must be an especially good witch, and I know she will help you, Dorothy. (GLINDA *enters.*)

GLINDA: I am Glinda, the Good Witch of the South. I have heard of how you landed here on the cyclone, child. What can I do for you?

DOROTHY (*Curtsying*): My greatest wish is to get back to Kansas, for Aunt Em will certainly think something dreadful has happened to me.

GLINDA: I am sure I can help you. But if I do, you must give me the Golden Cap.

DOROTHY: Willingly, for it will be of no use to me now. (*Gives her cap*)

GLINDA: I think I will need it just three times. (*To* SCARECROW) What will you do when Dorothy has left us?

SCARECROW: I will return to the Emerald City, for Oz has made me its ruler. The only thing that worries me is how to cross the tremendous mountain bordering your land. On our journey here, the Winged Monkeys carried us over.

GLINDA: By the Golden Cap I shall command the Winged Monkeys to carry you back to the Emerld City. (*To* TIN WOODMAN) What will become of you when Dorothy leaves?

TIN WOODMAN: The Winkies, in the land of the West, were very kind to me, and wanted me to rule over them after the Wicked Witch of the West was melted. If I could get back there again, I'd like nothing better than to be their ruler forever.

GLINDA: My second command to the Winged Monkeys will be that they carry you safely to the land of Winkies. I am sure you will rule the Winkies wisely and well. (*To* LION) And when Dorothy goes back to Kansas, Lion, what will you do?

LION: The beasts in the forest on the outskirts of your land want me to be their king. If only I could get back to them, I would spend my life there very happily.

GLINDA: My third command to the Winged Monkeys shall be to carry you to your forest. Then, having used up the powers of the Golden Cap, I shall give it to the King of the Monkeys, so that he and his band may be free forever after.

SCARECROW, TIN WOODMAN, LION (*Ad lib*): Thank you. You are so kind to us. (*Etc.*)

DOROTHY: Glinda, you are certainly as good as you are beautiful. But you have not yet told me how to get back to Kansas.

GLINDA: Your silver shoes have wonderful powers. They can carry you anywhere in the world. If you had known their power, you could have gone back to your Aunt Em the very first day you came here.

SCARECROW: But then I should not have had my wonderful brains. I might have passed my whole life in the farmer's cornfield.

TIN WOODMAN: And I should not have had my lovely heart. I might have stood and rusted in the forest till the end of the world.

LION: And I should have lived a coward forever.

DOROTHY: This is all true, and I am glad I was of use to these good friends. But now that each of you has what you most desire, and a kingdom to rule besides, I should like to go home.

GLINDA: All you have to do is knock your heels together three times and command the shoes to take three steps and carry you wherever you wish in the wink of an eye.

DOROTHY (*Joyfully*): I shall command them at once. (*Hugs* LION, SCARECROW *and* TIN WOODMAN) Goodbye, goodbye, everyone. You have all been such good friends, and I will never forget you.

SCARECROW, TIN WOODMAN, LION (*Ad lib*): Goodbye, Dorothy. We shall always remember you, too. (*Etc.*)

DOROTHY (*To* GLINDA): I am so grateful for your kindness. (*She stands solemnly and clicks heels together three times.*) Take me home to Aunt Em! (*Blackout, crash of thunder, and curtain quickly closes. Lights come up on apron of stage to reveal*

DOROTHY *sitting on the floor, with no shoes on, holding Toto. She stands up, looking dazed.*) Good gracious, here I am back in Kansas! (*Points offstage*) And there is Uncle Henry's new farmhouse, and there are the cows in the barnyard. Oh! I've lost the silver shoes. (AUNT EM *rushes in and takes* DOROTHY *in her arms.*)

AUNT EM: My darling child! Where in the world have you been?

DOROTHY: In the Land of Oz. (*They hug each other.*) Oh, Aunt Em, I am so glad to be home again. (*Quick curtain*)

THE END

A Doctor in Spite of Himself

by *Molière*
Adapted by *Joellen Bland*

Ingenious prescription mends broken hearts. . . .

Characters

SGANARELLE, *a woodcutter*
MARTINE, *his wife*
VALERE ⎱ *servants*
LUCAS ⎰
GERONTE, *their master*
JACQUELINE, *maid*
LUCINDE, *Geronte's daughter*
LEANDRE, *in love with Lucinde*

TIME: *The 1600's.*
SETTING: *A wood, played before the curtain.*
BEFORE RISE: SGANARELLE *and* MARTINE *enter, quarreling, from left.*

287

SGANARELLE: How dare you argue with me, Martine! I am your master!

MARTINE: You are my husband, Sganarelle. I did not marry you to be treated so badly.

SGANARELLE: *You? I* am the one who is miserable. With a complaining wife like you, how can I be anything else?

MARTINE: I have plenty to complain about! You have brought us to the poorhouse! You eat us out of house and home.

SGANARELLE: What? Do you deny me food?

MARTINE: You have sold everything in the house, even the bed!

SGANARELLE (*Smugly*): We'll have nothing to pack when we move.

MARTINE: You squander away all our money in the village!

SGANARELLE: Only to keep up my spirits! Do you want me to be unhappy?

MARTINE: Of course not. But what am I to do at home with four little children to feed? They cry for bread.

SGANARELLE: Nonsense! Give them a thrashing and a drink of water.

MARTINE (*Furiously*): I don't know how much longer I can put up with this.

SGANARELLE: If you insist on being angry, I'll leave you to give my ears a rest. I have wood to cut.

MARTINE: Yes, wood to cut and sell, but your wife and children never see the earnings! Scoundrel!

SGANARELLE: Scream at the trees, if you must! I'll go beyond the sound of your voice. (*Exits*)

MARTINE (*Pacing*): I must teach him a lesson! Once he was a good husband and father, but the company of bad fellows has ruined him. What can I do? (*Paces nervously.* LUCAS *and* VALERE *enter, but* MARTINE *does not notice them.*)

LUCAS: How are we to get out of this fix, Valère? We have been given an impossible order!

VALERE: Our master Géronte is the richest and most powerful gentleman in the province. As his servants, we must obey him. Besides, we love his daughter Lucinde as though she were our own, and her illness concerns us as much as it does her father.

LUCAS (*Sadly*): Poor Lucinde! It is terrible to have her marriage to Horace postponed because of this sudden illness!

VALERE: Lucas, she is so unhappy. Her maid Jacqueline told me something in confidence that might be the cause of her unhappiness.

LUCAS: What is it? (*Listens intently*)

VALERE: She said that Lucinde looked very favorably on that young fellow, Léandre.

LUCAS (*Surprised*): Léandre? A fine young man, to be sure, but he is penniless.

VALERE: True. Géronte would never consent to such a marriage, and I told Jacqueline to advise her mistress so. It is true that Horace is some thirty years older than Lucinde, but he will make her a perfect husband. He has a large fortune, and he loves the girl.

MARTINE (*Aloud, to herself*): I must think of a plan. I must! I must!

LUCAS: Poor Lucinde! Not a single doctor has been able to cure her. I hate to think of the beating we will get if we fail to find a doctor who can cure her!

MARTINE (*To herself*): Where are my wits? I can't seem to think of anything! (*Starts walking left, bumps into* VALERE *and* LUCAS) Oh! I beg your pardon! I didn't see you here, gentlemen.

VALERE: You look very upset. Are you in trouble, madame?

MARTINE: It is kind of you to ask. (*Sighs deeply*) My whole life is one of great trouble! I am looking for a solution to a very serious problem.

LUCAS: Why, so are we!

MARTINE: Indeed? Perhaps I can help you.

VALERE: It is you who are kind, madame. Our master has sent us to find a doctor who can cure a strange malady that has stricken his daughter.

MARTINE: What sort of malady?

LUCAS: The poor young lady has lost her power of speech.

VALERE: Alas, she cannot speak a word. Many physicians have tried, but none could bring her any relief. Her father is desperate.

MARTINE (*Aside*): Here is the answer to my problem! (*To* LUCAS *and* VALERE) How fortunate that you ran into me! I know a doctor who specializes in strange diseases.

VALERE (*Eagerly*): You do? Madame, where is he?

MARTINE: He is in the forest, cutting wood.

LUCAS (*Puzzled*): A doctor—cutting wood?

MARTINE: He is a very unusual man. You would never recognize him as a doctor, for he insists on dressing as a common wood-cutter and pretends he knows nothing about medicine.

VALERE: How odd!

MARTINE: Yes, but he is really a genius. He will often suffer a sound beating rather than admit he is a skilled physician.

LUCAS (*Bewildered*): I have never heard of such a thing.

MARTINE: He will not tend the sick unless someone beats him.

VALERE (*Astounded*): This is beyond belief!

MARTINE: But once he is subdued, he works wonders!

VALERE: Then we must have him! What is his name?

MARTINE (*Cautiously*): Sganarelle.

LUCAS: Is he really as skillful as you say? We cannot afford to make a mistake.

MARTINE: He can work miracles! A woman in our village was dying, and no doctor could save her. But Sganarelle took one look at her, put a little drop of something into her mouth, and she was up and walking around the room in a few minutes.

LUCAS (*Impressed*): Miraculous indeed!

MARTINE: And not two weeks ago, a boy fell off the church tower and broke every bone in his body. When Sganarelle was forced to attend him, he rubbed the child all over with a special ointment, and the boy jumped up and ran off to play.

VALERE: Incredible! We must find Dr. Sganarelle at once!

MARTINE (*Looking off right*): I believe he will spare you that trouble. I hear him coming this way. Good day, gentlemen! I must be going.

VALERE: How can we ever repay you, madame?

MARTINE: You have, by solving my problem! My heart is light now. Good day, gentlemen! (*Runs off left, laughing. After a moment,* SGANARELLE *enters, right, with a bottle, which he turns upside down.*)

SGANARELLE (*Disappointed*): Empty! How am I to work when I am so thirsty?

VALERE (*To* LUCAS): He doesn't look like a doctor.

LUCAS: Quite a shabby bumpkin!

SGANARELLE (*To himself*): Who are these fellows? Why are they looking at me?

LUCAS: Come, we must speak to him. (VALERE *and* LUCAS *start to cross toward him.*)

SGANARELLE: They are coming this way!

VALERE (*Approaching* SGANARELLE): Pardon, sir, is your name Sganarelle?

SGANARELLE (*Suspiciously*): Yes and no, depending upon what you want with him.

VALERE: We want to show him every courtesy, and beg his assistance in a very urgent and important matter.

SGANARELLE: In that case, I am Sganarelle, and I will be glad to help you if I can. I'm the best woodcutter in France!

VALERE: We are not interested in woodcutting.

SGANARELLE: But no one can cut wood better than I!

VALERE (*Puzzled*): Why, sir, does a man with your vast skill and learning insist on hiding his identity and concealing his talent?

SGANARELLE (*Astonished*): I don't understand you.

LUCAS: Don't try to deceive us. We know all about you.

SGANARELLE (*Suspiciously*): What do you know about me?

VALERE: That you are the greatest doctor in this province!

SGANARELLE: Doctor? Why, I'm not a doctor now, and I never was!

LUCAS (*To* VALERE; *knowingly*): He denies it.

VALERE: Just as the woman said he would. (*To* SGANARELLE) Come, sir, don't force us to do something for which we might be sorry later.

SGANARELLE: What are you talking about? (*Adamantly*) I tell you, I'm not a doctor!

LUCAS: Sir, we beg of you, admit you are a doctor and come with us at once.

SGANARELLE: How can I admit I am a doctor when I positively am not?

VALERE (*With resignation*): Then we must bring you to your senses. At him, Lucas! (VALERE *and* LUCAS *begin to pummel* SGANARELLE.)

SGANARELLE (*Falling to his knees*): Oh! Ow! Stop! Gentlemen, please, stop! I'll be anything you say, if you'll just stop beating me! (VALERE *and* LUCAS *stop.*)

VALERE: We have no wish to harm you.

SGANARELLE: Then why have you nearly killed me? And why do you insist that I am a doctor?

VALERE (*In disbelief*): Do you still insist that you are not a doctor?

SGANARELLE (*Protesting loudly*): I am a woodcutter! A poor, honest woodcutter!

LUCAS: I hate to do this, but we are desperate men! (VALERE *and* LUCAS *pummel* SGANARELLE *again.*)

SGANARELLE: Oh! Stop! Please stop! All right—as you please! I'm a doctor! I'm a doctor! (VALERE *and* LUCAS *stop, but still hold* SGANARELLE *by the arms.*)

VALERE: Are you the most skilled and learned doctor in the province?

SGANARELLE: Yes! Yes!

LUCAS: A doctor who specializes in strange diseases?

SGANARELLE: Of course! Whatever you say! (LUCAS *and* VALERE *release* SGANARELLE.).

VALERE: That's better. At last you've come to your senses.

SGANARELLE (*Holding his head*): Oh-h-h! I think you have knocked my senses to bits and pieces!

LUCAS: We beg your pardon, sir, but you won't regret admitting that you are a doctor. Our master, Géronte, will reward you generously when you have cured his daughter.

SGANARELLE (*Eagerly*): Reward?

VALERE: Just name your fee, and our master will gladly pay you any amount.

SGANARELLE: Any amount?

VALERE: Any amount!

SGANARELLE: Ah! (*Confidently*) Yes, now I remember distinctly. I *am* a doctor. (*Rubs hands together*) Now, what seems to be the problem with your master's daughter?

VALERE: She has lost her tongue.

SGANARELLE (*Jokingly*): But, gentlemen, I don't have it.

LUCAS: Ha! You will have your joke! A doctor with a sense of humor is much to our liking! (VALERE *and* LUCAS *lead* SGANARELLE *off right.* MARTINE *slips in from left.*)

MARTINE (*Aside*): This is turning out better than I expected! I will follow them and see this through to the finish. (*Laughing, she runs off after them. Blackout*)

* * * * *

TIME: *A short time later.*

SETTING: *A room in Géronte's house, elegantly furnished.*

AT RISE: GERONTE *is seated in chair, with* VALERE *and* LUCAS *on either side of him.* JACQUELINE *is dusting and listening in on the conversation.*

VALERE: Master, we have brought you the best doctor that can be found. We are sure you will be satisfied.

LUCAS: He has performed miraculous cures!

GERONTE: If he can make my darling Lucinde speak again, it will be the greatest miracle of all.

VALERE: You will see that he is rather eccentric, master. His mind wanders, and he likes to play the fool.

LUCAS: But he is very learned and he can speak quite elegantly when he wants to.

GERONTE: I don't care how he speaks, as long as he cures my daughter. Bring him to me at once!

VALERE (*Bowing*): Yes, master, at once! (*Runs out right*)

JACQUELINE (*Crossing to* GERONTE): Please, listen to me, master! I never fail to give you good advice. This doctor will fare no better than all the others. In my opinion, the best doctor you can give your darling Lucinde is a handsome young man for a husband—a man she truly loves!

GERONTE (*Angrily*): This is none of your business, Jacqueline!

LUCAS (*To* JACQUELINE): Hold your tongue, you silly! You'll only get yourself and your mistress in trouble.

JACQUELINE (*Ignoring* LUCAS): Master, there is not a doctor in the world who can do my mistress a bit of good. I tell you, a true and loving husband is the cure for her illness!

GERONTE: When I wanted to marry her off, she balked and gave me nothing but trouble.

JACQUELINE: Of course she did, master. You wanted her to marry an old man she doesn't love. Why won't you let her marry the man of her own choosing?

GERONTE: Such as?

JACQUELINE: Such as young master Léandre!

GERONTE: Nonsense! Léandre hasn't a penny to his name!

JACQUELINE: He is the only heir of a rich old uncle!

GERONTE: Money to come is nothing compared to money in hand!

JACQUELINE: But, master, I have always heard that happiness in marriage is worth far more than wealth.

GERONTE (*Loudly*): And I have always heard that a maid who doesn't tend to her work and hold her tongue may get her ears boxed!

LUCAS (*Taking* JACQUELINE'*s arm*): Come, Jacqueline! The master knows what is best for his daughter.

JACQUELINE: I'm not so sure about that! (*She returns to her dusting, as* VALERE *enters with* SGANARELLE, *who is dressed in a long black robe, and carries a black bag.*)

VALERE (*Bowing*): Master, here is Doctor Sganarelle!

GERONTE (*Rising and bowing*): I am honored to meet you, sir. I am in urgent need of your help. My daughter, Lucinde, has fallen victim to a terrible malady!

SGANARELLE: Lucinde! What a beautiful name!

GERONTE: I'll send for her. Jacqueline! Bring your mistress here at once.

JACQUELINE: Yes, master. (*To herself*) For all the good it will do!

SGANARELLE (*Looking at* JACQUELINE; *appreciatively*): Who is this pretty young woman?

GERONTE: That's Jacqueline, my daughter's maid.

SGANARELLE: If the mistress is half as pretty as the maid, I am most fortunate to be in attendance here! (JACQUELINE *frowns at* SGANARELLE *and exits left.*)

LUCAS (*To* SGANARELLE): Come, sir! Is this any way to behave?

SGANARELLE: Forgive me! I humbly await my patient with all my resources of medical science!

GERONTE: And where are they—your resources?

SGANARELLE (*Touching head*): In my head, sir! Where else? (JACQUELINE *leads* LUCINDE *in.*)

GERONTE: Here she is, my only daughter!

SGANARELLE: And how lovely she is. (*To* LUCINDE) Now, my dear, what is the trouble? (LUCINDE *points to her mouth*.) What? I can't hear you.

GERONTE: That is the trouble, sir. She can't speak, and no one can discover why. Her marriage has been delayed because her intended husband will not marry her in this condition.

SGANARELLE: What? He is an idiot! What man would refuse a wife who is always silent? Oh, if only my wife could have this affliction, how peaceful my life would be!

GERONTE: Come, sir. I want my daughter married at once. You see (*Hesitates*) . . . her intended husband is quite wealthy, and I don't wish to lose him. You must cure my daughter!

SGANARELLE: Yes, of course. (*To* LUCINDE) My dear, give me your hand. (*Takes* LUCINDE's *hand, looks at it closely, kisses it, then examines it again*) Ah! The young lady's pulse definitely indicates that she has lost the ability to speak.

JACQUELINE (*Aside*): Now, there's a clever man.

GERONTE: We know that. But how has this happened?

SGANARELLE: I assure you, sir, that the best medical authorities would agree there is some impediment in the use of her tongue.

GERONTE (*Impatiently*): Yes, yes! But what is to be done about it?

SGANARELLE: My advice is to put her to bed immediately and give her plenty of bread dipped in wine.

GERONTE (*Surprised*): The cure is as simple as that?

SGANARELLE: Sir, the combination of bread and wine is the surest cure for loss of speech. Parrots are fed nothing else, and you know how much they chatter!

GERONTE (*Beaming*): Why, you are right! (*Patting* SGANARELLE *on shoulder*) What a wonderful doctor you are! (*Turns to* JACQUELINE) Jacqueline, put your mistress to bed at once, and bring her as much bread dipped in wine as she can eat.

JACQUELINE: Yes, master. (*Aside*) This is ridiculous! (JACQUELINE *and* LUCINDE *exit left*.)

SGANARELLE: I will look in on her later this evening.

GERONTE: Will she be cured by morning?

SGANARELLE: Very likely. Now, I must go.

GERONTE: But first I must pay you, sir.

SGANARELLE: Yes, of course. I almost forgot.

GERONTE (*Giving him bag of coins*): You are too modest. I can't thank you enough! Now, I'd better be certain Lucinde gets the best wine in the house. Valère, Lucas, come with me! (GERONTE, VALERE, LUCAS *exit left.*)

SGANARELLE: I'd better be well away from here before dawn. (*Holds up bag of coins*) Doctoring pays much better than cutting wood. (LEANDRE *enters right, carrying bag which contains wig, beard, long robe and hat.*)

LEANDRE (*Cautiously*): Sir!

SGANARELLE (*Startled*): Who are you? What do you want?

LEANDRE: I need your help desperately! (SGANARELLE *crosses to* LEANDRE, *holds his wrist.*)

SGANARELLE: Ah! Your pulse is very weak.

LEANDRE: I am not ill, sir!

SGANARELLE: Then what do you want with me?

LEANDRE: My name is Léandre, and I am in love with Lucinde.

SGANARELLE: Aha!

LEANDRE: Lucinde loves me, too, but her father will not let me see her. If you will help me, I have a plan for speaking to her. Our happiness depends on it!

SGANARELLE (*Pretending to be angry*): You are asking me, a dignified, learned, famous physician, to stoop to some lover's intrigue?

LEANDRE: Please, I beg of you, not so loud!

SGANARELLE: You are a bold scoundrel. If Master Géronte knew you were here in his house he would—

LEANDRE (*Stuffing purse into* SGANARELLE's *hand*): Sir, this money is all yours if you will help me! (SGANARELLE *shakes purse, hears sound of coins, and tucks purse under his robe.*)

SGANARELLE: You're not really a bad fellow after all. What do you want me to do?

LEANDRE: First, let me tell you that the cause of Lucinde's illness is love.

SGANARELLE: Love! How is that?

LEANDRE: She only pretended to lose her voice, to avoid being forced to marry a man she doesn't love.

SGANARELLE (*Surprised*): Then she isn't really ill?

LEANDRE: No.

SGANARELLE: Then how can I cure her?

LEANDRE: Listen to my plan. I will disguise myself as an apothecary whom you have brought in on Lucinde's case. If you will teach me a few medical terms, I can convince old Géronte that I am a learned man.

SGANARELLE: But I know nothing of medical terms.

LEANDRE (*Confused*): What? But you are a doctor!

SGANARELLE: I am no more a doctor than you are an apothecary. I was forced into this masquerade. (*Laughs*) What a team we will make!

LEANDRE (*Shaking head*): You certainly fooled me. Well, let us see if we can get the old gentleman to release his daughter to my care. (*Looks off left*) Here he comes now. Quick! Help me get into my disguise! (LEANDRE *takes beard, wig, hat, and robe from bag.* SGANARELLE *helps him put them on.*) It's a good thing Géronte has seen me only once. He won't recognize me at all.

GERONTE (*Entering left*): Doctor, you are still here. Who is this gentleman with you?

SGANARELLE: This is my trusted apothecary, sir. He has an additional remedy I have prescribed for your daughter.

GERONTE (*Pleased*): Another remedy? Very good. (*Frowns*) I'm afraid the first one you prescribed is nearly choking her. (LUCINDE *enters left, with* JACQUELINE.)

JACQUELINE: Master, your daughter will not stay in bed. She insists on walking about.

SGANARELLE: Perhaps a little exercise will do her good. (*To* LUCINDE) My dear, this learned apothecary will tell you about his latest remedy. (*Pushes* LUCINDE *toward* LEANDRE, *then leads* GERONTE *to opposite side of room*) Now, sir, did you know that learned doctors are still debating whether women are easier to cure than men?

GERONTE: Really? How is that so?

LEANDRE (*Softly*): Lucinde, it is I, Léandre!

LUCINDE (*Hoarsely*): Léandre! How wonderful!

SGANARELLE (*Loudly, to* GERONTE): Indeed! Some physicians say yes, some say no. I say both yes and no. For, you see . . . (*Ad libs conversation with* GERONTE)

LEANDRE: Do you still love me, Lucinde?

LUCINDE (*Aloud*): Oh, there has been no change in my affection.

GERONTE (*Suddenly*): What's that? My daughter's voice! Lucinde, you can talk again! (*Runs over to her, embraces her*)

LUCINDE: Yes, Father. I can speak, and I have to tell you at once that I will have no one but Léandre as my husband!

GERONTE (*Angrily*): What? Is this the first thing you have to say to me?

LUCINDE (*Louder*): I am resolved to marry Léandre, or no one at all!

GERONTE: This is impossible!

LUCINDE (*Shouting*): I won't marry Horace! I absolutely refuse! Léandre will be my husband!

GERONTE (*Holding his ears*): Good heavens! What a noise! (*To* SGANARELLE) Sir, I beg of you, make her speechless again!

SGANARELLE: I'm afraid that is impossible.

GERONTE: Enough of this nonsense! Lucinde, I am your father, and I say that you will marry Horace this very night.

LUCINDE: Never! I will die first!

SGANARELLE: Sir, allow me. Lucinde's illness still affects her mind, but I believe I can cure her.

GERONTE: You can cure ailments of the mind, too?

SGANARELLE: Yes. Just leave it to me and my trusted apothecary. (*To* LEANDRE) You see how determined Géronte is that his daughter marry this Horace, even though her ardent affection is only for you. I'm afraid her case is serious, and there is no time to lose. Let me suggest a hasty dose of runaway purgative mixed with drafts of matrimony, as necessary. If she makes a fuss, be firm. But make her swallow it as gently as you can. Now, take her out and go in the direction of the church, while I talk to her father. Jacqueline, you may want to witness the cure. It's the only remedy.

JACQUELINE: Yes, sir!

LEANDRE (*Happily*): Thank you, Doctor! (LUCINDE, LEANDRE, *and* JACQUELINE *run out right.*)

GERONTE: What was that medicine you were prescribing, Doctor? Runaway purgative, and—

SGANARELLE (*Quickly*): Special medicines, sir, used only in an emergency like this.

GERONTE: She is so stubborn! Ever since I learned how madly in love she was with this Léandre, I have kept her shut up in the house.

SGANARELLE: A very wise move, sir.

GERONTE: I would not allow them to speak to each other. Though I have been told that Léandre was making every effort to see her.

SGANARELLE: He'd have to be pretty smart to fool you.

LUCAS (*Rushing in, right*): Master! Master! Oh, what a calamity!

GERONTE: What's the matter, Lucas? You're as pale as a sheet! Do you need the doctor?

LUCAS: No! This "doctor" has been your undoing!

GERONTE: What do you mean? Speak up!

LUCAS: Your daughter has just run off with the apothecary— whose real name is Léandre—and the doctor helped them.

GERONTE: What? (*Points to* SGANARELLE) This doctor?

SGANARELLE (*Nervously*): Now, sir, be calm. It was part of the cure.

GERONTE: A cure! You have betrayed me. (SGANARELLE *runs to door.*) Lucas, stop him! Don't let him get away! Hold him while I go for the sheriff. (*Runs off*)

LUCAS (*Holding* SGANARELLE): You'll be hanged for this, Doctor!

SGANARELLE: Doctor! *You* are the one who insisted I be a doctor!

MARTINE (*Entering right*): Sganarelle, is it you? (*To* LUCAS) Why are you holding the doctor?

LUCAS: To keep him here. He is going to be hanged!

MARTINE (*Upset*): Hanged? What has he done?

LUCAS: He has arranged for my master's daughter to run away with the wrong man!

MARTINE: Sganarelle, is this true?

SGANARELLE: Not to my way of thinking!

GERONTE (*Entering right*): The sheriff is coming. Now you'll get what's coming to you, you impostor!

SGANARELLE: Sir, I would gladly submit to a sound beating, if you'll only let me go afterwards.

GERONTE: A beating is too good for you! (LUCINDE *enters with* LEANDRE, *without his disguise.*)

JACQUELINE: Master, hear this young man, please.

LEANDRE: Sir, I am Léandre, and I've brought Lucinde back to you. We were going to run away and be married, but I don't want to steal your daughter—I would rather you give her to me, freely and willingly.

GERONTE (*Enraged*): Never! You penniless, impudent scoundrel.

LEANDRE: Sir, I wish to inform you that I have just received a letter telling me of my uncle's death. I am his only heir, and all his possessions are now mine.

GERONTE (*Softening*): Indeed? Well, sir, I am very glad to hear it. (*Beaming*) I insist that you marry Lucinde at once . . . with my blessing, of course!

LUCINDE (*Embracing* GERONTE): Oh, Father, thank you! I am so happy!

SGANARELLE (*Wiping his brow*): I hope, sir, that you will not wish to see me hanged now.

GERONTE (*Brusquely*): Just get out of my sight! I've had enough cures for one day. Lucas, show him out. (LUCAS *takes* SGANARELLE *by the arm.*)

SGANARELLE (*Pulling away from* LUCAS): I'm going! Come, Martine. I've had enough doctoring.

MARTINE: Aren't you going to thank me? I'm the one who procured for you the honor of being a doctor.

SGANARELLE: Yes, and because of you I received a terrible thrashing and was almost hanged!

MARTINE: Perhaps you would rather be a woodcutter, then?

SGANARELLE: Aye, that I would, for it's a work I know.

MARTINE (*Slyly*): And perhaps you would like to be a good husband and father again, to the wife and children who need you.

SGANARELLE: Yes, that too, Martine. I want to go home and never think about doctors again!

LUCINDE (*Loudly*): But you were a wonderful doctor, Sganarelle. You cured me, and Léandre and I shall never forget you! (*Curtain*)

THE END

Pride and Prejudice

by Jane Austen
Adapted for round-the-table reading by *Deborah Newman*

Matchmakers lose, love wins out, in this classic comedy of manners. . . .

Characters

NARRATOR
MRS. BENNET
MR. BENNET
JANE
ELIZABETH
MARY ⎬ *their daughters*
LYDIA
KITTY
DARCY
BINGLEY
SIR WILLIAM
CHARLOTTE
MISS BINGLEY
LADY CATHERINE

NARRATOR: It is a truth universally acknowledged that a single man in possession of a good fortune must be in want of a wife. However little known the feelings or views of such a man may be on his first entering a neighborhood, this truth is so well fixed in the minds of the surrounding families that he is considered the rightful property of some one or another of their daughters. Mrs. Bennet, the ambitious mother of five daughters, was merely pointing out this truth when she announced to her husband that Netherfield Park had at last been let. Mr. Bennet received the announcement with his customary silence.

MRS. BENNET: My dear Mr. Bennet, do you not want to know who has taken it?

MR. BENNET: Eh? Well, my dear, *you* want to tell me, and I have no objection to hearing it.

MRS. BENNET (*Enthusiastically*): His name is Bingley, and he's from the north of England.

MR. BENNET: Is he married or single?

MRS. BENNET: Oh, single, my dear, to be sure! A single man of large fortune—four or five thousand a year. What a fine thing for our girls.

MR. BENNET (*Quizzically*): How can it affect them?

MRS. BENNET: My dear Mr. Bennet, how can you be so tiresome? You must know that I am thinking of his marrying one of them.

MR. BENNET: Is that his design in settling here?

MRS. BENNET: Design! Nonsense, how can you talk so? But it is very likely that he *may* fall in love with one of them. Therefore, you must visit him as soon as he comes. It will be impossible for *us* to visit him if you do not.

MR. BENNET: Surely you are overscrupulous. I dare say Mr. Bingley will be very glad to see you, and I will send a few lines by you to assure him of my hearty consent to his marrying whichever of the girls he chooses.

MRS. BENNET: Mr. Bennet, you have no compassion for my poor nerves.

MR. BENNET: You mistake me, my dear. I have a high respect for your nerves. They are my old friends. I have heard you mention them with consideration these twenty years.

MRS. BENNET: Ah, you do not know what I suffer.

MR. BENNET: But I hope you will get over it and live to see many young men of four thousand a year come into the neighborhood.

MRS. BENNET: It will be of no use to us if twenty such should come, since you will not visit them.

MR. BENNET: Depend upon it, my dear—when there are twenty, I shall visit them all.

NARRATOR: Mr. Bennet was among the earliest of those who waited on Mr. Bingley. Mrs. Bennet was delighted beyond all measure with his action. And soon she was made deliriously happy by the news of a ball at Netherfield to which she and her daughters were invited. This threw the whole Bennet household into a frenzy of preparation, which was slowed down momentarily when Mrs. Bennet heard that Mr. Bingley was to bring twelve ladies and seven gentlemen down from London for the ball. But when the Bingley party entered the room, it consisted of only five altogether: Mr. Bingley, his two sisters, the husband of the eldest, and another young man.

MRS. BENNET: Jane, fix your hair.

JANE: Yes, Mama. Oh, Lizzy, isn't Mr. Bingley handsome?

ELIZABETH: He has a pleasant countenance.

MRS. BENNET: Such charming manners. Jane, he is looking at you. Smile and fix your gown.

MARY: Who is the other young man, Mama?

LYDIA: Isn't *he* wicked looking!

KITTY: Lady Lucas says his name is Darcy—and that he has *ten* thousand a year.

MRS. BENNET: Lydia, Kitty! I cannot have you discussing such things at a ball. . . . *Ten* thousand, did you say?

ELIZABETH: His money has scarcely helped his countenance. A most forbidding, disagreeable face.

MRS. BENNET: Elizabeth Bennet! Mr. Darcy looks like a noble gentleman.

NARRATOR: But if Mrs. Bennet looked upon Mr. Darcy with all the favor her ambitious heart could bestow, Mr. Darcy looked upon Mrs. Bennet and her family with the utmost disfavor. He danced only with Mr. Bingley's sister, and then declined to be introduced to any other lady in the room. He was the proudest, most disagreeable man in the world, and Mrs. Bennet fervently hoped that he would never come again.

BINGLEY: I say, Darcy, I hate to see you standing about by yourself in this stupid manner. Hadn't you better dance?

DARCY: I certainly shall not, Bingley. You know how I detest it, unless I am particularly acquainted with my partner. Your sisters are engaged, and there is not another woman in this room whom it would not be a punishment for me to dance with.

BINGLEY: I would not be so fastidious as you are for a kingdom, Darcy. I never saw so many pleasant girls in my life. Why, some are uncommonly handsome.

DARCY: *You* are dancing with the only handsome girl in the room, Bingley.

BINGLEY: Yes, Miss Jane Bennet is the most beautiful creature I ever beheld. But Darcy, there is one of her sisters—Miss Elizabeth Bennet. She is very pretty, and I dare say very agreeable. Do let me ask Miss Jane to introduce you.

DARCY: Hm-m. She is tolerable, Bingley, but not handsome enough to tempt *me*, and I am in no humor at present to give consequence to young ladies who are slighted by other men— she does not yet have a partner, does she? You had better return to Miss Jane and enjoy her smiles. You are wasting your time with me.

BINGLEY: I shall return to Miss Jane—with pleasure!

SIR WILLIAM: Oh, there you are, Mr. Darcy!

DARCY (*Coldly*): Sir William.

SIR WILLIAM: What a charming party this is. I always say there is nothing like dancing. I consider it one of the first refinements of polished societies.

DARCY: Certainly, sir, and it has the advantage also of being in vogue among the less polished societies of the world. Every savage can dance.

SIR WILLIAM: Ha, ha. What a wit you are, Mr. Darcy. (*Calls*) My dear Miss Elizabeth, are you not dancing? Come, Mr. Darcy, you must allow me to present this young lady to you. You cannot refuse to dance when so much beauty is before you.

ELIZABETH: Indeed, Sir William, I have not the slightest intention of dancing.

DARCY: But will you do me the honor, Miss Elizabeth?

SIR WILLIAM: You excel so much in the dance, Miss Elizabeth, that it is cruel to deny me the happiness of seeing you dance. And though Mr. Darcy dislikes the amusement in general, he can have no objection, I am sure, to oblige us for a while.

DARCY: Well, Miss Elizabeth, shall we? (*Pause*) I said, Miss Elizabeth, will you do me the honor?

ELIZABETH: I heard you the first time, Mr. Darcy, but I could not immediately determine what to say in reply. You wanted me, I know, to say "yes" that you might have the pleasure of despising my taste. But I always delight in overthrowing this kind of scheme. I have, therefore, made up my mind to tell you that I do not want to dance at all—and now, despise me if you dare.

DARCY: Indeed, Miss Elizabeth, I do not dare.

NARRATOR: The evening passed pleasantly for the whole Bennet family. Mrs. Bennet had seen her eldest daughter much admired by the Netherfield party; Mr. Bingley danced with Jane twice. Mary, who honored the company with a solo, heard herself mentioned to Miss Bingley as the most accomplished girl in the neighborhood. Kitty and Lydia had been fortunate enough to have partners all evening, which was all they had yet learned to care for at a ball. And Elizabeth, who had overheard Mr. Darcy's conversation with Mr. Bingley, delighted in repeating it, to the extreme consternation of her mother.

KITTY (*Giggling*): Oh, Lizzy, do tell it again. Only *you* could have said that to Mr. Darcy.

LYDIA: Elizabeth Bennet, does Mama know you refused Mr. Darcy?

ELIZABETH: She does not. And you must keep my secret, Lydia.

JANE: But Mama does not approve of Mr. Darcy.

ELIZABETH: No—not of *him*. But, Jane—think of his estate, Pemberly. And ten thousand a year. I think Mama looks upon him kindly in spite of herself.

MRS. BENNET: Jane! Oh, here you are. My dear, you don't know what good luck. Look—a message from Caroline Bingley. She wishes to have you come and dine with her tonight.

JANE: How nice.

MRS. BENNET: Yes. But Mr. Bingley and that—that awful Mr. Darcy will be away. That is unfortunate.

JANE: May I have the carriage, Mama?

MRS. BENNET: No, my dear, you had better go on horseback. It seems likely to rain, and then you must stay all night.

ELIZABETH: That would be a good scheme if you were sure they would not offer to send Jane home.

MRS. BENNET: But the gentlemen will have Mr. Bingley's chaise. And Lady Lucas has informed me that they have but one at Netherfield.

JANE: I would much rather go in our carriage, Mama.

MRS. BENNET: But your father cannot spare the horses.

ELIZABETH: Mama, if you asked him he would give them to you. He always has before.

MRS. BENNET: Elizabeth, I told you I am sure your father will need the horses. Oh, Jane, my darling, what an opportunity! I am sure you will be asked to stay the night—and in the morning, your Mr. Bingley will be there!

MARY: Mama, I must say that I do not think this is exactly right. Just the other day, in my reading . . .

MRS. BENNET (*Interrupting*): Nonsense, Mary. You will ruin your eyes with your reading. Come, Jane, let us see what you have to wear.

NARRATOR: Mrs. Bennet was a true weather prophet. It not only rained, it thundered, and with each clap she grew more cheerful. Jane did not return that night; the morning brought a message from her saying she had been soaked to the skin en route to Netherfield and was forced to remain in bed. Elizabeth set out at once for Netherfield to nurse Jane.

But if Jane had found the company at Netherfield very much to her liking, Elizabeth could see nothing in it to admire—with the exception of Mr. Bingley, who was all goodness and thoughtfulness. Miss Bingley proved to be a most obnoxious hostess. She soon impressed upon Elizabeth that her brother was to marry Mr. Darcy's sister, and that she, of course, would, in turn, marry Mr. Darcy. Miss Bingley took every opportunity to woo Mr. Darcy with her charm, and thus Elizabeth felt no surprise when, one afternoon in the library, Miss Bingley turned to Mr. Darcy and, with her most charming smile, said:

MISS BINGLEY (*Coyly*): How delighted Miss Darcy will be to receive such a letter, Mr. Darcy. Pray tell your sister that I long to see her.

DARCY: I have already told her so once by your desire.

MISS BINGLEY: And tell her I am delighted to hear of her improvement on the harp—and pray, let her know that I am quite in rapture with her beautiful little design for a table. I do admire your sister. She is so accomplished.

BINGLEY: It is amazing to me how young ladies can have the patience to be so very accomplished as they all are.

MISS BINGLEY: *All* young ladies accomplished! My dear brother, what do you mean?

BINGLEY: They all sing, play the spinet, or paint. I am sure I never heard of a young lady without being told of her accomplishments.

DARCY: The word accomplished can be applied to any woman today who sings, paints, or plays the spinet. Those arts hardly deserve to be called accomplishments. I cannot boast of a half dozen ladies in the whole range of my acquaintance, who are *really* accomplished.

ELIZABETH: Then, Mr. Darcy, you must comprehend a great deal in your idea of an accomplished woman.

DARCY: Yes, Miss Elizabeth, I do. No woman can really be considered accomplished who does not excel in music, singing, drawing, dancing, and all the modern languages; and besides she must possess a certain something in her air and manner of walking, the tone of her voice, and her manner of speech. . . And to all this, she must yet add something more substantial, in the improvement of her mind by extensive reading.

ELIZABETH (*Tartly*): I am no longer surprised at your knowing *only* six accomplished women, Mr. Darcy. I rather wonder now at your knowing *any*.

DARCY: Are you so severe upon your own sex as to doubt the

possibility that any woman can possess all these virtues?

ELIZABETH: *I* have never seen a woman of such capacity, application, and elegance as you describe.

MISS BINGLEY: I believe, Mr. Darcy, that Miss Elizabeth Bennet is laughing at you.

ELIZABETH: And, of course, Mr. Darcy is not to be laughed at. Though I dearly love a laugh, I hope I never ridicule what is wise or good, and certainly Mr. Darcy's picture of the ideal woman must be both. Follies, nonsense, whims and inconsistencies do divert me, I own, and I laugh at them whenever I can. But these, Mr. Darcy, I suppose, are precisely what you are without.

DARCY: Perhaps that is not possible for anyone, Miss Elizabeth. But it has been the study of my life to avoid those weaknesses that would expose one to ridicule.

ELIZABETH: Such as vanity and pride, Mr. Darcy?

DARCY: Yes, vanity is a weakness, indeed. But pride—where there is a real superiority of mind, pride will always be a good regulation.

MISS BINGLEY (*Coolly*): Well, now, Miss Bennet, your examination of Mr. Darcy is over, I presume? And pray, what is the result?

ELIZABETH (*In a mocking tone*): I am completely convinced that Mr. Darcy has no defect. He admits it himself with no disguise. And now, if you will excuse me, I must go to Jane. Good afternoon.

BINGLEY: I shall go with you, Miss Elizabeth. (*Pause*)

MISS BINGLEY: Well! I must say, Miss Elizabeth is never at a loss for words. You know, Mr. Darcy, I must confess I could never see any beauty in her. Her face is too thin, her complexion has no brilliancy, and her features are not at all handsome. I remember when we first came to Netherfield, how amazed we all were to find that she was a reputed beauty. And I particularly recollect your saying, "*She* a beauty! I should as soon call her mother a wit." (*Pause*) Mr. Darcy!

DARCY (*Bemused*): Eh?

MISS BINGLEY: Why, I do believe you've not heard a word I was saying. What were you thinking about—with that faraway look in your eyes? Pemberly, perhaps?

DARCY (*Thoughtfully*): No, Miss Bingley. I have been meditating on the very great pleasure a fine pair of eyes in the face of a very pretty woman can bestow.

MISS BINGLEY (*Simpering*): Oh, Mr. Darcy. And what lady has the power to inspire such reflections?

DARCY: Miss Elizabeth Bennet.

NARRATOR: Mr. Darcy would have found little to admire in Elizabeth Bennet's eyes a few nights later when she chanced to meet a Mr. Wickham, attached to the regiment near her home. Mr. Wickham, a charming and debonair young man, brought up the subject of Mr. Darcy soon after he had been introduced, informing Elizabeth that he had grown up with Mr. Darcy, and had, in fact, been provided for by Mr. Darcy's father. But Mr. Darcy, feeling that Wickham was beneath the Darcy family, had deprived him of this money. Mr. Wickham found a ready and sympathetic listener in Elizabeth, whose eyes flashed as she declared to him that she hoped she would never meet Mr. Darcy again.

The next morning brought a message for Jane from Miss Bingley which seemed to grant Elizabeth's wish. Miss Bingley regretfully informed Jane that the whole Netherfield party was on their way back to town—without any intention of coming back. To Elizabeth, Miss Bingley's designs were quite clear. But she found herself strangely upset by this departure. Mrs. Bennet was inconsolable—to have come so near, and to have lost all. Her constant complaints made the household so unbearable that Elizabeth was glad to accept an invitation to visit her friend, Charlotte Collins, whose husband was the pastor of Lady Catherine de Bourgh. At the end of the first week of Elizabeth's visit, Mr. Darcy, Lady Catherine's nephew, arrived at the estate totally unexpected.

CHARLOTTE: Elizabeth, come over to this window. Here he is again—your Mr. Darcy. Elizabeth, he must be in love with you. Surely that is the only reason he comes to visit us so often.

ELIZABETH (*Sharply*): Charlotte, please do not call him *my* Mr. Darcy. And stop talking such utter nonsense. He comes to pay you and his aunt, Lady Catherine, his respects.

CHARLOTTE (*Calmly*): No, Elizabeth, I say he must have some feeling toward you. Else why would you always meet him when you are walking? And you yourself know that he made a special effort to talk with you at Lady Catherine's ball.

ELIZABETH: Mr. Darcy talks to me just to plague me and despise me the more.

CHARLOTTE: Elizabeth, I am not dressed to greet him. Please, you must talk to him until I return. (*There is a brief pause.*)

DARCY: Miss Elizabeth, the maid told me I would find you in here.

ELIZABETH (*Coolly*): Yes, Mr. Darcy, she was correct.

DARCY (*With a rush of feeling*): Miss Elizabeth—oh, in vain have I struggled, but my feelings will not be repressed any longer. You must allow me to tell you how ardently I love you.

ELIZABETH (*Astonished*): Mr. Darcy!

DARCY: You are surprised. Yes, I must confess, so am I. I realize that there will be obstacles—family obstacles. But I love you, and that I cannot overlook. It makes me forget all else. That you are inferior to me—that, in a sense, such a marriage would be degrading to me—I know. And I have considered your background fully. I am aware of much that is lacking. But I wish to marry you in spite of this.

ELIZABETH (*Coldly*): Mr. Darcy, in cases such as this the usual custom is to express gratitude for the sentiments avowed. If I could feel gratitude, I would now thank you. But I cannot—I have never desired your good opinion, and you have certainly bestowed it most unwillingly. I am sorry to cause pain to anyone. But after my refusal, you can have little difficulty in overcoming the feelings which you tell me have long prevented the acknowledgment of your regard for me.

DARCY (*Upset*): Miss Elizabeth—is this all the reply I am to have the honor of expecting? I might, perhaps, wish to be informed why, with so little endeavor at civility, I am thus rejected.

ELIZABETH (*Firmly*): I might as well inquire why, with so evident a design of offending and insulting me, you choose to tell me that you love me against your will, against your reason, and even against your character. I have every reason to think ill of you, Mr. Darcy. You have ruined, perhaps forever, my sister

Jane's happiness by taking away Mr. Bingley. (*Hotly*) Oh, do not deny it! You have been most unfair in your conduct to Mr. Wickham. From the very beginning of my acquaintance with you, your manners impressed me with the fullest belief of your arrogance, your conceit, and your selfish disdain of the feelings of others. I had not known you a month before I felt that you were the last man in the world whom I could ever be prevailed upon to marry.

DARCY (*Hurt*): You have said quite enough, madam. I perfectly comprehend your feelings, and have now only to be ashamed of what my own have been. Forgive me for having taken up so much of your time, and accept my best wishes for your health and happiness. Good day.

ELIZABETH (*Angrily*): What an unbearable man!

CHARLOTTE: Elizabeth, was that Mr. Darcy departing in such a hurry?

ELIZABETH: It was.

CHARLOTTE: Oh, dear. I did so hope to have a word with him. Did he say anything of consequence to you?

ELIZABETH: No, Charlotte. Mr. Darcy said nothing of consequence.

NARRATOR: The next day, Elizabeth received a letter from Mr. Darcy.

ELIZABETH (*Reading from letter*): "My dear Miss Elizabeth. Be not alarmed on receiving this letter. It does not contain any renewal of those sentiments which were so disgusting to you yesterday. But you charged me with two offenses of a very different nature, and I wish to clear them, if only for my own sake. As to ruining the happiness of your sister, I can only say that such a thing would always be farthest from my mind. Mr. Bingley is indeed in love with your sister. But it has never occurred to me that *she* favored him, and when he asked me I expressed that opinion.

With respect to your accusation of my having injured Mr. Wickham, I can only refute it by laying before you his whole story. Mr. Wickham grew up in the bosom of my family. But when my father died, Wickham left for the society of London; he became a mere idler, asking for money when he needed it, and otherwise doing nothing but enjoy himself. He then tried to elope with my sister, Georgiana, who was all of fifteen at the time. I am sure you will understand when I tell you I foiled that attempt. Soon after this, he tried again with the daughters of some of my friends, each time making sure that the young woman in question could turn over to him a large bank account. I have since had nothing to do with Mr. Wickham. I will only add, God bless you. Fitzwilliam Darcy."

NARRATOR: Directly after Mr. Darcy's letter had arrived, another letter came for Elizabeth. It was from her sister Jane, and the news was not good. Lydia had run off with Mr. Wickham, and the couple could not be found. It was hoped that they planned to be married. Elizabeth hesitated, reread Mr. Darcy's letter, and then set off for Lady Catherine's estate in search of Mr. Darcy. She was taken aback by his kindness. He promised to set out for London at once to find the couple. Elizabeth, her mind much more at ease, made plans to return home, and an hour later Mr. Darcy's chaise was seen setting out for London.

A letter finally came for the anxious Bennets from their uncle in London: the couple had been found, and Wickham had been persuaded to marry Lydia on payment of ten thousand pounds. Mr. Bennet was perturbed at owing so much money to his brother-in-law, but Mrs. Bennet was overjoyed; she would at last have a married daughter. The family eargerly awaited the arrival of the bride and groom. Lydia ran into the house into the open arms of her parents and sisters.

LYDIA: Oh, Mother, how happy I am to see you. And Jane and Lizzy! How good to see you again.

MRS. BENNET: Oh, Lydia, my Lydia. A married woman! But where is your husband?

LYDIA: Mr. Wickham is tending to the horses. He will be in directly. And what a charming man he is. I only hope, Lizzy, that you have half my luck.

MRS. BENNET: How well you look, my dearest Lydia.

LYDIA: This *is* a fine gown, isn't it? (*Rambling on*) You must all come to Brighton. I shall get all of my sisters fine husbands before the winter is over.

ELIZABETH: I thank you for my share of the favor, Lydia, but I do not particularly like your way of getting husbands.

MRS. BENNET: Jane, my dear, you must come and help me in the dining room. Lydia, you stay right here and rest yourself, and Elizabeth shall talk to you.

LYDIA: Lizzy, you've never had an account of my wedding. Are you not curious how it was managed?

ELIZABETH: No, Lydia. I think there cannot be too little said on the subject.

LYDIA: Lizzy, you are so strange! But I must tell you how it went off. We were married at St. Clements. It was agreed that Uncle and Aunt and I were to go together, we would meet Mr. Wickham there at eleven. All the time I was dressing, Aunt was talking away, just as if she were reading a sermon. And then, just as we were about to leave, Uncle was called away on business. I was so frightened, for he was to give me away, and I thought he would never get back. Fortunately, he returned in fifteen minutes. I recollected afterwards that if he *had* been prevented from returning, the wedding need not have been put off. Mr. Darcy might have done just as well.

ELIZABETH: Mr. Darcy!

LYDIA: Oh, yes—he came with Mr. Wickham. But, gracious me! I quite forgot. I ought not to have said a word about it. It was to be such a secret. (*Happily*) But look! Here comes my darling husband up the walk. I must run to him.

NARRATOR: Elizabeth, burning with curiosity, wrote at once to her uncle. The answer came back soon. Mr. Darcy had not only found Lydia and Wickham, he had paid off all of Wickham's debts and made the necessary financial arrangements with him. The contents of this letter threw Elizabeth into a flutter. It was difficult to determine whether pain or pleasure bore the greater share. Mr. Darcy had done all this for Lydia—a girl for whom he had neither regard nor esteem. Elizabeth's heart whispered that he had done it for *her*. Her spirits were scarcely quieted when the news came that Mr. Bingley was returning to Netherfield with Mr. Darcy. Mr. Bingley visited the Bennet home at once, and the purpose of his visit was made evident: he proposed to Jane. In the general rejoicing that followed, Elizabeth had no chance to speak to Mr. Darcy, and he soon left the country for London. Elizabeth did, however, have the honor of a visit from Mr. Darcy's aunt, the Lady Catherine de Bourgh.

LADY CATHERINE (*Haughtily*): You can be at no loss, Miss Bennet, to understand why I have come so far.

ELIZABETH (*Calmly*): Indeed, Lady Catherine, I am not able to account for your visit at all.

LADY CATHERINE: Miss Bennet, I have heard a report that you plan to marry my nephew, Mr. Darcy. That must of course be an impossible falsehood.

ELIZABETH: If you believed it to be impossible, I wonder you took the trouble of coming so far. What could your ladyship intend by it?

LADY CATHERINE: To insist upon having such a report universally contradicted!

ELIZABETH: Your coming here to see me and my family will be a confirmation that such is already the case.

LADY CATHERINE: Miss Bennet, I insist upon being satisfied. Has my nephew made you an offer of marriage?

ELIZABETH: Your ladyship has declared it to be impossible.

LADY CATHERINE: Mr. Darcy is engaged to my daughter. Now, what have you to say?

ELIZABETH: Only that if he is so, you can have no reason to suppose he will make an offer to me.

LADY CATHERINE (*Angrily*): Obstinate girl! Tell me, once and for all, are you engaged to him?

ELIZABETH: I am not.

LADY CATHERINE: And will you promise me never to enter into such an engagement?

ELIZABETH: I will make you no promise of any kind.

LADY CATHERINE: You are, then, resolved to have him?

ELIZABETH (*Stiffly*): I have said no such thing. I am only resolved to act in that manner which will, in my opinion, constitute my happiness without reference to *you,* or to any other person so wholly unconnected with me.

NARRATOR: Lady Catherine left the Bennet home, having failed her mission to intimidate Elizabeth. Time passed, and Mr. Darcy soon returned from London.

DARCY (*Calling*): Miss Elizabeth. Miss Elizabeth! Your mother told me you were out here in the garden.

ELIZABETH: It is good to see you again, Mr. Darcy.

DARCY: Thank you. It is good to see you.

ELIZABETH (*Impulsively*): Mr. Darcy, I have been silent too long. I can no longer help thanking you for your unexampled kindness to my poor sister. Ever since I have known about it, I have been most anxious to tell you how grateful I feel. Were it known to the rest of my family, I should have not merely my own gratitude to express.

DARCY: I am exceedingly sorry that you have been informed of what may, in a mistaken light, have given you uneasiness. I thought your aunt and uncle were to be trusted.

ELIZABETH: You must not blame them. Lydia first revealed it to me, and of course, I could not rest until I knew all. Let me thank you again and again, in the name of my family.

DARCY: If you *will* thank me, let it be for yourself alone. I shall not attempt to deny that the wish of giving you happiness led me on. Elizabeth, my—my feelings and wishes are unchanged about you. But one word from you will silence me on this subject forever.

ELIZABETH: Mr. Darcy—I—my feelings have undergone a change.

DARCY (*Eagerly*): Then it is true! Lady Catherine told me what had passed between you. It led me to hope. . . . I knew enough of your disposition to be certain that if you had absolutely, irrevocably decided against me, you would have acknowledged it frankly and openly.

ELIZABETH (*Laughing*): Yes, you know enough of my frankness to believe me capable of *that*. After abusing you so abominably to your face, I could have no scruple in abusing you to your relations.

DARCY: What did you say of me that I did not deserve? You called me proud, I believe. And so I was. But you—you, my Elizabeth, have humbled me. I hope I have proven that to you.

ELIZABETH: Oh, let us not talk of all that. I—I was prejudiced and until your letter came, I thought you were the most disagreeable man alive.

DARCY: Then my letter helped?

ELIZABETH (*Archly*): You intended that it should. (*Playfully*) Mr. Darcy, tell me, how could you fall in love with me? What set you off in the first place?

DARCY: I cannot fix the hour, or the spot, or the look, or the words which laid the foundation. I was in the middle before I knew that I *had* begun.

ELIZABETH: My behavior to you always bordered on the uncivil. Did you admire me for my impertinence?

DARCY: For the liveliness of your mind.

ELIZABETH: You may as well call it impertinence at once. The fact is that I aroused and interested you because I was so unlike other women. Shall you ever have the courage to announce to Lady Catherine what is to befall her?

DARCY: I shall have to write to her. But right now I must go in and speak to your father. The sooner, the better!

NARRATOR: So off went Mr. Darcy to ask Mr. Bennet for Elizabeth's hand. Elizabeth remained in the garden, soon to be joined by her mother.

MRS. BENNET: Good gracious, Elizabeth! That disagreeable Mr. Darcy is in the library with your father. Why must he be so tiresome, always coming here? Your father will not wish to talk to him very long.

ELIZABETH (*Happily*): I shall be glad to take him off Father's hands, Mama.

MRS. BENNET: No, I think I shall attend to it myself.

NARRATOR: Mrs. Bennet strode out, determined to send Mr. Darcy on his way. Within minutes, Mr. Bennet hurried to Elizabeth's side, a worried look on his face.

MR. BENNET: Lizzy, I must speak with you. Are you out of your senses to be accepting Mr. Darcy? Have you not always hated him?

ELIZABETH: I do not hate him now, Papa. I *love* him.

MR. BENNET: Lizzy, I have given my consent, but I must ask you if you are resolved to have him.

ELIZABETH: Papa, I cannot tell you all he means to me—how he has changed, and how I have changed. It would take too long. But you must know that all the arrangements—financial and otherwise—for Lydia's wedding were taken care of by Mr. Darcy. And he is such an angel that he never wanted us to know.

MR. BENNET: Then he is worthy of you.

MRS. BENNET: Elizabeth! You must help me. I cannot get Mr. Darcy to leave. He is a most horrible, proud creature!

MR. BENNET: Mrs. Bennet, may I advise you that you are speaking of your future son-in-law?

MRS. BENNET (*Astonished*): My future—but—Lizzy! Is this true?

ELIZABETH: It is, Mama.

MRS. BENNET (*Happily*): Oh, my darling Lizzy. How rich and great you will be! What jewels, what carriages you will have! I am so happy. Such a charming man—so handsome, so tall. Oh, my dear Lizzy! Pray apologize for my having disliked him so much before. Three daughters married. Ten thousand a year. What will become of me? I shall go distracted!

MR. BENNET: Elizabeth, I do not know what to make of your mother. If you did not get married, she would lose her mind, and now that you are, she has promised to lose it anyway.

THE END

Production Notes

FITNESS IS THE FASHION

Characters: 4 male; 7 female; 1 male or female for Officer Cannon; as many male and female extras as desired for Other Teenagers.

Playing Time: 25 minutes.

Costumes: Liz, Jay, Mrs. Smith, Joan, Sandy, and Other Teenagers wear exercise outfits—leotards and tights or shorts and T-shirts. Charles wears jeans, shirt. Granny wears dress at first, then changes into leotard. Mr. Smith wears suit. Mrs. Milligan wears casual clothes, then changes into shorts and shirt. Officer Cannon wears uniform.

Properties: Letter; book; dress on hanger; briefcase; suitcase; two badminton racquets.

Setting: The Smiths' family room. A sofa is against wall up center. At left is cassette player with tapes piled near; in front of it is coffee table holding magazines, bowl of fruit, and plate of cookies. Desk, telephone, and chair are at right. Other furniture (chairs, end tables, lamps) has been pushed toward walls to make room for exercising in center. Exercycle and weight scale are down right. Ankle or wrist weights and other equipment are piled on table left. Door left leads outside; door right to other rooms.

Lighting: No special effects.

Sound: Popular music on tape; doorbell.

JOE WHITE AND THE SEVEN LIZARDS

Characters: 4 male (Joe White, Mike Video, Braggart McTaggart, and Shadow); 1 female (Fenella); 26 or more male and female extras for all other parts. Parts of Three Voices and Batter, Runner, Catcher, Third Baseman, and Outfielder may be doubled, if desired.

Playing Time: 25 minutes.

Costumes: Joe White wears a ragged shirt, baggy baseball pants, and old cap. Braggart McTaggart, silver uniform, with a sequinned W on the back, and cap with sequins. The Lizards wear ragged baseball uniforms. Other ball players and Narrator wear regular baseball uniforms with W or E on the back, as required. Mike Video is dressed in loud sport coat and slacks, and has a bow tie. Shadow has sunglasses, black trench coat with turned-up collar, and dark gloves. Fenella is dressed in jeans and shirt. Ghost Umpire wears an umpire's uniform with white ghost make-up on his face. Groundskeeper wears white polo shirt, white pants, and baseball cap. Rooters, T-shirts with W on the front, dark shorts, and baseball caps. Signmaker may wear an artist's smock and beret. Photographer wears a trench coat.

Properties: Book, three bats wrapped in cellophane and tied with satin bows, dustcloth, toy trumpet, signs reading WORLD SERIES—WESTERN HEMISPHERE VS. EASTERN HEMISPHERE; BRAGGART MCTAGGART—GREATEST OF THE GREAT!; DEATH VALLEY. LOWEST POINT IN THE U.S.; PLAY BALL!; and SHUTOUT!; camera, pennants, two apples, the poisoned apple painted bright red with sparkle dust, purse, contract, pen, soda bottles, basket full of soda bottles, cactus, dilapidated mitts, baseball, crooked bat, package, microphone, three good mitts, masks and chest protectors for Catcher and Ghost Umpire.

Setting: A baseball stadium, with home plate, third base, and pitcher's mound. Chairs or bleachers extend across back center, with benches for the dugout in front of the chairs. In Scenes 1, 2, and 3 there is a backdrop of empty stadium seats; in Scene 4 a similar backdrop shows a stadium and scoreboard reading WESTERN HEMISPHERE—1, EASTERN HEMISPHERE—0.

Lighting: Flickering lights and blackouts.

Sound: Fanfare, slide whistle, popping sounds, wind, bottle smashing.

KID AVALANCHE

Characters: 3 male; 8 female.

Playing Time: 30 minutes.

Costumes: Modern, everyday dress. When Kid first enters, he wears jeans, turtleneck, and sneakers. He changes to girl's top and shorts. At end of play, he wears black lace gown over shorts and top, and his head is covered with shawl and black veil. Abby wears black uniform and white apron. Uncle Tetley wears safari jacket, pants, boots, and sun helmet. Petunia and Marigold wear leotards, shorts, and sneakers.

Properties: Boxes; bags, suitcase with large sticker reading YMCA, and holding boxing gloves, gym shorts, athletic shirts, and socks; legal document; dinner bell.

Setting: The living room of a dorm. Door center leads to hall and street; door left leads to kitchen and other rooms of the house. Down center are sofa and table with magazines. Up right is stereo. Dressmaker's dummy is up left, with boxes and bags nearby. Dummy's cover is on sofa. Other chairs and tables complete furnishings.

Lighting: No special effects.

Sound: Spanish dance music, as indicated in text.

A CASTLE IN SPAIN

Characters: 4 male; 4 female.

Playing Time: 30 minutes.

Costumes: Modern dress. Scene 1: Peter, Jill, Tommy, and Roseanne are dressed in patched jeans and faded shirts; Jennifer wears dress. Mr. Holloway wears artist's smock. Scene 2: children and Aunt Harriet wear night clothes and robes; Señor Garcia wears a toreador costume. Later, Tommy and Jennifer, as ghosts, wear sheets, and Jennifer wears a white lace mantilla over her head.

Properties: Lanterns, easel, canvases, paint brushes, paint box, palette, toy mouse, life-like hen, hair ribbon, stack of mail, white lace scarf, flute, flowers, school books, unseen wire attached to painting on easel, broom, apron, leather polish, rag, pen, checkbook, pitcher, glass, covering for painting, credential papers.

Setting: The barn studio and home of the Holloway family. At center rear is sliding barn door. At left of door is large studio window. At left is

view of loft with hay hanging over the edge and ladder standing against it. Upstage right is door leading to other parts of the barn. At right are six horse stalls that serve as bedrooms for the family; wooden plaques with names hang above each door. Room, though untidy with books and toys scattered around, is cozy, furnished with table and odd chairs, a couch, chest of drawers with cracked mirror above it, and decrepit easy chair. Ox yoke and saddles adorn walls. Through open door is a view of the countryside.
Lighting: No special effects.
Sound: Hen cackling; flute.

SOCIETY PAGE

Characters: 2 male; 6 female.
Playing Time: 30 minutes.
Costumes: Modern dress.
Properties: Pencils, pads, paper, pictures, purses for Mrs. Jesperson, Violet, and Sally, glue, camera, tripod, photographic equipment, galley sheets, book, wrapped parcels (some of them containing bottles), newspapers, coat for Violet, soda cans.
Setting: The cluttered society office of a newspaper. Two large desks are placed diagonally at center. Each has a telephone, typewriter, papers, glue pot, large black-and-white photographs, etc. There are two chairs near them. There are several wastebaskets overflowing with papers. Up right is door leading outside, up left a door to darkroom, and down left a door leading to inner office. Water cooler is up left.
Lighting: No special effects.

P.R.—PLANET RELATIONS

Characters: 2 male; 5 female.

Playing Time: 30 minutes.
Costumes: Cmdr. Siggzy wears a metallic jumpsuit, silver face makeup. Others wear everyday clothes.
Properties: Books, notebook, glass of water, pencil, papers.
Setting: The Adams living room. Upstage center is front door. At left and right of the door are windows. Up right is a small table holding a telephone and a vase of flowers. Down right is a large sofa. At center is a coffee table flanked by chairs. Books and magazines are on table. Down left is a chair. At left is a door leading to rest of house.
Sound: Beeping; doorbell.

MISS CAST

Characters: 5 male; 3 female.
Playing Time: 35 minutes.
Costumes: Everyday clothes for all except Judy, who wears all black, and always wears sunglasses. At the end of Scene 2, she changes into simple party dress and removes sunglasses. Nancy, Ray, David, and Bill also change into party clothes at end of Scene 2.
Properties: Knitting; script; newspaper; movie magazines; bottle of weed spray.
Setting: Johnson living room. Sofa and chairs are center; card table with model airplane parts on it is up right. Phone is on end table. Exit right leads outside; exit left to rest of house. There is open window in rear wall.
Lighting: No special effects.
Sound: Telephone and doorbell.

BUFFALO BILL'S WILD WEST SHOW

Characters: 5 male; 8 female; 11 male and/or female.
Playing Time: 20 minutes.

Costumes: Western period dress for all. Buffalo Bill, cowboy hat, western shirt, vest, beard and moustache. Annie Oakley, fringed dress festooned with medals won by sharpshooting, white cowboy hat and boots, holster with gun. Villain, black cape, top hat, moustache. Railroad Quartet, overalls and flannel shirts, floppy black hats, boots. Dinah, dress with apron. Lilly and Milly, brightly colored dresses with feathers in their hair. Four Horses, ears, tails, manes. Daisy and Mrs. Bluntpound, fancy dresses. Mr. Bluntpound, shirt, vest, string tie, derby.

Properties: Toy guns; Kentucky Fried Chicken bucket (rubber chicken may be substituted); belt; pocket mirror; over-sized plastic cigar; three small stools; small table; glass of milk; map; paper full of holes; cardboard stagecoach (large enough for four actors to hide behind, with door cut in center); two purses; small picture; coins; stick horse.

Setting: Stage is bare. If desired, it may be decorated with a Western mural, or several large cacti.

Lighting: No special effects.

Sound: Gunshots; villain music; can-can music.

The Homiest Room

Characters: 3 male; 2 female.

Playing Time: 20 minutes.

Costumes: Everyday casual clothes.

Properties: Comics; knitting; book; camera and accessories; reflectors; plate of cookies; letter containing check; magazine.

Setting: Saunders living room. Furniture is comfortable-looking, though a bit worn, except for a very new-looking chair up right. The chair has a high straight back and is upholstered in an attractive fabric. Up center is fireplace with mantel above it and mirror over mantel. In rear wall right is door leading outside; in center of left wall, another door leads to rest of house. Downstage from new chair, against wall, stands large, old-fashioned desk with books, papers, clock, and telephone. There is chair on either side of fireplace, and other chairs and tables placed around stage.

Lighting: No special effects.

Sound: Telephone.

The Gypsy Look

Characters: 3 male; 3 female.

Playing Time: 20 minutes.

Costumes: All wear casual, modern clothing. Nora puts on bright scarf and hoop earrings, as indicated, and Sue change into slacks, bright shirt, sash, head scarf, one hoop earring, and wears moustache, as indicated.

Properties: Dry cleaning; purse; books; hoop earrings; small suitcase.

Setting: Living room. At center is table with books, papers, basket of apples and dish of candy on it. Down right is large easy chair. Several smaller chairs and other furniture are placed around room. Exits are up left and right.

Lighting: No special effects.

Sound: Doorbell.

The Mystery of the Gumdrop Dragon

Characters: 2 male; 4 female; 11 male or female for Guards, Page, Court Scribe, Town Crier, Clowns, Wizard, Gatekeeper, and Gumdrop Dragon.

Playing Time: 20 minutes.

Costumes: Traditional court attire. Prince and Princess are dressed in white. Sir Sourball, a suit of "armor." Court Scribe, tights, short jacket, and cap with quill. Town Crier, black cape and hat. Clowns, clown costumes. Wizard, long cloak and hat decorated with astrological symbols. Gumdrop Dragon, green papier-mâché costume, trimmed with candy.

Properties: Handkerchief; roll of paper; inkwell; toy white rabbit; wand; chains.

Setting: Throne room in the Kingdom of Candyland. Princess's throne is center, and chairs are at either side. Table with inkwell is at right.

Lighting: Lights dim, for moonlight, as indicated in text.

Not Fit for Man or Beast

Characters: 4 male; 3 female.

Playing Time: 25 minutes.

Costumes: Little Nell wears a shabby but somewhat fancy dress and has long blonde curls. Maw wears a long old-fashioned dress and a shawl. Forsythe wears a black suit, slouch hat, and a gun holster, and has a long handlebar moustache. Baby Face wears a checkered suit, loud tie, and derby hat. The Widder Clancy wears slacks, a fancy blouse, and long earrings. Handsome Hal Herbert wears an elaborate cowboy outfit with two holsters, a silver star on his shirt and a coiled lasso attached to his belt. Paw is dressed shabbily and has a long bushy beard; a gold collar button is in the front of his collarless shirt, and he wears a wet ten-gallon hat.

Properties: Large sack, 2 official-looking pieces of paper, large red handkerchief, deck of cards, small pieces of kindling, match, toy guns. If desired, a paper cup of water may be concealed in crown of Paw's ten-gallon hat.

Setting: The interior of a shack in the Old West. A door is at upstage center and a crude window at right of door. Near the right wall there is an old-fashioned stove and downstage from it a deep woodbox. There are a few rustic chairs and a rough table with an oil lamp.

Lighting: For a fire, a light may be turned on in back of a patch of red paper on the wall. Also, flashes of lightning, as indicated in the text.

Sound: Sounds of storm, mooing and galloping as indicated.

The Gala Garage Sale

Characters: 4 male; 6 female; male and female extras.

Playing Time: 20 minutes.

Costumes: Modern. Professor Gribble wears spectacles, brown coat, blue tie, gray trousers, and derby.

Properties: Three identical umbrella stands, tea kettle, telescope, shopping bag, sea chest with metal handles and initials "AU" on front, money.

Setting: Garage interior. Exits right and left. Table down center with garage sale items, including coffee mill, pillow, unstrung tennis racket, vase, money box, woman's hat, and metronome. Empty table down right. On other tables, left, assortment of household articles, clothing, dishes, books, etc. Up center, large sign reading, A WHALE OF A GARAGE SALE!

Lighting & Sound: No special effects.

Meet Miss Stone-Age!

Characters: 1 male; 4 female.

Playing Time: 10 minutes.

Costumes: Rocky wears a top hat and black bow tie around bare neck; he

has imitation animal-skin costume. Others wear animal skin costumes, spike heels, sashes with names of regions, etc. Glenda has tiara, dark glasses.
Properties: Hand microphone, bouquet of roses, 3 papier-mâché clubs; papier-mâché stone wheel, large slab of "stone," chisel, slip of paper.
Setting: Beauty pageant stage, with risers, curtains, chairs, etc.
Lighting: No special effects.

A PERFECT MATCH

Characters: 2 female; 1 male.
Playing Time: 15 minutes.
Costumes: Everyday clothing. Alice wears watch.
Properties: Briefcase filled with papers; ring.
Setting: Office. Desk, covered with papers, is center. Telephone and intercom are on desk. One chair is placed behind desk and two chairs are arranged in front of it.
Lighting and Sound: No special effects.

HARVEY THE HYPOCHONDRIAC

Characters: 2 female; 3 male.
Playing Time: 15 minutes.
Costumes: Modern dress; Abby wears jogging suit in Scene 4.
Properties: Newspaper; small paper bag; bottle of champagne; dishes, glasses, and silverware; handkerchief.
Setting: Living/dining room of Tyler family. Dining table and chairs are left; couch and coffee table are right. Exit left leads to kitchen; exit right, to front door. Scene 4, on street in front of Tyler house, may be played before curtain.
Sound: Doorbell.
Lighting: No special effects.

SWINE JUST WANNA HAVE FUN

Characters: 3 female; 1 male.
Playing time: 20 minutes.
Costumes: Pigs wear caps and gowns over high school football jerseys, pink jogging pants, sneakers. Pig noses: disks of reinforced pink construction paper with two dots for nostrils, attached with spirit gum; or, store-bought rubber pigs noses that attach with elastic bands. Tails: straighten and connect two wire hangers end-to-end and wrap around waist, leaving a foot hanging in back to twist into a corkscrew, then thread it with pink sponge rollers. Wolf wears black pants and shirt, white shoes with spats, white gloves, and black visor with black ears attached.
Properties: Trophy, three suitcases, three books with large labels reading, THE THREE LITTLE PIGS, COSMOS, and GET RICH, YOU PIG; telephone, box labeled ACME TACKS, filled with nails to rattle and sealed so that they won't spill out; rope; bowl with popcorn; deck of cards; three tin pie plates; three cans whipped cream; three long feathers; rug. Houses are made of refrigerator-sized boxes, with one side removed. Small cardboard boxes to hold telephone and books.
Setting: Played in front of curtain, then on bare stage with optional New York City skyline backdrop.
Lighting and Sound: Tape recording of "Pomp and Circumstance" and graduation announcer. No special lighting effects.

GREAT CAESAR'S GHOST!

Characters: 4 male or female.
Playing Time: 10 minutes.
Costumes: Roman togas. Caesar

wears laurel wreath on head.

Properties: Pad, pencil, crystal snow ball.

Setting: Caesar's office. Desk and chair are center. There are several other chairs around room.

Lighting: No special effects.

Sound: Knock at door.

THE MIDNIGHT RIDE OF . . . WHO?

Characters: 4 male; 2 female.

Playing time: 20 minutes.

Costumes: Appropriate dress of the Revolutionary War period. Longfellow may wear cutaway coat, flowing black tie.

Properties: Several sheets of blank paper (Longfellow's poem can be written out on a sheet, if desired), quill pen, bottle of ink, silverware, riding whip, tricorn hats.

Setting: Area down right contains desk and two chairs. At center is the Revere house, with a table, on which are several pieces of silverware, and a few chairs. Riding whip and tricorn hat are placed on another smaller table. There is a window in backdrop.

Lighting: Lights are raised and dimmed as indicated in text, to denote the area of action.

Sound: Horse's hooves, whinny, as indicated in text.

THE IMPORTANCE OF BEING EARNEST

Characters: 5 male; 4 female

Playing Time: 30 minutes.

Costumes: Late nineteenth century dress.

Properties: Silver cigarette case, pencil, diary, pen, books, large black handbag, and small leather case containing calling card.

Setting: Scene 1, an elegant nineteenth century drawing room with sofa, chairs, desk, etc. Tea table holds tea set, tea cups, two platters of tea sandwiches, and a small bell. Doors at right lead outside; door at left lead to music room. Scenes 2 and 3, a garden, with pots of flowers, an iron settee, two iron chairs, and a table covered with books. Entrance right leads to house, and gate at left leads to street.

Lighting: No special effects.

SHE STOOPS TO CONQUER

Characters: 4 male; 4 female.

Playing Time: 35 minutes.

Costumes: Traditional late 18th century dress. Mrs. Hardcastle, Miss Neville and Kate wear long dresses with "looped-up" skirts or bustles. Hoops are worn under skirts. Flowers or lace caps are worn in the hair, which is drawn up into a chignon and carefully arranged. Kate's Maid, and Kate herself, in maid's costume, wear simple ankle-length printed cotton dresses, with plain long white aprons, white fichus around the neckline of the dresses, and white mob caps. Their hair is pinned up. They have white cotton stockings, and simple buckled shoes. Mr. Hardcastle, Marlow, Hastings and Sir Charles wear powdered or unpowdered wigs, with short queues. They wear long coats over waistcoats and breeches. All men wear boots.

Properties: Traveling bags, tray and three cups of chocolate.

Setting: An old-fashioned 18th century English parlor, with the look of a rustic country house. Setting should be representational, with most furniture painted on backdrop, and only a few elegant chairs, tables, etc., on stage. A painted screen is upstage, at one side. There are several exits.

Lighting: Lights dim, as indicated in Scene 1.

THE WIZARD OF OZ

Characters: 6 male; 6 female. Narrator and Munchkins may be male or female. Male and female extras. The Wizard of Oz in his various disguises may be played by different actors if desired.

Playing Time: 30 minutes.

Costumes: Dorothy wears everyday dress and carries a basket. The Witch of the North and the Wicked Witch of the West wear traditional witches' costumes, with pointed hats and long black cloaks. The Wicked Witch has a golden cap. Glinda wears a long, flowing white dress. The Munchkins wear odd, old-fashioned blue costumes. The Scarecrow wears a baggy shirt and overalls, and a straw hat; wisps of straw stick out of his costume. The Tin Woodman wears a silvery costume and helmet, and carries an ax. The Cowardly Lion wears a lion costume with a long tail. The Soldier wears a green uniform. The Winged Monkeys wear monkey costumes with wings attached; the King of the Monkeys has a crown. The Wizard of Oz wears a beast costume, and then an old-fashioned suit. Lovely Lady wears a long, colorful gown. Aunt Em wears an old-fashioned long dress with an apron.

Properties: Toy dog, silver shoes, oil can, four pairs of green spectacles, papier-mâché head attached to a string, broom, bucket of water, cup, powder, green bottle of liquid, green dish, small red paper heart, yellow rug. Ball of fire may be constructed from a circular piece of oak tag

painted red and orange, with pointed flames drawn at the edges. This may be suspended by a string from the ceiling, or supported on a stand from below.

Setting: Scene 1 takes place in a cornfield. There is a backdrop depicting the front of Dorothy's house. Later a stool with a pole on it is brought on for the Scarecrow. Scenes 2 and 4 take place in Oz's throne room. There is a large throne at center and a folding screen is at one side. The furnishings may be lavish and should all be green. Scene 3 takes place before the castle of the Wicked Witch of the West; a backdrop depicts the front of the castle. Scene 5 takes place in Glinda's castle. Simple but attractive furnishings may be used. Some of the furnishings used for Oz's throne room may be used for Glinda's castle as well.

Lighting: Lights dim and black out as indicated. Spotlight is used for Narrator.

Sound: Rumbling of cyclone; crash of thunder; bell.

A DOCTOR IN SPITE OF HIMSELF

Characters: 5 male, 3 female.

Playing Time: 30 minutes.

Costumes: Seventeenth century period. Peasant dress for Martine and Sganarelle (Sganarelle adds long black robe in Scene 2); simple outfits for Lucas and Valère, richer outfits for Géronte, Lucinde; maid's dress, apron and cap for Jacqueline, simple outfit for Léandre, with disguise of wig, beard, long gown, and hat.

Properties: Bottle, feather-duster or cloth for Jacqueline, black doctor's bag, coins, bag containing wig,

beard, long robe, hat, purse containing coins.

Setting: Before Rise: A wood, somewhere in France. This is played before the curtain. If desired, some
cut-out trees or shrubbery may be
placed across the front of the stage.
At Rise: A room in Géronte's house,
elegantly furnished with two or
three arm chairs, one or two small
tables, draperies over doors at right
and left.

Lighting: No special effects.